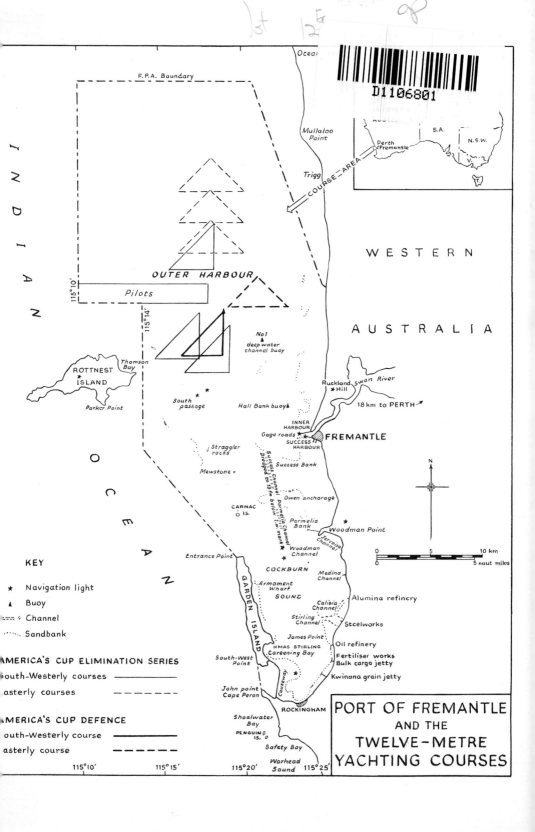

PORT OF FREMANTLE AND THE TWELVE-METRE YACHTING COURSES

AMERICA'S CUP '87

AMERICA'S CUP '87

Keith Wheatley

KEY PORTER BOOKS

For Sarah, who had faith, and Harry Bear, who was too old to come to the party.

First published in Great Britain by Michael Joseph Ltd.
27 Wrights Lane, Kensington, London W8 5DZ
1986

Canadian Cataloguing in Publication Data

Wheatley, Keith
  America's Cup '87

ISBN 1-55013-011-0

1. America's Cup races.   I. Title.

GV830 1987.W48 1986   797.1'4   C86-094742-5

Key Porter Books
70 The Esplanade
Toronto, Ontario
Canada M5E 1R2

ISBN 1-55013-011-0

Printed and bound in Canada by
T. H. Best Printing Company Limited

86 87 88 321

Contents

Acknowledgements

The America's Cup is a fortunate event in the quality of the journalists and writers who come to cover it. All I can claim to have brought is the newcomer's fresh eye and a small knowledge of sailing. My understanding of the cup has been underpinned by the work of such seasoned Newport veterans as Barbara Lloyd of the New York Times, Bruce Stannard of the Bulletin and Bob Fisher of the Guardian. In both their books and their reporting of sailing's premier regatta they set a standard that the rest of us can but steer for.

List of Illustrations

Foreword

Perth, Australia, is about as far as you can go from here and still be in civilization. And very civilized it is, too — a lovely modern city with Beach Boys scenery and a tea and cakes temperament. But a lot of things about Perth make it very different from home. When it's tonight here, it's tomorrow there. Christmas is a beach holiday, and all the rest — you know the Australian pitch. And when winter blahs are setting in up in our northern backyards, down under in Perth, there's going to be the most-ballyhooed event in the history of sailing circuses.

Canadians will be watching with both enthusiasm and jealousy. We're envious that it is the Aussies, our colonial cousins, who have beaten the Yanks and earned the right to host this wing-ding. It is their party, and they are the favourites. While the Australians go into this at better than even odds, we'll be cheering for our Canadian entry, fingers crossed that the *Canada 2* sailors and support team can somehow do the impossible. Or, if not the absolute impossible, maybe get to the semi-finals, or the quarter finals. We'll be hoping.

It's been a rough road to this festival of 12-metre madness for the Canadian squad. From two confident, big-talking syndicates we've come to one optimistic entry. Although the boat itself is reported to be very fast, it only recently arrived in Australian waters, while most of the challengers and all the defenders have been working out in the difficult Indian Ocean conditions for some time. Canadian skipper Terry Neilson is a superb sailor, an Olympic medalist and a leader, but he has no America's Cup experience and his crew is mostly rookies. Though they are individually talented sailors, only a few have raced twelves in big league competition. We have the only boat with a hockey stick for a flagstaff and a hockey player on the crew.

At this point in the evolution of America's Cup racing, we are led to believe that the making of a winner is a perfect science made up of boat design by computer, crew training by psychologists, and fundraising by Swiss gnomes. It would be easy to conclude that the odds are against the Canadians, particularly when you consider the heavy competition they'll be facing.

However, the upcoming America's Cup series is unpredictable; no one is sure what to expect since the wing-keeled white boat defeated the red one off Newport some three years ago. Each syndicate, even the Aussie defender camp, has nasty chinks in its armour. There are ego clashes, nervous backers, crew hassles and more guesswork than anyone admits to. All these elements have converged on Perth and its port city of Fremantle, where the Cup will actually be won. Even the cities are wrapped up in political issues and power plays that could only be precipitated by the sudden arrival of America's Cup gold.

I can remember one moment in the 1983 America's Cup that struck me later as significant. It occurred at the fall boat show in Toronto, in the line-up for an ice cream truck on a Saturday. Not many historical events have left their mark on me in ice cream line-ups, so I recall this one particularly vividly. It was the third race and Dennis Conner had already won two in succession. *Canada 1* had long since been dispatched to the footnotes and one could assume that the Aussies were about to fade to black, too, secret winged keel or no.

Someone had a small radio and we in the line were listening as John Bertrand and his John Denver-inspired zealots pulled out on the weather leg. *Australia II* continued leg after leg to gain over *Liberty* and won by a margin of three minutes. The crowd was delighted; still, no-one would have bet even their ice-cream cone on what was about to happen. Even after the challenger victory it remained inconceivable that Americans could be defeated — no challenger had even won two races. And, in fact, the Aussies did lose the next race before their amazing three-in-a-row march to the Auld Mug.

Later we viewed that America's Cup upset as the sports miracle of all time. We saw that New York Yacht Club brass were not gods in straw hats but a scared family ready to do anything they could, even change the rules while the contest was in progress, to keep their prized bauble. And on September 26 Dennis Conner cried. Australia went mad. The world turned upside down.

Which brings us to this edition of the Cup and this book. It's a weird, wonderful concoction of sports excellence, show biz, money and malarky that's shaping up on the other side of the globe. *America's Cup* peeks behind the curtains, over the top-secret keels, and under the war-room rugs to present a portrait of a contest more fascinating than any ordinary sailing event. This story of what's gone on until now will make it that much more intriguing to watch our Canadian boat and the others fight it out over four months. It's going to be thrilling for some and heartbreaking for a lot of others. The only thing that's certain is that anything can happen — 1983 and the events leading to this year's racing have proved that.

John Morris
Toronto, 1986

Chapter 1

Where Wealthy Men Gather

International yachting differs from those other sports sufficiently glamorous to make newspaper headlines in one important respect. A rich man with a spare-time interest in sailing can, through the application of money, ego and publicity, turn himself into a sporting titan. The viewing and reading public may see a tycoon at the helm of his ocean racer as it wins, say, the Fastnet Race and the image will be indelible. In the unlikely event of it being reported that the hero lay prostrate on his bunk throughout the four-day classic and it was only as the vessel approached the finishing line that his clammy hand grasped the wheel, that same public would not wish to know.

Something about the notion of one man and his boat, be it ever so vast, appeals directly to the collective consciousness. Prince Philip and Edward Heath both gave up yacht racing many years ago, but to many people either name instantly produces a mental photograph of the intrepid mariner against a backdrop of sea and sky. Herbert von Karajan is almost as well known at the helm of his sloop as he is on the conductor's rostrum, yet ill-health has for a long time restricted his sailing.

Wealthy men can, of course, buy control of soccer clubs or

baseball teams, but they are never going to trot out on to the pitch. Nor will the crowd, or the media, be interested in hero-worshipping the chairman if his team wins the cup final or the World Series. Enzo Ferrari is, perhaps, better known than most of his drivers, but not everyone can be born into a motoring dynasty. His fellow Formula One constructors and team bosses have generally spent a lifetime around oily engines, yet still the glamorous young men at the wheel hog the headlines. And jumping from the Mercedes into a Formula One cockpit on the back straight of the Nurburgring is more likely to provide death than glory.

Yachting, though, can make a weekend competitor an international figure. In the last America's Cup at Newport, Rhode Island, in 1983, the English and Australian press portrayed the struggle between the yachts of two of the challenging countries as an epic struggle between Peter de Savary and Alan Bond, the millionaires bankrolling *Victory '83* and *Australia II* respectively. Both were invariably interviewed on the Atlantic dockside after each race, resplendent in club blazer and white ducks, although they had followed the entire proceedings from a launch – watching through binoculars or on television. Indeed, two years earlier, during the Cowes Week staging of the 1981 Admiral's Cup, de Savary and Bond made a now notorious bet. After a great deal of fine Burgundy in an Isle of Wight restaurant the rivals wagered US$10,000 in gold on the outcome of a race between their two boats the next day. To the horror of their professional crews they wanted to helm the yachts themselves. 'Peter's a good club sailor but not for the real stuff,' said one when told of the plan. 'His job is to stay on the dock and keep the cheque book dry.' Bond's crew reacted in much the same way.

Sir Thomas Lipton is a name that few of the many millions of people around the world who occasionally brew a cup of Lipton's tea would be familiar with. Those customers who do recognise the name probably do so because of his obsessive pursuit of the America's Cup before the Second World War, rather than the subtle blending of orange pekoe or the skilful management of the family grocery empire. In a succession of fast J-class racers named *Shamrock I–V*, the provisions magnate squandered millions, probably more even in real terms than today's competitors at Fremantle, near Perth. His yachting exploits made him a household name, yet he never won the Cup.

Nearer our own time is the case of Sir James Hardy. There can hardly be an adult Australian, bar teetotallers and the Band of Hope, who has not tasted a glass of wine from the broad and excellent Hardy family vineyards in South Australia. Yet is he 'Jim the Vigneron' to the Australian public? No. Without ever coming close to winning the 'Auld Mug', as the America's Cup trophy is known, in over twenty years of involvement, Sir Jim features in a whole generation's mental scrapbook as the man standing on or near a twelve-metre yacht, usually saying to an interviewer: 'Next time . . .'

It would be both churlish and untrue to assert that these men and others like them have supported and subsidised a sport that demands vast amounts of their time and money in pursuit of column inches, appearances on television and the easy celebrity that goes with such things. They are in the grip of an obsession. But fame is as much a part of the cocktail as a bar-taut genoa sheet or a ridiculously dainty twelve-metre bow bobbing and dipping through early morning waves. Possibly it is the most addictive component of the mixture. Poverty, fright and even boredom have made men give up yacht racing, yet the thrill of sporting fame, of parity with the blessed young gods of pitch and wicket, is seldom willingly surrendered.

In the past decade there has been an additional factor at work. Around the Cup gather a small group of wealthy and powerful men. Some are rich in their own right. Others manage the funds of huge corporations. It is an elite. Membership conveys a patina, an image, which is worth a great deal when walking into the office of an international merchant bank and asking for a line of credit that will finance the ambitious takeover of a company twice the size of one's own. The Hong Kong Bank of Australia, a subsidiary of the giant Hong Kong and Shanghai Bank, is the largest independent sponsor of the Bond syndicate – an A\$1 million investment. The company says he is a valued customer, but it is undeniably true that a decade before winning the Cup Bond would have had to have asked politely for a loan of A\$1 million, let alone a donation. In the takeover-mad 1980s a line of credit is the path to glory and the Cup has shown itself to be no bad patch in which to cultivate borrowing power.

In some instances a club or syndicate can subsume the admittedly powerful egos of its members and become an aggregate obsessive. The New York Yacht Club, shattered by the loss to the Australians of the Cup they had held for 132 years, is one example. When textile magnate Arthur Wullschleger, designated the America II project director for the recovery of the Cup, could say in 1984, 'We don't have a budget as such. We intend to spend whatever it takes to win back that Cup. Money is the least of our worries,' one heard echoes of Kennedy's determination to put a man on the moon – irrespective of what it either cost or proved. Will Wullschleger become famous over the next six months from October 1986? Probably not exactly a household name, but a fair bit better known than he would have been back at the loom in North Carolina.

In wrath the New York Yacht Club acts more like an angry millionaire despot than a committee of vastly successful grown-up businessmen. When Dennis Conner, one of the world's top twelve-metre helmsmen, stepped ashore in Newport from his boat *Liberty* after losing the final Cup race and hence the trophy itself to *Australia II*, his patrons, as one man, turned their backs on the profoundly shaken skipper. If the traditional threat to replace the Cup in its glass case with the head of the losing helmsman was abandoned it was probably not through delicacy of feeling but because of the presence of too many television cameras. However, Conner's considered reaction was not to wash his hands of the whole daft business, but instead to cross the continent to his home town of San Diego and lead the Sail America syndicate into the coming series.

What of the interested but non-obsessed participant? Ted Turner, founder and operator of the successful twenty-four-hour television news service Cable News Network, has been one of America's best twelve-metre helmsmen and Conner's arch-rival. When told of his opponent's non-stop practice schedule prior to Newport, Turner could only drawl: 'Can you imagine? A grown man who sails *every* day?' Perhaps not surprisingly he has decided that Fremantle can carry on its aquatic jamboree without him.

These are the figureheads, the men that even the strap-hanging passenger on the Clapham omnibus has vaguely heard of. But while they step in and out of helicopters, throw high-society balls with Royal Marine bands and wheel and deal with fellow millionaires, some fairly ordinary tradesmen and sons of toil are out on the ocean pulling and hauling and grinding and sweating to make it all happen. One thing the rival syndicates can tacitly agree on is the need to encourage an unquestioning Corinthian idealism among the young men who sail the boats. Ethics are not at stake here, just the simple fact that if crew salaries, transfer fees and superannuation came into play, the costs would kill even the most expensive sporting event yet devised.

At Newport in 1983 the crew of *Australia II*, whose win in the promotional and image terms was of literally inestimable value to Alan Bond, were paid A$15 a day each. Their wage has not gone up since. 'I often ask myself is it fair that the poor little buggers who go to sea in one of the wettest boats ever evolved get only fifteen dollars a day when these large corporate sponsors are pouring millions of bucks into what is essentially advertising?' pondered Warren Jones, executive director of the Bond syndicate. 'It's almost a travesty to think that the million-dollar sponsorship is going to trickle down to pay some guy fifteen dollars a day. But that's how the system works. I'm almost feeling guilty.'

It is no secret around the waterfront that there was unhappiness in the aftermath of Australia's Cup win. Winning skipper John Bertrand confirms that he received no cash bonus for the victory, and only just broke even on his personal finances over the campaign as a whole. Some crew members went thousands of pounds into debt to make their participation possible. Although he says he feels no bitterness, Bertrand will not be helming for Bond or anyone else in the forthcoming series. Jones maintains that a new system drawn up since 1983 will ensure that a helmsman who sails for Bond's syndicate will get at least £50,000 – if he wins. Bertrand did, of course, go on to make at least US$1 million from his bestselling autobiography *Born To Win*.

In America, crewing aboard a twelve-metre in the Cup has always been a traditional pastime for the well-born Ivy League jock with a year or two to kill between Yale and Wall Street. Asked what it indicated to him when considering hiring young men that they had sailed in the Cup, a distinguished Manhattan banker simply said: 'It is an act that defines a lifetime.' With expansion of interest in the Cup to include California, and even an attempt from landlocked Chicago, the stranglehold of the social register upon the event is dwindling. As the focus of American corporate wealth and growth shifts to the sun belt – a long way from saltwater – the long-term effect, should the trophy return to the New York Yacht Club's panelled halls, will be fascinating.

For Britain, the army and the navy have always been discreet suppliers of husky young men to toil aboard soaking wet twelve-metre yachts. The public should not, of course, gain the impression that it pays taxes to provide millionaires with 'foredeck gorillas', so the commitment is kept as far from the spotlight as possible. At

Newport in 1983 a good half of Peter de Savary's Victory syndicate were on loan or long leave from the armed forces. When *Victory '83* needed a new mast from England urgently, it arrived by that most exclusive of shipping lines, the Royal Navy. HMS *Invincible* just happened to be paying a courtesy visit nearby, and who would notice a ninety-foot length of extruded aluminium amongst the operational turmoil of an aircraft carrier? Certainly the world's press didn't. (Prince Andrew was among the crew guarding this vital piece of cargo.) No other country takes such an indulgent attitude with its soldiers and sailors; still, it seems a safe assumption that only Britain still has cavalry regiments whose members get hunting leave – complete with an army horse.

This recruitment from the somewhat closed world of top yacht clubs and the military provides a contrast with the Australian method of finding a crew. The Australia II syndicate threw a national net as widely as possible to scoop up those with the time and the talent to sail for the America's Cup. Those with potential on paper were invited to attend the team's Fremantle headquarters for a short period of actual training and racing. In this way 200 applicants in November 1984 were whittled down to thirty-five by Easter of 1985. Parallel approaches were used by the South Australia and Kooka-burra syndicates – although the latter took the precaution, under-standable for a newcomer to twelve-metre racing, of paying their helmsman and other key crew sufficiently large salaries to ensure their loyalty. Of the A$5.5 million initial Parry budget (it later escalated to A$20 million), around ten per cent was allocated for expenditure on 'crew costs'. Lawrie Smith, the British yachtsman who steered *Victory '83* at Newport, was hired by Kookaburra for three months in early 1986 at a fee of A$4,000 a week – somewhat more, pro rata, than the managing director's salary.

What of the town that these young hopefuls and heavyweight professionals were arriving in? Fremantle is the port at the mouth of the Swan River – Perth is up-river, twelve miles away by road on the Stirling Highway (named after the naval captain who founded the colony of West Australia in 1829). It is a small city, bounded to the north by the river, to the east by a high ridge giving splendid sea views, and to the west by the Indian Ocean. Going south it hugs the freight tracks and dribbles away in a smattering of small weatherboard and iron houses towards the heavy industry of Kwinana, West Australia's unlovely answer to Scunthorpe or Gary,

Indiana. The population lives by the sea in both senses of the word. As the principal dock for the state during its early years and the main outlet for its wealth during the gold rush period a century ago, Fremantle had an importance vastly out of proportion to its modest population of 20,000. The solid, square-shouldered and stuccoed buildings of the West End commercial and shipping district, the best preserved volume of Victorian architecture anywhere in Australia, speak eloquently of the days when ships queued for wharf space and empty warehouses were as rare as hotels with a vacant room.

The harbour still moves an increasingly valuable volume of containers each year, but as a major source of employment it is finished. Hundreds now work on the wharves where thousands of 'lumpers' once toiled. Profitable maritime activity has shifted half a mile south to the fishing harbour, where Portuguese and Italian immigrants and their children have built a thriving industry on catching and exporting crayfish. Three hundred or so crayboats are based here, the bulk of their delicate catch going to Japan and the Far East. Around the town examples of grandiose marble and terracotta villas, such as would be unremarkable in the suburbs of Naples or Ancona, testify to the handsome incomes which these delicate crustacean cousins of the lobster have provided. Fremantle is as much Italian as it is Australian. *Il Globo* is displayed on every newsstand and, since most of its delicatessens and small grocery shops are run by Italians or their descendants, eight different grades of olive oil are more readily available than barbecue sauce.

Despite a vigorous and healthy underlying pulse, it is superficially a sleepy little town. 'You could fire a cannon from one end of the High Street to the other at noon and probably not hit anybody,' said Fred Robinson, the social worker appointed at an early stage by the state government to alleviate the harmful effects of the Cup upon 'Freo', as it is affectionately known to every one of its inhabitants.

During the past decade Fremantle, once the gateway to Australia for hundreds of thousands of immigrants who poured from their £10 berths aboard scruffy ships into the impersonal, Ellis Island vastness of the passenger terminal, has opened its arms to a new kind of immigrant. Craftspeople, university lecturers, born-again divorcees, artists, writers, gentleman builders and mid-rank media folk drifted to the town by the VW-ful. For refugees from Australia's neat green sprawling suburbs and the easily available dream of a brick house on a quarter-acre block, the cheek-by-jowl jumble of Fremantle's largely pre-First World War cottages and terraces proved irresistible. Furthermore, it was cheap. As the numbers of trendies swelled, the warm feeling of living next door to a stevedore or a machine operator from the huge biscuit factory, 'real people' as the newcomers would put it, was enhanced by the knowledge that there were also neighbours with whom they would feel at home sharing a bottle of Cabernet Sauvignon living just down the street. And all the while property values crept gratifyingly upwards.

The group who embodied the changes most visibly were the Rajneeshis – 'Orange People'. Their 'ashram' (commune) was based in the old Trades Hall – a fine old building virtually on the waterfront. Distinguished by the custom of dressing always in the colours of the rising or setting sun and carrying a photograph of their now fugitive leader, the Bagwhan, around their necks, the Rajneeshis became a very familiar part of the Fremantle street scene. To a hard-nosed, largely working-class community which had never had very much and had worked hard for that, the sight of these young, almost exclusively middle-class and well-educated drop-outs was a severe provocation. When less exotic newcomers began to eat in the Rajneeshis' cheap but excellent vegetarian restaurant and to employ their building company for its reliability and workmanship, suspicion began to harden into dislike. More worrying still was the unholy alliance between a new breed of entrepreneur developers, who wanted to take the town towards a very different future, and the Rajneeshis, who were to build it for them.

When the Cup was won for Australia at Newport in September 1983 it did not take long for realisation to dawn in Fremantle that something very big indeed was coming its way. A process of gentrification and redevelopment that might have taken a generation to accomplish was going to happen in a period of three years. Business rents began to creep up, ludicrous lease agreements were asked for semi-derelict shops and, in the background, big fish cruised, looking for parcels of land. It was in the housing market that the first casualties occurred. Graffiti shouting 'Don't lose your house for the Cup' began to appear; at about the same time estate agents started to send circulars to householders offering them alternative accommodation if they would offer their homes for rental during the six-month period of the yacht racing. Landlords with apartment blocks began to daydream of emptying them for rehabilitation and then rental to the affluent 'yotties' and the tourists who would come in their wake. As the months went by they stopped daydreaming and did it.

Action produces reaction and a counter-alliance began to emerge. The physically dispossessed, losing their rented flats and houses, started to combine with the mentally evicted, the middle-class newcomers who had fallen in love with a charming seedy town that now looked set to become Australia's St Tropez. Community pressure groups were formed. One leader of such a group ran for mayor in the local elections on an anti-Cup ticket. He was not elected, but nor was he disgraced by the poll. A street theatre troupe emerged and began to perform morality tales against the regatta. Television producers, by now almost more numerous than stevedores in the streets of south Fremantle, saw a story on their doorsteps, and documentaries on such earnest themes as 'The Future of Freo' acquired researchers, film crews and budgets. As the bureaucracy and the media cranked themselves up for a new round of issue politics, saving Fremantle developed into almost as big a growth industry as the building, maintenance and racing of twelve-metre yachts.

Meanwhile, Perth was up with the ball and running in a very different direction. Never a city to pay much attention to the past when a bigger and brighter future could be glimpsed around the corner, it embraced a new age of boosterism. If there was ever a litter problem in the wide streets running down to the Swan River, it could probably be blamed on discarded prospectuses with the application page torn out and despatched to some hopeful new company on the city stock exchange's booming Second Board. When a triumphant Bond and his crew brought the Auld Mug home from Newport in October 1983, the motorcade from Fremantle to Perth was watched by 450,000 people, half the city's population. Those who know a bit about the inhabitants reckon that the other fifty per cent were probably at home planning a hotel or a real estate development for the 1986/7 defence. Six huge new hotels have opened in the past year alone, with more tower cranes sprouting from the corner of every block.

Biggest of all, and illustrative of the can-do mentality, is the casino and resort project on the shores of the Swan, opposite the business district. Two years ago (1984) it was nothing more than an optimistic set of applications. No major Australian city had a casino, despite a national addiction to gambling in all its forms. When permission was granted to middle-rank local entrepreneur Dallas

Dempster to go ahead, he promptly mortgaged everything his prosperous family possessed and borrowed A$30 million from the bank to fund his share of the project. When shares were offered by prospectus to the West Australian public – equity, it is to be remembered, in an untried company operating in a new field planning to build a huge A$100 million complex to a punishing schedule on a rubbish tip that first had to be reclaimed – they were fifty per cent over-subscribed on the first morning. Plans to allocate stock to institutions in Sydney and Melbourne had to be abandoned; the locals swallowed the lot. Their grandfathers had had the gold boom, their fathers the nickel boom. Now they were to have the Cup boom.

Shares sold at a ninety per cent premium of the fifty-cent issue price within hours of Burswood Management going public. Mr Dempster's sixty million units were worth A$55 million, and he got his title deeds back from the bank. Another giant had joined Bond, Holmes à Court, Ralph Sarich, Denis Horgan and Peter Briggs in a city that produces multi-millionaires the way others grow traffic jams. On a parallel course to the entrepreneurs and wheeler-dealers, and unbeaten in speed of growth, the bureaucracy flourished. Any newcomer to Australia tends to bring with him among his mental baggage the image of a freewheeling society, minimally regulated. What he finds is a proliferation of government and administration that would make a Scandinavian, even a Frenchman, feel at home. Almost every ministerial portfolio and ministry, save defence, is duplicated between the state and federal governments. A vigorous layer of local government sits beneath these two, blaming Canberra or the state capital as often as possible for local shortcomings. Within weeks of its arrival in Australia, the Cup had acquired a thick coating of bureaucratic barnacles. After a year the government felt obliged to publish an official guide to the committees and departments that had mushroomed from Cup spoors. No one could understand it.

Western Australia appointed a minister for the Cup. Canberra allocated around A$32 million in grants for spending in Perth and Fremantle in the build-up to the Cup, and thought that it too ought to have a minister to oversee the spending. Ministers need advisers and officers, so in early 1985 Captain Beresford Noble, as chief-of-staff, with a team of aides beneath him, was hired. Supporting them were six major committees representing marinas, communications, law and public safety, transport, urban planning and, finally, visitors and tourists. Many individuals at the centre of things sat on more than one committee, not to mention the sub-committees. They were always in meetings, and anyone wanting to see them had to make an appointment for an hour earlier even than the rising time of the young crewmen on the twelve-metre yachts.

It was, too, a flourishing time for 'consultants'. Large sums were involved and the mighty engine of government had never before been harnessed to yacht racing. If in doubt, hire an expert – or someone who appears to be one – became the watchword. At the operational level – for example, of the young and enthusiastic senior public health engineer whose conclusions over Fremantle's effluent problem had to be checked at vast expense by a consultant, because the engineer knew nothing about yachting – the reliance on 'here today, gone tomorrow' outsiders became a considerable irritant. What he knew, he knew, and he knew about shit. Some public servants left their jobs to become consultants. They were close enough to the action to seize the opportunity of boarding the gravy train whilst there were still seats to be had.

In some ways the public service began to mirror the invidious distinction found among military personnel between those who have seen action and those yet to hear bullets whizz past their ears. Functionaries who could put America's Cup after their names found themselves acquiring more staff and bigger offices, and travelling to faraway places such as Sardinia and Bermuda – destinations not normally found on a civil service itinerary. This new elite hardly endeared themselves to colleagues still struggling with subsidies to wheat growers or laundry facilities in the hospital service. Whether it was pure pique or whether distance lent detachment is impossible to say, but public servants on non-Cup duties began to wonder out loud at middle-class dinner parties and social gatherings whether the whole Cup extravaganza was really worth all the effort and dislocation it involved. 'Don't lose sight of the fact that this is not an international event. It's not the Olympics where, by custom and practice, each team represents a whole nation,' a very senior civil servant said over a year before racing began. 'This is a group of extremely rich individuals who have come to play with their boats off our coast and we are breaking our backs for them.'

Personal wealth may have been apparent around the twelve-metre syndicates but, without exception, each of them was looking very hard for corporate sponsorship to meet the extraordinary costs of their campaigns. Few millionaires wish to empty their wallets into the wet and bottomless bilges of a twelve-metre yacht. Those who have done it before, like Alan Bond and Peter de Savary, were particularly aware that the 1986/7 Cup series was going to be a beast so large and ravenous of money and resources that it could suck in and destroy individuals, no matter how wealthy. De Savary decided to stay out, despite an initial involvement in the entry. Accordingly, in the seven countries sending teams to Fremantle the syndicates went searching for companies that, in return for a name on a bow, sweater, or spinnaker, would part with hundreds of thousands of dollars to keep the whole game rolling. Initially the yachtsmen were confident that single big sponsors could be found who would underwrite their whole campaigns; a minimum cost of around US$10 million for most teams; more for some.

No one found these fairy godmothers. Each syndicate had stories of how they had been a hair's breadth from landing the big one. Philip Tolhurst, legal director of the British syndicate, maintains that their greatest chance of a single big sponsor was sabotaged by a call to the company concerned from a sceptical Royal Thames Yacht Club member. In the early days relations between the club and the Challenge syndicate were far from harmonious, and some RTYC men thought it would be better if the whole business was quietly disposed of without the pain of going to Perth.

The wave of euphoria and national pride that swept Australia in the immediate aftermath of Bond's victory at Newport failed to turn into a rush of supporting dollars. By mid-1985 the Australia III syndicate had still to find half the financial support they needed, and the biggest backer at that stage was still Bond's local vehicle, the Swan Brewery. The ten-dollar bills of ordinary Australians joining the Defence Club was a very important source of revenue, as was the licensing of the boxing kangaroo logo that has almost become an alternative national flag for Australians.

In Europe the most successful fund-raising syndicate was the Yacht Club Italiano of Genoa. By Easter of last year (1985) they had ten sponsors who had donated A$1 million each. The list read like a *Who's Who* of Italian business, with Aermacchi and Perugina among the best-known. Paradoxically, the giants of German industry, particularly the motor sector where support had been promised, found themselves unable to come forward to support the Potsdamer Yacht Club's campaign (it would have been the first in the distinguished history of German yachting and from a club where the Kaiser sailed). PYC reluctantly dropped out of the Royal Perth's field of vision. The biggest pledged sponsor, Porsche, had counted on the 1987 Cup taking place at Newport. In the USA they sold thousands of cars, in Australia next to none. Porsche pulled out.

In the United States the willingness of corporate America to jump into the big seas off Fremantle proved far less than the twelve-metre community had expected. The New York Yacht Club may have been able to use endless photographs of its skipper John Kolius posing behind a soft-top Cadillac – the club's first business sponsor – but elsewhere around the country syndicates were throwing in their hands because of lack of money. 'We were all banking on much bigger participation from the TV networks, but that doesn't seem to be happening,' said Dennis Conner of the San Diego syndicate in mid-1985. Of course, the television companies were very much watching pre-start manoeuvring in Western Australia where the thorny subject of who would get the television rights and for how much was very much on the table for discussion. Sitting right there at the head was Mark MacCormack, legendary founder of International Management Group – agents to Angela Rippon and the Pope.

MacCormack was a small-town, small-time lawyer in Cleveland, Ohio, until he discovered Arnold Palmer. The latter was already a top golfer; MacCormack's genius was to turn him into an industry – endorsing products, selling his own brand of clubs, making personal appearances to open supermarkets and occasionally playing in golf tournaments. The name Arnold Palmer became worth millions of dollars, a percentage of them accruing to his agent and promoter. What could be done with one sportsman in a single sport could be done elsewhere. Once most of the top tennis stars had signed with International Management Group, MacCormack's vehicle, Wimbledon became virtually his tournament – to the discomfort of the old guard at the All England Club. Probably his greatest coup was to secure the marketing rights for Pope John Paul's triumphal tour of Britain in 1982. Of course, IMG made nothing more than its operational costs out of the event (all royalties went to the Catholic Church to cover the huge costs of the operation) but the prestige of having fronted for Christ's vicar on earth was not thrown away by IMG.

Staff inside the organisation tell the story of a routine meeting with MacCormack in late September 1983 when the news came through that the Australians had achieved the unthinkable and wrested the America's Cup from the vice-like grip of the New York Yacht Club. No one around the boardroom table was particularly interested in yachting and the discussion continued along its previous lines. Suddenly MacCormack, who had been doodling on the yellow legal notepad that goes everywhere with him, announced that yacht racing was the future and that IMG ought to go down to Australia to see if marketing rights could be secured. 'No one paid much attention really,' said an executive who was present. 'However, the next day we found that Mark was already on an aeroplane heading for Perth.'

Once in the West Australian capital he found that the Royal Perth Yacht Club were already embroiled with domestic sponsors and television arrangements – but that the international field was wide open. Very quickly the rights to market and broadcast the largest and costliest regatta in history to the rest of the world were secured by IMG. Payments would go to the club, with a percentage taken by MacCormack.

From a television viewpoint the problems of broadcasting the Cup were complex from the outset. Firstly there are almost three events: the elimination series to find the defender of the Cup, the elimination series to choose the challenger for the Cup and, lastly, the best of seven races' final between these two yachts. The audiences for each of these would be different. Australian audiences for the defender series would be huge, international interest small. The reverse would be true for the challenger series, and the task of persuading Australian networks to cover four months of races that were of little interest to them would be formidable. Viewer interest in the final itself was potentially vast, but that was six months and hundreds of races away. And even then there was the risk of a final between South Australia and New Zealand – a race that would turn off 100 million TV sets.

Secondly, there was the question of physical access to the course both by sea and air. Clearly it would be impossible to allow any TV station with the desire to do so to just climb into a helicopter or launch and start filming. Early on in the planning stage the Royal Perth Yacht Club decided that it would opt for pooled coverage by a combination of the four Australian networks rather than sell exclusive rights to any one organisation. The rationale for this was that none of the commercial channels has transmitters which covered the whole of the country. The Australian Broadcasting Corporation, which does have that coverage, could not afford to mount such a vast outside broadcast operation. 'We felt that this event belonged to the whole of Australia and that everyone should get a chance to see it,' explained Noel Robins, world-class yachtsman and executive director of the Royal Perth's America's Cup committee. 'That led us to suggest the pool arrangement.'

It was the signal from this joint broadcasting effort that MacCormack had the rights to sell to TV stations around the world. Estimates of its worth varied, with some observers saying US$10 million and IMG's man in Perth maintaining that the real figure was more like US$1 million. What remains certain is that they will be the only pictures taken close to the sailing action, and Mr MacCormack will have his finger on the switch.

What the sponsors hope to buy through supporting the America's Cup — and some sceptics maintain they are getting nothing at all, merely pouring money away in the great tradition of Sir Thomas Lipton — is that most intangible and perishable of commodities, a glossy high-quality image. No one could imagine that the public would believe the yachts were better sailed by crews fuelled on high-grade Scotch whisky. Of course not. It was the sleek patina of ultimate sport at ultimate expense that made White Horse whisky decide that it was worth a A$400,000 payment to the Royal Perth Yacht Club, via MacCormack, to become the official whisky of the twelve-metre series. If sales boom beyond a certain point as a consequence of media coverage of what is happening off Fremantle, then a bigger royalty will be paid — the A$400,000 is only a minimum guarantee.

At another level pure altruism with a dash of condescension operates. Westpac, Australia's biggest banking corporation and a vastly profitable company, decided at a very early stage after the Newport victory that they would be one of the Royal Perth's principal corporate sponsors, at a cost of A$350,000. No one within the bank seemed terribly interested in what they would actually receive for the equivalent of the annual operating costs of a small outback branch. 'We prefer to look upon it as a gesture of help from a large organisation to a small one trying to run a large event,' said one of the Westpac directors rather grandly to a syndicate chief who was seeking sponsorship for his half-built twelve-metre yachts.

Yet when push comes to shove, as Australians are fond of saying, this is not always an attitude that can be justified, either to more junior staff or to the bank's small shareholders. These people know that they are not going to be the ones entertained to long, languid lunches on long, equally languid launches at the Royal Perth Yacht Club, or offered a suite for the weekend on the cruise liner *Sea Goddess* which Westpac has chartered and moored in Fremantle harbour for the duration of the Cup. These facilities, and others of a similar nature made possible by a sponsor's financial backing of the yacht racing series, offer an opportunity for the genuinely exclusive entertaining of highly rated clients and customers. After all, the Ritz is open to all those with a sufficiently well-padded bank account, but the committee boat at the start line of an America's Cup race is a little harder to gain access to.

Yet a great deal of the interest and razzmatazz around the Fremantle Cup series has rested on the belief that for the first time in 135 years this esoteric, expensive yet engaging sport has mass appeal. No yacht race in history has ever before found an audience in the way that television brought the final duel between Dennis Conner and John Bertrand into viewers' lives around the world. Victory for Australia, of all countries, made flesh the notion that egalitarian, unstuffy outdoor people who tried harder could triumph over the blue blazers and absurd boaters of the New York Yacht Club. Initial entries from nearly thirty yacht clubs around the world showed that the days of the Newport cartel, an influential insider group awash with old money from the very cream of international yachting, amusing themselves every three or four years with a little summer struggle over the Auld Mug, were finished or, at the very least, numbered.

Sponsors would have fled from the idea of being seen to bankroll such a tiny and indulgent group. White Horse are clear that they would have supported no Cup prior to this one. At the higher reaches of the mass market much commercial success depends upon creating the illusion that one is catering for an exclusive and discerning minority that is desirable yet absolutely minute numerically, whilst in reality supplying the product to a larger and affluent minority who perceive themselves as somewhat special. However, groups and minorities, however glamorous, can be too small, and the old America's Cup clique would certainly have fallen into that category.

This sort of yachting has been, since 1983, up there with the aspirational glamour pastimes such as skiing – good to get behind and fine for the image of an up-market company. Yet if the hundreds and thousands of dollars spent were to be tangibly beneficial the company needed to get its high-level contacts right out there on the start line with the insiders, where once only an Ivy League background and blue blood registered. Without that ambience the America's Cup wouldn't have the cachet that has brought it this far. Many sponsors are trapped in a dilemma. Their customers know high-level junketing when they see it and know too that they are paying for it. Yet one cannot pretend that twelve-metre racing is World Series baseball, available to allcomers for the price of a seat. No wonder that some of the men signing the cheques are wondering what they have got into and what they are going to get out of it – and in some cases, how they can get out of it.

Chapter 2

Have You Got What It Takes?

One of the main elements in the America's Cup's unique sporting flavour is the prevalence of defeat – for 132 years no one knew what it was like nor what resources it might take to win the Auld Mug. Of course, some fine skippers, excellent crews and first-rate yachts defended the Cup for the New York Yacht Club over that period. Yet when one realises that the best challenger in the Cup's history (until *Australia II*'s victory) was Tommy Sopwith in *Endeavour*, who managed to win two of the seven races against the Vanderbilt syndicate's *Rainbow* in 1934, it becomes clear that the home side enjoy enormous advantages. Since the best-of-seven formula was adopted in 1930, there has been a complete whitewash (a four-nil defeat of the foreign boat) no less than seven times out of the twelve challenges for the Cup. Pressure on the defending crew has not been of the highest order. History and statistical analysis told them that they had only to draw on their depth of experience in home waters, sail competently around the course in a sound boat, and let the overseas challenger self-destruct for the Auld Mug to remain safely on its pedestal at the New York Yacht Club's headquarters on West 44th Street, Manhattan. The successful crews from the NYYC could not answer the burning question: 'What does it take to win the Cup?' Their experience of hanging on to it was of a different and, ultimately, lower order.

Alan Bond earned the knowledge the hard way. 'When I first challenged with *Southern Cross* in 1974,' he has recalled, 'I did not realise how much there was to learn before any challenger from a distant shore could beat the Americans with their highly trained crews, massive financial backing and important home-water advantages. As we went into successive challenges in 1977 and 1980 we built up our expertise in many areas, including our management ability arising from protests, disputes and interpretations of the rules. By the time we reached our fourth challenge in 1983 we knew what it took to win.'

The crux of the tangible logistical problem is to put together a team and a construction programme that must develop over a period of between two and three years, a timespan more usually found in building developments than sport, and bring them to a crescendo in just a few weeks under enormous external pressure, both from publicity and from the other competitors. John Bertrand, the first challenging skipper in history to win the Cup, has thought long and hard over four campaigns going back to 1970 about the obstacles to success.

'The only thing I can liken it to is sending a rocket ship to the moon,' said Bertrand, 'except that all the way through the development you know that you must blast off on a certain date. There are no excuses and it's a race with the Russians and about three other countries.' Commentators often try to draw a comparison with Formula One motor racing, but Bertrand believes that campaigning a twelve-metre in the America's Cup is on a different plane of complexity, because there are more people involved and it is over a longer period of time than a Grand Prix season. 'It is over three years and then it comes down to two months' racing – without any warm-up sessions.'

When it comes to the question of what it takes to win the Cup Bertrand is an incomparable source – he is the only man to have done it. Untroubled by modesty, he is direct but neither vain nor arrogant. His decision not to sail in the 1987 series and attempt to defend the Cup he so dramatically won is characteristic of a comfortable, roomy, but not overblown ego. 'I've done it four times, my first campaign was in 1970 with Sir Frank Packer – Jesus Christ, there was a tough old bastard. You've got to be prepared to sweat blood and I was ready to do that while we climbed our Everest. You go for it and you put your life on the line and your family on the line. After four tries and finally climbing Everest I feel, well, what else is left? Do you keep defending it for the rest of your life or do you stop and go into new directions? How many times do they want me to climb the mountain? We've done it, we've been up there and that was the whole point of fourteen years of trying.'

Without a doubt he is annoyed by accusations that he doesn't want to be the man to lose the trophy it took so long to win. 'Say whatever you like. How many times am I supposed to win the damned thing?' Even more irritating to Bertrand are the people who presume that he is under a moral obligation to sail again to show that it was no fluke. 'The fact is we've done it. It certainly wasn't a fluke and we're very proud of what we've achieved.' He would also be among the first to stress the importance of having the right boat, first-class sails and fittings, and top-rate shore facilities to create a successful campaign. His great-grandfather, Thomas Pearkes, sailed as engineer with Sir Thomas Lipton in two of his *Shamrock* challenges. There can have been few jobs more 'nuts and bolts' than keeping a huge J-class yacht in racing trim.

Newport in 1983 represented both a triumph and a crisis for those who held up the hardware as pre-eminent among the problems of twelve-metre racing. Ben Lexcen, the Sydney-based designer responsible for the Bond syndicate's boats, had produced two yachts for the series, *Challenge 12* and *Australia II*. The former was traditional, fast and efficient; the latter was more radical and possessed a 'secret' keel – later to be unveiled with its now famous 'wings'. It made the boat sail faster to windward, tack through the wind more quickly, and also point higher – that is, it was able to sail more nearly straight into the wind than its rivals. On other points of sailing, particularly with the wind at the stern, *Australia II* possessed no clear advantage.

In the early days of testing the two boats off Perth there was a time when *Challenge 12* would effortlessly pull away from her supposedly faster rival whenever the two boats turned away from the wind and hoisted spinnakers. Aboard the winged wonder senior syndicate people began to feel that, as so often with 'design breakthroughs', they had bought a pup. While the slide rules and calculators came out one sailor began to think about seaweed. A notoriously heavy and prolific kelp infests the Indian Ocean in this area. Could the highly inventive, state-of-the-art, forward-sloping keel have collected a bunch of distinctly low-tech weed? *Australia II* was turned head-to-wind and drifted slowly astern. As she did so a giant haystack of sea grass slid out from its resting place at the tip of the keel. Downwind speed now came up to expectations.

Leaving aside such humorous but minor problems, the new boat was an enormous breakthrough in design. She was a car with one more gear than her rivals. Thousands of hours of tank-testing and model-making had produced a boat that could do what no other had managed in 132 years. This was a triumph for the researchers and theoreticians. But it also brought a crisis which arose from the belief that a successful challenge for 1987 could now only be founded upon more computer hours and endless days dragging models up and down the world's ship tanks in an effort to produce another great leap forward. Such work was enormously expensive and ate into budgets that also had to cater for crew training, transport and accommodation. Yet what was the alternative? Everyone in the twelve-metre community had had it drummed into them at Newport that several tons of lead sculpted on a computer graphics screen had achieved what six generations of the world's most expert yachtsmen had consistently failed to do – win the America's Cup.

For example, the British challenge for 1987 is firmly rooted in tank-testing and computer research. While the Australian and American syndicates have jostled and queued around the pools of the Netherlands Ship Model Basin at Wageningen, where Lexcen lived with his wife Yvonne for four months and did the initial work on *Australia II*, the British work began early in 1985 at the National Maritime Institute in Feltham. By May that year Herbert Pearcey, an aerodynamicist who designed the breakthrough 'supercritical wing section' on the Harrier, Trident and VC10 aircraft and who heads the research team, was able to say confidently, 'I don't know whether anyone has ever used a combination of one-third and one-tenth scale models in a tank as systematically and as comprehensively as we have.'

Such confidence is not unusual among scientists who feel they have been given the experimental tools and the budget to get on with the job. At the NMI the British team were testing the designs of David Hollom, whose early work has mostly been on the hulls of world-class model yachts. Seventy miles away in the New Forest village of Beaulieu, veteran twelve-metre designer Ian Howlett has also been drawing hulls for the British effort. His models are tested at the Woolfson Unit at Southampton University, where Howlett himself was once in charge of tank-testing. In spite or, perhaps, because of that experience, he can be sceptical about the benefits of running expensive models up and down giant bathtubs and recording the results with the most costly monitoring equipment that money can buy.

'A tank is a tank,' says Howlett, who at thirty-six has designed twelve-metres for the Cup challenges in 1973, 1976, 1980, 1983 and now 1987. On the last three occasions money was found to pay him and actually build the craft. *Victory '83*, Howlett's boat for Peter de Savary, was acknowledged as perhaps the fastest and best-designed conventional boat of its kind in the world. In Italian hands it won the world twelve-metre championship off Sardinia in 1984. 'You can plough the model up and down the water, suck side-force data up on to magnetic tape, squirt it through a computer and end up with nothing better than an eye watching a needle on a dial. It comes down to the expertise of the people doing the testing – not how big the tank is. Yachts are very different to big ship models.' Howlett is cynical, funny and speaks in truncated, Runyonesque spurts.

'Very tough to get good results. It's not an exact science. Very easy to screw up right through. Plenty have done.' He believes that bad results are worse than no results. Better for an experienced designer to trust his hand and eye. 'The guy who's got a really good feel for it and goes straight in there is going to be in pretty good shape,' in his view. Howlett is a classic example of the personality where science meets art, and fuses. Too great an emphasis on one will cause him to recoil and fervently embrace the other – at least in public.

To a man in love with beautiful boats the concept that owners or syndicates can throw a mountain of data and money at a team of scientists whose primary expertise is a tank or a computer and say, 'This week's problem is to design a radical twelve-metre,' is rank heresy. Skippers such as Bertrand and the legendary Dennis Conner and owners like Alan Bond have consistently made the point, largely to one another, that when the contending twelves cross the start line formed by the America's Cup buoy and the NYYC committee boat they tend to be about as fast as one another. A tenth of a knot would be a big discrepancy. There is an explanation for this – a reason why you don't get similar situations in offshore racing, where frequently a new boat will be so startlingly superior to its rival that for a season it will clean up everything in sight.

'Most of the boats one draws never really get assessed,' believes Howlett. He is sitting in the studio of his thatched cottage-cum-workshop, the drawings for some of the world's most famous twelve-metre boats lie stacked on the shelves. More have been processed and 'squirted', to use a favourite word, into the computer. Not more than a mile or so away the tiny riverside hamlet of Buckler's Hard sleeps in the evening sun. Here the oaks of the New Forest were hewn and trimmed to build the frigates and four-deckers that made the British Navy the most feared and powerful nautical institution in the world. 'Ocean racers and the rest of them are in such a low state of tune that their design limits don't really get explored,' continued Howlett. 'You've got to design something pretty bad not to be able to run with the pack. With twelve-metres everything is a notch or so up. One boat is slower than another – then the world knows about it. These twenty-five-ton machines are being raced in a similar state of tune to Olympic dinghies. No other big yachts ever are in my experience.' He continues to expand the view that designers are of comparatively little importance – Howlett's own words.

Nearly thirty years ago, in 1958, critics treated the British challenger *Sceptre* as a boat absolutely without hope because of just one aspect of her design. '*Sceptre* was condemned for having a bluff, full bow that couldn't go through waves,' explained Howlett. Yet it was identical to the most successful modern boats. 'I've got the drawings here behind me.' He waves a long, thin arm back at a map chest.

Where he believes that radical designs have the most impact is in their psychological effect on the opposition, who immediately believe they are playing the game with one card short in their hand. A widespread and credible (though unproven) theory in the twelve-metre world is that the winged keel of *Australia II* had as many drawbacks as plusses while the boat was in the water: loss of downwind speed, a tendency to wobble, and so forth. The beneficial effect, again not susceptible of measurement, was that the American opposition at Rhode Island, and to a lesser extent the other would-be challengers, felt that they started each race lacking a secret weapon. The secrecy and media hype surrounding the winged keel were crucial factors here; it wouldn't have been enough for the keel simply to be new.

Howlett was the first to make this sort of play in twelve-metre racing. 'The writing was on the wall when we did the bendy mast in *Lionheart,*' recalls the young designer. That boat was the British challenger at Newport in 1980, and though conventional in her hull lines she had a mast that was less of a static skyhook and more of a moving, twisting part of the sail. 'The Americans had never seen anything like it before and didn't know how to build one. They were really rattled and manipulated a protest – a sixty-page document – through Baron Bich, the French challenger. Bond and the Aussies were there and this experience became, I believe, a major factor in the way they played the game with the keel in 1983.'

Two elements are important here. The first is that in the rarefied, utterly irrational world of the America's Cup the opposition both fear and want any new development, even before its contribution, positive or negative, has been tried and assessed. Most of the secrecy surrounding the 1987 Cup – *Kookaburra*'s submarine-style pen with the steel walls, the double chain fence of the New York Yacht Club, and so forth – is there to create a background where the announcement or even rumour of a new go-faster, revolutionary sailing widget cannot be checked or weighed, only feared.

The second and more insidious problem of a radical new development comes for the crew of the boat. Howlett again: 'I don't think I was completely honest in my assessments of the results from that mast. The press were blowing up about the boy wonder with the bendy mast and I wanted to believe in it. Both myself and the crew would have done better to concentrate in other areas. Because we had a gimmick we forgot about the simple stuff that every club sailor knows – getting round the marks right up close, taking wind shifts . . .' According to Howlett, whose ear was pretty close to the ground in Newport, Lexcen's keel was on the verge of being scrapped because skipper John Bertrand didn't believe in it. Certainly the latter's autobiography, *Born To Win,* makes it clear that he had grave doubts about the all-round benefits of the new keel.

Design breakthroughs of a radical nature are clearly a double-edged sword. They can hypnotise the crew that possesses them into suspending their better judgement about the exact benefits obtained, just as much as they may intimidate the opposition into believing that they are sailing a boat that lacks the newest equipment necessary to win. Furthermore, and most dangerous of all, if the crew with the gold filigree halyard or the butter-muslin spinnaker want to maintain their psychological advantage they are obliged to stick to the gimmick come hell or high water.

It may be that the publication of Bertrand's frank and controversial book last year (1985) will knock away some of the credulity of twelve-metre sailors and owners. He makes it clear that while acres of newsprint and yawning hours of television drove into the minds of public and opposition the ineffable, unbeatable superiority of the wonderboat from down under, he and the boys out on the water were facing real problems from their yacht. Tight turning and tacking were fine and dandy on the start line, but on the reaches and square runs, where the wind is abeam of or behind the boat, the opposition would come waltzing right past them – most notably *Azzurra*, the lovely blue Italian boat. On any point of sailing *Australia II* had a tendency to wobble beneath the feet if not absolutely perfectly balanced. When the crews from other Australian boats sailed on her, as they sometimes did, they often found it difficult to stand up and keep their footing against the shake.

When questioned at after-race press conferences about why his boat had looked slow on a particular day Bertrand would just smile enigmatically or mutter something about sail testing. And the willing suspension of disbelief went on. The boys with the cameras, notebooks and microphones went away from the cramped sweatbox of the Newport Armoury and pumped out more kilobytes of information about the invincible white boat with the secret weapon nine feet below the waterline. If lies weren't directly told it was certainly true that no one in Bond's camp came out and said, 'The boat is dead-dog slow on certain points of sailing and we're desperately worried about it.' Who can say where creative psychology ends and pure gamesmanship takes over? More pertinently, what really takes one crew to victory in the America's Cup and leaves another, with a faster boat, floundering?

'It's the intangible psychological aspect that is crucial,' believes Bertrand. 'The tangible areas – the keel, the fund-raising, the management, the technology – you can put all that in place, it's easy. You put it all on paper and do a critical path. It's quickly possible to see if you're two weeks or two months out of tune. All these are the things you can make happen with money and expertise.

'At the eleventh hour, when the technology is finalised and the syndicates are all in place, the learning curve becomes very flat.

Everything happens at about the same speed when you get to the starting line. It's pretty much the same at the Olympic Games – it's the same at any major event I've ever competed in. You'll get, say, six competitors out of the world with theoretically an equal opportunity of winning and it's the same, exactly similar, with the America's Cup. The imponderable, the unmeasurable, is motivation: the character of the people, the strength of mind, whatever you want to call it.' Perhaps it is no accident that the crew of a twelve-metre is eleven men – that crucially sized group found in so many sports from cricket to soccer, and significantly very nearly the same numerically as the army platoon, the unit out of which devotion, heroism, understanding and ultimately victory has always sprung. Bertrand is unusually fond of military metaphors and one of his greatest friends on *Australia II* was 'The Major', a Brisbane army officer with a background in intelligence but with muscles that didn't come from reading cable traffic. 'SAS, for sure,' thought his fellow crewmen, although they didn't ask.

In conversation, Bertrand draws heavily on military analogies to explain the flavours and feelings of leading an America's Cup crew. Asked whether he and his shipmates went partying after the last race with the Cup, so to speak, in their hands, Bertrand replied: 'I'd liken the America's Cup to spending something like four months fighting for your life behind enemy lines in Vietnam – then a parachute rescue team comes in and you are reprieved. You don't have a party. They stick you in a bloody rehabilitation hospital to get you back to the real world.' On another occasion Bertrand spoke with awe of the day when he was privileged to meet the commander of the F14 fighter squadron on board the aircraft carrier USS *Nimitz* (it was probably a big day for the fighter jock, but it is interesting that the yacht skipper felt he was being granted the favour). 'The pressures of decision-making for those guys, dicing with the Russians – and unofficially it's all happening up there – is exactly the same as America's Cup racing,' observed Bertrand. 'Our life's on the line. Five hundred million people are watching.'

The two literary focuses that matter most for Bertrand are Richard Bach's novel of anthropomorphic flying aspirations, *Jonathan Livingstone Seagull*, and the microscopic analysis of the behaviour of American military fliers, Tom Wolfe's book *The Right Stuff*. Both are ultimately to do with the pursuit of personal excellence for its own, holy sake, taking the mind and body into areas where the real world is little more than a vaguely glimpsed backdrop. Oddly enough, in view of Bertrand's experience aboard the floating city of the *Nimitz*, Wolfe's study of the right stuff grew largely out of his 1975 magazine essay 'The Truest Sport: Jousting with Sam and Charlie'. It observes the obsessive, cool and laconic introspection of carrier-based fighter pilots flying into combat over Hanoi. The central character, John Dowd, had been a top basketball player before he began flying F–4Bs for Uncle Sam.

'Now that he was in the military, however, Dowd, like many service athletes, began to get a funny feeling . . . Now that he was in the Navy, something about sports, something he had never thought about, became obvious. Namely all team sports were play-acting versions of military combat,' wrote Wolfe. From the other side of the window and in a less sophisticated manner, Bertrand has seized the same thought.

In the early 1980s a veteran Hollywood B-movie director named Sam Fuller enjoyed something of a cult success with his movie *The Big Red One*. It followed the fortunes through training, D-Day and the fighting slog across Europe to Berlin of just one platoon from the US Army's elite soldiering group, the First Infantry Division. It had the usual quota of bullets and bombs, indeed Fuller uses action as well as anyone who ever looked down a camera lens. But what attracted a huge audience from a generation generally unreceptive to the charms of war movies was the skilful and intuitive portrayal of a group of comrades under immense stress, yet caring for one another, motivating their fellows, and through this both surviving and winning. Tenderness producing the hard will to triumph is a fascinating phenomenon, either afloat or in the ghastly killing ground of Europe, 1944.

Curiously, though, one of the most fragmented, overwrought and unhappy teams at Newport for the America's Cup in 1983 also had the largest component of military personnel and hardware. This was Victory '83, the British syndicate. Apart from Peter de Savary, the largest contributor was the UK taxpayer. This unofficial secret even had a codename, 'Charleston Reprise' (phonetic talk for yes), by which the subject was always referred to lest any passing media pick up on a good theme to fill a lay day and cause questions to be asked in the House of Commons. A large proportion of the sixty or so personnel were on secondment from the army, navy or the Royal Marines. Within the Victory team there was intense rivalry, backbiting and much factionalism. It came from the top downwards and seemed to prove that although the virtues and disciplines of Mars might be necessary to put together a crew capable of winning the America's Cup, one did not obtain them simply by throwing military men in a boat together.

A group of scruffy Aussies, anarchic and in many ways unyielding to authority because of the particular nature of Australian culture, were the ones who found their way towards that group discipline from which the individual may be set free to rise far above his workaday limitations. It was in the psychology of sailing that the key to unbolting the Auld Mug and taking it back to Perth would be found.

Internal haemorrhaging is a favourite phrase of Bertrand's. He uses it constantly to refer to why some teams win and others lose, particularly towards the end of a competition when the noose is tightening. 'It's when the pressure gets so intense that the syndicates and the people defeat themselves without reference to what the opposition are doing to them,' explained the champion skipper. 'The British did that in Newport. We did not defeat them. Their boat was actually very, very good. *Victory '83* could have won the 1983 America's Cup in my opinion. When de Savary started sending people home and switching skippers, going for publicity and not wins, it all fell apart.' Ian Howlett, the designer who could have become as famous a yacht designer as Ben Lexcen but for the phenomenon that Bertrand describes, is an all-out advocate of the importance of psychology in winning at twelve-metre games.

'The whole of each twelve-metre campaign is about avoiding bad decisions. There are people everywhere who want to do the wrong thing and take you down a blind alley,' offers Howlett. 'All the impetus is for bad decisions.' It is to counteract these tendencies that Howlett always wants to be at the race site, helping them wind up, thinking about how to do the job rather than pottering at a drawing board. 'Twelves are primarily a problem of human relations right the way through. You need a bunch of people who get on well and have respect for each other. Not very many of them have to be great sailors.

'If you're winning races easily the psychological poise and strength comes without real effort. If you're losing races, eyes are looking round for a reason. Let's chop it, let's change it. The sailors like to find a mechanical reason for the problem. People driving the boats don't like to say, "I blew it". If you're the helmsman at a press conference after a losing race are you going to say, "Yes, I was a bit slow off the starting line. A few too many wines last night. I was feeling a bit rough."? Much easier to say that number four genoa could be fuller in the top and we need a new rudder. It's basically a question of getting the guys driving the boats to accepting responsibility.' And, of course, only in a strong but compassionate team where the members feel warm and confident towards one another will men find the honesty and directness to accept blame and not let it haunt them on the morrow, when the two giant boats are diving and pecking on the ten-minute gun.

'It's the psychology of winning that's the toughest area to overcome,' says Bertrand. 'That's the area you can't buy with time and money. It's experience and the quality of the people. The difference between winning and losing among the top three competitors at the Olympic Games is how they perceive themselves. The self-image on the starting line – whether you reckon you're going to get whipped by two centimetres or whether you believe you're going to blitz the other guy by the same amount.' This has to be true for each of the men on the boat, not just the skipper standing at the stern with the wheel in his hand. Talking with Bertrand about how the crew worked together the word democracy comes up endlessly. Anyone could say anything to anyone – at least concerning the sailing of the boat. The only hierarchy was founded on excellence. Aboard *Australia II* the youngest winch-grinder, invariably known as 'boat-niggers' in sailing circles, would say to Bertrand, 'Come on John, sail the boat. The wind's left, left.' Aboard Dennis Conner's boat *Liberty* the crew were the best drilled and toughest in the world, faster than *Australia II* in almost every manoeuvre. But hardly anyone except the navigator and tactician dared speak to the imperious Conner. In the weekend before the final race, when the Cup series hung at three all, the crew of *Liberty* toiled to shift lead in and out of the keel, trying to find optimum displacement for the expected conditions. Conner disappeared to play golf for the entire weekend. Yet, despite the discipline, in that final race the crew of *Liberty* blew up completely, particularly the barrel-chested skipper, the finest match-racer in the world. Why?

'Because he faced a competitor that he respected – myself – and he was outgunned in the decision-making process. We had eleven men thinking and feeling as one on board our boat,' answers Bertrand.

'Half-way through the America's Cup one of the *Liberty* crew came up to me, of all people, and said: "I couldn't think of a better guy to lose the America's Cup than Dennis Conner." For a *Liberty* crew member to say that knocked me flat. In my opinion, if I had asked one of our guys to cut off his right arm to win the America's Cup he would have had no hesitation in doing it. That was the kind of incredible strength of character we had in the group. Love and loyalty.' If the minds and attitudes of the men who sail twelve-metre yachts are the final determinants of who wins, it makes good sense to put as many resources into that area as into well-cut sails and high-lift keels.

For this reason Bertrand began to look around for a professional psychologist, preferably one with sports experience, to fill in and expand on the areas where he instinctively felt he must take the crew's thoughts. He eventually met Laurie Hayden, a psychology lecturer at a Melbourne college and the man who worked on the heads of Carlton United, one of the most successful Australian Rules football teams. The two men's thoughts on the problems of initial motivation and, later, stress control coincided exactly. Using Hayden did not make Bertrand popular with the syndicate hierarchy. 'Because the whole thing smacked of going to a shrink a lot of the senior people felt intimidated by it and didn't want to know about Laurie. Bondy said to me one time, well he intimated it really, "Maybe I've made a mistake with Bertrand. If he needs someone to help him with his head, maybe he's not tough enough." My analysis was that we spend millions on keels and sails and we practise for thousands of hours going from one tack to the other, so why don't we work on our minds as well?'

Opposition did not lessen as the period of working up *Australia II* wore on. 'This guy's just excess baggage,' Bond said of the psychologist at one point. In order to secure the right to use Hayden, the skipper sent the management a long and forthright memo. It was written to obtain a small tactical victory, but in fact it contains the essence of Bertrand's competitive philosophy. Since he is the only man in history to win the America's Cup, unless one goes back to John C. Stevens and the romp around the Isle of Wight, it is worth quoting at some length:

> The key to motivation is that it comes from within the group. It is extremely important that this is recognised and worked on. Assuming all our other bases are covered – yacht design, tuning sails, boatspeed potential, physical toughness – then the final mental toughness and approach through the 45-odd races will mean the difference between

winning and losing. Although every winning elite athlete is an amateur sports psychologist himself, to get professional outside help will be a major asset and far superior to whatever any of us within the management can achieve. This has already been proven in other sports. We are not reinventing the wheel.

Bertrand had his way and Hayden came aboard, although never fully trusted by the top brass.

Almost anyone who has played team sports, at any level, will have experienced those episodes when everyone on the side feels elevated, confident and invincible, with skill and timing flowing through them without conscious effort. It is at these times that the total achieved becomes far more than the sum of individual talent and effort. It was Bertrand's belief that through constant training of the mind as well as the muscles this state of grace could be reached regularly and predictably, just as an ignition key will always start a well-tuned car. He was proved right at Newport, when a boat that he felt was technically deficient in many areas defeated the most efficient racing machine and helmsman in the world.

It seems doubtful whether the lessons have sunk into the twelve-metre sailing community. The feint that began accidentally and was later developed deliberately – of *Australia II*'s invincibility because of her winged keel – seems to have hypnotised the professional racers, just as it swept up the media and through the watching public. In September 1985, with just a year to go to the beginning of the elimination series which foreign yacht would challenge for the Cup, all the emphasis was still on how many millions of dollars each syndicate was spending on tank-testing hulls or computer assistance in sail design. Dennis Conner's design team for the San Diego syndicate took to holding their meetings in a lead-lined, soundproofed room at the Lawrence Livermore weapons research institute on the University of California's Berkeley campus. The room, swept daily for 'bugs', is normally used by scientists working on nuclear fusion or President Reagan's Star Wars defence plan. Some of the personnel are interchangeable. 'The technology is just incredible,' said yacht designer Gary Mull, who left the San Diego group to join the San Francisco-based St Francis Club challenge. 'Our guys are in the absolute stratosphere of excellence. The only other time you can get to work with people like this is on Pentagon projects. The Russians would give zillions to have them working for them.'

Mull's St Francis colleague Albert Calderon, an aerodynamicist and hydrodynamicist of standing equal to Britain's Herbert Pearcey, usually works for NASA, but felt good about designing twenty-five-ton racing dinghies. 'The America's Cup has ceased to be a totally sporting event,' he declares. 'Now it has become a totally technical programme. We felt the challenge of competing with the top research groups in the world. It's not really sailing that brings us into this, we are seeking the frontiers of technology. It is a science challenge that we regard as one of the most important.'

Only among the top American sailors did a note of caution and scepticism about the pre-eminence of hi-tech in the coming campaign begin to creep in. The scientists, designers and syndicate backers around the world were still going flat out for a bigger bang. Tom Blackaller, the veteran US twelve-metre sailor, as effervescent as Conner is dour, is skipper and leader of the St Francis Yacht Club's syndicate, and is already worried at the way the Cup shows signs of changing from a sailing regatta to a research competition. 'The guys who sail these boats are only eighth or ninth in the pecking order,' Blackaller told a Californian interviewer. 'In Fremantle the wind is so constant, so predictable that this is going to be a flat-out speed contest, a drag race. The guy who comes up with the fastest design is going to win. That's why we are spending untold millions on research. What we've got here is a race between boffins.' There doesn't seem to be much scope there for the qualities that Tom Wolfe and John Bertrand would respond to – good old boys risking life and limb to douse a spinnaker in under ten seconds, holding a tack to within three feet of a rival twelve-metre on a reciprocal course, and, above all, grace under pressure, that magical Hemingway formula which has never been bettered.

In France the Marseilles-based syndicate headed by Olympic gold-medallist Yves Pajot committed itself to a massive research programme that would precede and take precedence over anything that happened on the water while the crew were trialling on the Ben-Lexcen-designed *Challenge 12*, bought from the Melbourne syndicate after the 1983 Cup. The backers of the 'Challenge Française pour l'America Cup' determined the shape of the campaign almost from the outset. Aerospatiale, the leading French company in space and aviation, is deeply involved with hull design and construction. The car and industrial technology company Matra has produced a computer program that governs the entire campaign. So all-embracing is it that a sheet trimmer can virtually look up the breakfast he'll be eating on a given day during the series. The French government space agency, equivalent to NASA, is assisting the syndicate in the areas of both sail-making and meteorology.

Pajot is deeply committed to the concept of on-board computerisation and believes it will provide the key to winning the Cup. 'We are convinced that any edge in design, equipment and information will be the difference between success and failure in Fremantle,' he says. On the other side of France the La Rochelle syndicate, skippered by his younger brother Marc, has taken a less laboratory-orientated approach. Its designer Phillipe Briand is also a top sailor, world champion in one-tonne and half-tonne classes. 'By racing the boats I design, I have a better feel for them and the chance to understand what they do,' Briand believes.

In Italy the Consorzio Italia, rivals to the Aga Khan's Azzurra syndicate, numbers the Gucci empire among its backers, but the design work owes more to high-tech than high chic. Aermacchi, Italy's leading aerospace company and creator of the Macchi jet fighter which is now in use with air forces around the world, are both sponsors and designers of the boat *Italia*. Other sponsors include dairy and meat companies. 'But there will be no salami or milk on our sails. This is a very technical, competent challenge,' says Flavio Scala, reserve helmsman and a syndicate executive.

In New Zealand Kiwi designers Ron Holland and Bruce Farr, both successful expatriate yacht designers, possibly the best-known names in the world in that field at present, worked on the twelve-metre for the homeland with home-based Laurie Davidson. Yet despite their monumental track record in designing fast, race-winning boats, all the emphasis from the Kiwi camp was on research and more research. In Perth the Kookaburra syndicate backed by West Australian millionaire Kevin Parry, a former furniture manufacturer and retailer who took off into semi-conductors and semi-submersibles, has made the twelve-metre effort an operating division of the Parry Corporation with its own board and all that implies. The research effort that goes into the development of mini-submarines to work the world's growing number of offshore energy fields has been harnessed to the creation of three boats that the rugged Parry hopes will go faster than those of his arch-rival in West Australian tycoonery, Alan Bond.

All this effort can be traced back to the focal point of *Australia II*'s radically new, winged keel, which grew out of thousands of hours of tank-testing by designer Ben Lexcen at the Netherlands Model Ship Basin. Bond, syndicate director Warren Jones, manager/grinder John Longley and John Bertrand flew to Holland under conditions of great secrecy after the 1981 Cowes Week race to Dinard. They travelled through the night via military airfields, helicopters and hired cars until they reached the basin where a proud Lexcen revealed his breakthrough – a third-scale model with a winged keel. Bertrand, terrified of Bond's willingness to fall in love with novelty, describes his reaction in *Born To Win*. 'Under stress I usually have two principal expressions of alarm. When I saw that winged keel, and everything seemed suddenly to have roared into life, if not Technicolor, I just stood there and used them both. "Jesus Christ!" I said. "Holy Shit." Had I not told them so many times? Give me a similar boat and we'll go out and sail it better.'

In fact, something not so far from that happened in the end. *Australia II* proved to have as many drawbacks as advantages, and Bertrand firmly believes that it was the quality of the men sailing her that won the day. Not all observers agree. Arthur Wullschleger, project director of the New York Yacht Club's 1987 attempt to get the Auld Mug back and a veteran of many a Newport Cup, put it pithily: 'That boat saved Bertrand's ass. Conner says that if he'd been sailing it he would have won the series four-nil and I believe him.' Bertrand makes it clear, however, that the myth of winged-keel invincibility suited three groups in particular very well: they wanted to believe in it.

Australia had become a nation of yachting converts. People who had never even been on a boat in their lives were reading up about the Herculean struggle off Newport, Rhode Island. The fascinating thing about their interest, however, is that it revolved around a total myth – that *Australia II* was a boat that was about twice as fast as the American's *Liberty*, that she was secretly powered by a mysterious keel with wings, and that essentially all the crew had to do was sit on her and she would carry them to victory . . .

The myth, however lacking in truth it may have been, happened to suit everyone perfectly. The press, of course, loved it because it was easy to understand such a marvellously simple concept – it saved them the trouble of having to understand the almost unfathomable complications that surround twelve-metre racing yachts.

It also suited Dennis Conner and his henchmen, because it

provided for them a perfect excuse for losing the America's Cup, should it come to that.

The third myth-lover was Bertrand. He knew that *Australia II* was not in any way unbeatable, and he also knew that the boat had the Americans rattled when they really should not have been.

What no one could have foreseen was how a myth manipulated in the media stew of Newport would come to be universally believed and would then determine the entire pattern of the next America's Cup. Every hour in that lead-lined room in southern California, every metre that a twenty-foot model is towed down a quarter-mile tank comes back to that fundamental confidence trick in Rhode Island.

Can the scientists be blamed if, to a yachtsman, they sound detached and almost bored by the tradition and romance of the Cup? It could be argued that at each successive regatta there have been design breakthroughs – and reverses – created in the past by designers in oilskins with a pencil between their teeth. On the whole the boats will get faster, if only by the most marginal increments, as the technologists in white coats get their hands on more and more of the processes leading up to an America's Cup defence. Men who have never been sailing in their lives, like Britain's top researcher Herbert Pearcey, will say to interviewers: 'Sailing is new to me in the sense of personal involvement, but the sea is the sea and the wind is the wind. The aeronautical and hydrodynamic factors are the same as in many other applications.'

The men who created the myth are less afflicted by the need to create a 'rocketship' than other Cup syndicates. Since September 1984 *Australia II* has been ploughing practice furrows up and down Gage Roads, off Fremantle, where the races will be held. 'We're having fun and we're getting better every day,' said manager John Longley, a grinder on board *Australia II* at Newport and a veteran of Cups back into the 1970s. A tousle-headed giant of a man who loves sailing enough to train all day aboard a twelve-metre and then jump off the dock at teatime to go off for an hour on a windsurfer, Longley is so active aboard a boat that he can appear to be at both bow and stern virtually simultaneously. 'It's very lucky to be in the position we're in – a bunch of guys who love sailing twelve-metre boats and having the best ones to do it on.' The attitude in this camp is emphatically not one of waiting for a wonderboat to come off the drawing board of Ben Lexcen and then go out and cruise it to victory.

Everyone hoped that *Australia III* would prove even swifter than her older sister, but if that turned out not to be the case . . . 'Well, we've still got the boat that beat Conner at Newport and we're having fun.'

John Bertrand parted company from the syndicate in a blaze of controversy over some of the claims and attitudes in his book *Born To Win*. The harmony necessary to sail a highly strung, sixty-foot racing boat cannot be achieved if some of the crew are near to blows. Nevertheless, some of the philosophy that developed under the leadership of Bertrand and psychologist Hayden runs on without them.

One thing is certain: the process of attuning a winning crew to one another and making them comfortable with each other's strengths and weaknesses cannot be accelerated simply by applying more resources. You cannot throw cash at this problem and solve it. 'You can't buy time,' as Bertrand puts it. 'Other people are going off to work, making their fortunes or just their careers, and it's a wet day in Fremantle and you don't feel like going sailing. That's when the importance of philosophy and psychology becomes vital. Discipline would make the guys go out on the boat, but you can't just do that and sail up and down – people need to be all charged up for it to have any value. This part of the programme is possibly the most vital of all.'

It's all a question of human relations, as Ian Howlett would say back in his New Forest den. 'Yacht designing has always been a fashion business, half art with a dash of science. I'm not sure that will stay true – the number-crunching is getting much too powerful. A world that believes in maths like that, I think it's a little dangerous.' Of course, the cynical might just say that this year's fashion is for massive research programmes. Howlett fears that Fremantle will be full of improbable claims and counter-claims about magically fast keels. 'It's a bit dull and all to do with psychology really,' he said, leaning into his third pint of nut-brown bitter in a little pub near Palace House in Beaulieu. 'The guy that has a glass keel might have the edge. Find me some glass as dense as lead and I'll win you the America's Cup. The opposition would be so terrified they'd fall off their boats.'

Chapter 3

Fremantle Booms Again

In 1829 the Royal Yacht Squadron was thriving and successful. Yachting had begun to be as popular in New York Harbour as it was on the Solent. The Squadron members were comfortably off businessmen and aristocrats who lived in sophisticated cities and could spend large amounts of time and money racing boats. In the New World entrepreneurs were building railways and canals and making money; on the other side of the Atlantic the gentry sold their ancestral lands for the same purposes and they too made money. On the other side of the globe the Aboriginal inhabitants had barely seen a white man, let alone dreamed of a railway.

On 2 May 1829, Captain Charles Fremantle, in command of HMS *Challenger*, filed a report to his masters at the Admiralty that he had on that day 'Taken of formal possession of the whole of the west coast of New Holland in the name of his Britannic Majesty.' It was Fremantle's third visit, his first being in 1827. Yet he was not, by over a century, the first European to land in what would eventually become the home of the America's Cup. The Dutch explorer Willem de Vlaminhg visited the Swan River area in 1697 and stayed long enough for his imagination to be enthralled by its unique population of black swans. Eighty years earlier in 1616, his countryman Dirk Hartog had become the first white man to set foot in the continent that was to become Australia. He landed 500 miles to the north of the Swan in the bleak and inhospitable area now known as Shark Bay. The remote Dirk Hartog Island still bears his name. For whatever reasons, the Dutch failed to exploit their discovery. It was English settlers who disembarked from the merchantman *Parmelia* that followed Captain Fremantle's careful soundings in through the reefs and shallows. The sixty-eight pioneers stepped from small ship's boats on to the beach below what is now the Round House at Fremantle. Their hardships will not be easily fathomable to the competitors and guests who use the new America's Cup marina, constructed by the West Australian government not two cables from that first landing place. A contemporary account may give some spur to the imaginative:

> They arrived in the depth of winter; few or no tents had been provided for their accommodation and no sort of cover had been prepared on shore. The weather, even for winter, being unusually severe, the unfortunate women and children were exposed to the most harassing privations and frequently had to sleep under umbrellas as the only covering from the deluges of driving rain that swept up from the Indian Ocean. Champagne cases, pianos and even carriages were later used in improvising temporary dwellings. Only with the greatest difficulty could those unfortunate people, unused as they were to rough colonial life, light fires for cooking purposes.

Communication with Britain could take up to a year and the optimistic settlers who sailed in the *Parmelia*'s wake could have no idea of the difficulties they would face on that bleak white beach in the chilly drenching southern winter. Each month more ships arrived: *Marquess of Anglesey, Euphemina, Lion.* Around fifty colonists and their effects would be aboard each one, plus government stores and livestock. Lieutenant Breton, a young Royal Navy officer, has left this fragment from his journal of life during a visit to the infant town of Fremantle:

> Tents and huts in every variety; goods of all descriptions scattered about in disorder; the emigrants employed, some in cooking their provisions, and others in sauntering about or landing their effects; many looking very miserable and a few equally happy. Different kinds of animals, just landed, and showing evidently how much they must have suffered during so long a voyage; such was the scene I witnessed

on landing at the spot on which the future principal seaport of Western Australia was to stand.

Notwithstanding the chaos on shore during those first few months, the more visionary among the newcomers could see the vast potential of the spot they had come to. After his third visit, during which the annexation took place, Captain Stirling wrote in his diary:

> The richness of the soil, the bright foliage of the shrubs, the majesty of the surrounding trees, the abrupt and red coloured banks of the river occasionally seen, and the view of the blue summits of the mountains from which we were not far distant, made the scenery round this spot as beautiful as anything of the kind I have ever witnessed.

It was clear to all that although Fremantle could be developed as the colony's mouthpiece and gateway, her heart must be inland, further along the river towards the rich farmland at Guildford. Three months after the first landing Perth was established. The site was proclaimed by the chopping down of a tree on a parcel of land set aside for military barracks. The choice of name was a piece of typical nineteenth-century unctuousness. Sir George Murray, Secretary of State for the Colonies, had been born at Perth in Scotland.

Australia's oldest established family business, wine and spirit merchants Lionel Samson, was begun in those first few months. Lionel was one of the first four settlers to buy a plot of land in the area just back from the beach. His descendants still run the business from the same site, a record of continuity of tenure unequalled anywhere else in Australia. However, even this rock-like certainty has been moved to some extent by the advent of the America's Cup. Bill Samson, great-grandson of the founder, is preparing to sell part of the firm's site for Cup development. It is possible that the disruption to normal life during the races may force the Samsons to move their operation elsewhere. From arrival by boat to eviction by boat in four generations.

One of the best accounts available of the first ten years of the Swan colony is from George Fletcher Moore, an Irish gentleman farmer and lawyer who came out to Fremantle with the earliest party. In his old age he permitted to be published his early journals. *Diary of Ten Years' Eventful Life of an Early Settler in Western Australia* was issued in London during 1884 and has been invaluable ever since.

When Fremantle was a year old Moore drew it this way:

> A bare barren-looking district of sandy coast; the shrubs down for
> firewood, the herbage trodden bare, a few wooden houses, many
> ragged-looking tents and contrivances for habitations – our hotel, a
> poor public house into which everyone crowded – our colony, a few
> cheerless dissatisfied people with gloomy looks, plodding their way
> through the sand from hut to hut to drink grog and grumble out their
> discontents to each other.

During the Cup period the last few phrases would probably find a
contemporary echo as the syndicates congregate and disperse in
different bars and pubs bemoaning the Western Australian government or a troublesome spinnaker – whichever comes to hand.
However, by the last month of 1832 (two years later) Moore was
able to write of a very great physical difference in his surroundings:

> Now there is a town laid out in regular streets of stone houses with
> low walls, and in some places palisades in front; two or three large
> well-kept inns or hotels, in which you can get good clean beds and
> private rooms.

By the late 1830s the town had become established enough to
support two competing whaling companies. Whenever a whale was
reported in the channel two boats would pull for their lives from
Fremantle beach, harpoonist standing poised in the bow. Very often
they would have a rival in the form of one of the American whaling
boats, out on a long voyage from Boston or Salem. Ferocious
competition off Freo between US and Australian mariners is not a
phenomenon discovered in the last eighteen months. The whales,
too, are still around, and several practising twelve-metres have
found themselves surrounded by four or five huge spouting mam-
mals.

By 1837 there existed a stable and thriving settlement, not yet
grand enough to escape the wit of Captain John Stokes RN, who
visited that year. He wrote:

> Fremantle, of which it was drily said by the quartermaster of one of
> HM ships who visited the place. 'You might run it through an hour
> glass in a day', is but a collection of low white houses scattered over
> the scarce whiter sand.

At this stage of settlement the Swan River was the only practical
means of communication with Perth, twelve miles inland. Since
Fremantle was on the south shore and the fledgling capital on the
north (and the river had yet to be bridged), travel by horseback or

buggy was impossible in the early years. A ferry was established a mile or two up-river, but until reliable roads were built between the port and the administrative centre it made more sense to travel by water than bludgeon through the raw bush on foot. Fremantle had one serious drawback as a port. A huge coral bar blocked the rivermouth, covered by only two and a half feet of water at high tide. No ship could enter the river, which would have been an advantage both from the point of view of unloading and shelter. The anchorage just off Arthur's Head, where the first landing took place, was acceptable in fine weather and in the prevailing south-westerly wind, but if it blew up and shifted into the north then it was a dangerous spot. Landing settlers, cargo and stock via a lighter was a slow and hazardous business. It was not until 1837 that the Fremantle Whaling Company was able to build a small jetty out from beneath Arthur's Head.

Proposals to tackle the problem of the bar and create a protected rivermouth harbour were floated almost from the first days of settlement. There were two obstacles. First, the technical difficulty and cost. A plan in 1830 for a 1,000-yard breakwater and blasting of the bar was estimated to cost £165,000 – an absurdly high sum for a tiny remote colony that was still only taking its first breaths. The second problem was more intangible, but harder still to overcome. Fremantle was at this stage bigger than Perth, but the establishment of the governor and his retinue of colonial government at the latter site was the 'writing on the wall' for the people of Fremantle. They feared that once the bar was removed and the Swan became navigable as far up-river as Perth, their town would wither and die, as ships took to sailing right up to the capital and unloading there.

The town's prominent citizens, led by local papers such as the *Fremantle Herald*, became adept at stalling harbour proposals or finding sufficient problems with them so that the project fell into doubt once more. It was over half a century later in 1897 that the bar was successfully blasted and a harbour created by Charles Yelverton O'Conner, an engineer of genius and an Antipodean counterpart to Isambard Kingdom Brunel. His 400-mile water pipeline across the dry interior to the Kalgoorlie goldfields was a wonder of the nineteenth-century world.

The small jetty below Arthur's Head was linked to the High Street and the rest of the town by a tunnel through the rocky outcrop that separated the community from Bather's Beach and the visiting ships.

The Round House, erected in the earliest days as a small gaol on top of the limestone head, supplied prison labour to dig the connecting tunnel. The prominence of the Round House and its use as a prison from the beginning of Fremantle history often leads people to assume that the settlement began as a penal colony, like New South Wales or Tasmania, populated by the flotsam and jetsam from British prisons. However, on the Swan River they were freemen and proud of it. Many of the first settlers, like George Fletcher Moore, were men of substance and professional qualification back in Europe, and they had taken a huge, but voluntary, gamble in coming to the newest and most isolated of His Majesty's colonies.

However, the middle classes may have been willing to take a punt on coming to the Swan River, but the opportunity and motivation to do so was lacking among labourers and tradesmen. One of the recurring themes in Moore's journal is the chronic shortage of workmen and the very high wages they could consequently demand from those settling new land and building homesteads. By the 1840s, a decade or so after the landing at Fremantle, the labour shortage was beginning to hamper the colony's economic development. A petition was circulated in 1848 and despatched to London requesting that West Australia be designated a penal colony. Official opinion in Perth was against such a move, but after canvassing various district magistrates as to the possible use for ticket-of-leave men, Governor Fitzgerald decided to ask Whitehall for prisoners. Western Australia was gazetted a penal colony in November 1849, and in June 1850 the *Scindian* arrived at Fremantle carrying seventy-five convicts. This was an enormous source of controversy in the colony. Many felt humiliated that they had been forced to embrace a system that the rival colonies on the east coast of Australia had already been able to discontinue. Pragmatists, however, pointed out that they were getting decent men as prisoners, mainly guilty of white collar crimes, not the murderers and cutthroats sent to Sydney and Hobart. Above all, their labour was desperately needed. Their first job was not to plough for men like Moore, but to build their own accommodation. On 4 August 1851, work began on the huge limestone gaol that still dominates Fremantle's skyline, sitting on the ridge above the port like a town of its own behind watertowers and walls.

Three days earlier in that same week, on 1 August 1851, an event occurred off England's south coast that would have a profound effect on Fremantle generations later. The schooner *America* arrived in Cowes harbour after a twenty-day voyage from New York, via Le Havre; the passage time included four days becalmed. The *America*'s owners knew they had a fast boat on their hands. They had come to race around the Isle of Wight for a Royal Yacht Squadron trophy that would become the America's Cup.

Early in 1851 a group of London businessmen interested in the growing sport of yachting despatched an invitation to their New York counterparts to bring over for the Great Exhibition one of the New York pilot schooners – boats famous on both sides of the Atlantic for their grace and speed. The invitation passed to George L. Schuyler, who formed a syndicate with John C. Stevens, commodore of the burgeoning New York Yacht Club, to build a new boat. Other members included Edwin Stevens (brother of John), James Hamilton, J. Beekman-Finlay and Hamilton Weekes. Work was already in progress when a second letter arrived in Manhattan, this time from the commodore of the Royal Yacht Squadron. It did nothing so vulgar as to suggest a race, but merely hinted that the members of that august body would be interested to see what the New World could come up with. Stevens knew a hawk from a handsaw and replied with colonial bluntness that, 'we propose to avail ourselves of your friendly bidding and take with good grace the sound thrashing we are likely to get by venturing our longshore craft on your rough waters'. He knew quite well that the invitations by now had next to nothing to do with the elevated conceptions of the Great Exhibition and everything to do with the British vision of themselves as the finest and most experienced yachtsmen afloat.

George Steers was the best designer on the US east coast and he drew *America*. She was to weigh 171 tons and measure ninety-four feet overall, with a twenty-three-foot beam and an eleven-foot draught. Like a modern Cup yacht her widest beam was aft of midships. Her builder, William Brown, who had a yard on the East River, gave a price of $30,000 for constructing the yacht. So enthusiastic did he become that he made the extraordinary offer of waiving the bill if she did not prove faster than the opposition. The NYYC, never slow to come forward, accepted with alacrity.

The club's next move should have the ring of familiarity to anyone with a knowledge of its tactics down the years. *America* was raced in New York Harbour against another Stevens yacht, the *Maria*. The latter was an all-out, smooth-water racing machine, very lightly built, whereas *America* was planked in oak and constructed to endure an Atlantic crossing. *Maria* wiped the harbour floor with the new boat, whereupon Stevens went back to William Brown and screwed the bill for building her down to $20,000.

Nevertheless, Stevens was so elated with her performance and potential that he began offering huge wagers to anyone who could beat *America*. As she lay in Cowes Roads during the first weeks of August, having already thrashed *Lavrock*, one of the top British yachts, in an informal race down the Solent on the last leg of her inbound passage, *America* could not find a competitor. Stevens' offer of a £50,000 bet frightened yachtsmen off – even the British aristocrats with their passion for wagers and huge gambling stakes. Eventually a wager of $10,000 flushed out the *Alarm*, a fellow contender for the Isle of Wight race, but somehow the contest never materialised. The syndicate turned down the chance to join in a regular Squadron race on 13 August, preferring to wait for a challenge from a single yacht. It never came. In a tart comment upon the lack of boldness shown by British sportsmen, *The Times* ran an article stating that the presence of *America* at Cowes was like 'the appearance of a sparrow-hawk among a flock of wood-pigeons or skylarks . . . her apparition off West Cowes among the yachtsmen seems to have been completely paralysing.'

Stevens' fellow syndicate members were all for taking *America* home, but they decided to have one last fling at a squadron regatta. It was to take place on 22 August for an undistinguished trophy known as the '100 Guinea Cup'. The course was to be simply around the Isle of Wight in a clockwise direction passing to seaward of the Nab light vessel. One contemporary commentator described the fifty-three-mile course as 'notoriously one of the most unfair to strangers that can be selected'. Certainly the prospect of the race drew Derby Day crowds to Cowes. *The Times* reported:

> There must have been upwards of 100 yachts lying at anchor in the Roads, the beach was crowded from Egypt Point to the piers, the Esplanade in front of the Club (the Royal Yacht Squadron) thronged with gentlemen and ladies, and the people inland who came over in shoals with wives, sons and daughters for the day.
>
> Booths were erected all along the quay, and the roadstead was alive with bathers, while from the sea and shore rose an incessant buzz of voices, mingled with the splashing of oars, the flapping of sails, and the hissing of steam from the excursion vessels preparing to accompany the race.

Even grander spectators were out on the water that day. Queen Victoria and the Prince Regent were aboard the royal yacht, waiting to see the leading yachts round the Needles and head up the last leg for the finish off Cowes. As *America* passed by, well in front of a straggling field, her crew doffed caps, cheered and made merry, despite being in the middle of a race.

The syndicate's yacht had by no means made the running around the course. *Arrow*, owned by Joseph Weld, led the field initially, but hit Bembridge Ledge, a treacherous reef at the eastern end of the Isle of Wight. *Alarm*, the boat that had earlier accepted *America*'s wager, went to her assistance and dropped out of the hunt. *Volante* then led for some time, but sprang her bowsprit and allowed *America* to push out in front – where she stayed. As with modern racing for the Cup, the concept of a wonderboat is fine – but it is helped enormously by other people's gear failures and navigational mishaps. *America* crossed the line twenty-one minutes ahead of her nearest competitor, *Aurora*. There was, of course, a protest – a tradition that shows no sign of changing. The owner of the yacht *Brilliant* claimed that *America* had sailed a false course by passing inside the Nab rather than to seaward. The New York syndicate's successful defence was that the committee of the Royal Yacht Squadron, fine gentlemen but poor organisers, had managed to publish two conflicting sets of course instructions – one passing inside the Nab and the other outside. The protest failed.

Stevens received the Cup and a visit from the Queen. What followed has become almost as traditional in the history of the Cup – a vast and morbid inquest in the British press about how such a defeat could have come to pass. Correspondents with nautical pseudonyms filled the letters page of *The Times*, and the gentlemen's magazines overflowed with analytical articles on such technical matters as flying jibs and unlaced mainsails.

A different but equally heated controversy filled the correspondence columns of a newspaper called *The Inquirer* that week. The Swan River colony, now twenty-two years old, was still struggling to survive, but could at least support a regular weekly newspaper, *The Inquirer* – a 'West Australian Journal of Politics and Literature', as its masthead put it.

Convicts – how to treat them, where to put them, and whether they should be there at all – was the only topic of debate in Perth and

Fremantle during that America's Cup August. *The Inquirer* managed a minor scoop by obtaining an answer from the prime minister's private secretary in Downing Street concerning a rumour that the colony's supply of convicts was to be stopped almost before it had begun. After explaining that the muddle arose from the misreporting of a speech by Prime Minister Lord Grey in the House of Lords concerning the arrangements for convict stations in Gibraltar and Bermuda, Mr B. Hawes (the PS) continued most helpfully:

> The intention is to use every endeavour to make the presence of the convicts conducive to the prosperity of the colony, and gradually to increase their number, so far as the means of rendering them useful may present themselves, but to avoid any such large or sudden influx of convicts, as it must be evident would be productive of serious inconvenience and injury to the settlement.

The paper was glad to note that in another part of the same letter Whitehall confirmed that a number of free emigrants would be assisted to travel to the Swan — a quid pro quo for the colony taking prisoners. But clearly the arrival of men with broad-arrow suits was having its effect upon a small community. *The Inquirer* reported the formation of the settlement's first police force of two men, four 'pensioners' and a superintendent. They were to patrol the streets constantly (which gives a fair indication of how many streets there were), each man having his own beat, and were to be relieved every eight hours. There were to be no uniforms initially, but the men would wear 'some distinctive badge — a white stripe on the arm, we believe. Extremely shrill whistles will be provided for sounding an alarm.' It was a start, and also the beginning of a new and less innocent era. 'We hope that before long we shall have similar bodies formed wherever convicts or ticket-of-leave men may be stationed,' said the paper's editorial cautiously.

Attitudes to the convicts varied greatly among the settlers. An initial party of ten had been happily and usefully employed cutting drains in the farming areas round about Guildford — ten miles east of Perth and nowadays in the shadow of the airport. But at Fremantle a drama involving convict labour occurred. The *Saucy Jack*, a small cutter, was due to sail north to Shark's Bay and Dampier's archipelago, a rough trip of around 2,000 miles, in search of guano for use as fertiliser. Five ticket-of-leave men from the north Fremantle depot were to be embarked to dig and then load whatever guano was found. However, at the last minute the master, Mr Wills, balked at taking convicts on an expedition to the unexplored north and the scheme foundered.

The other preoccupations of the 2,500 citizens of the settlement were becoming somewhat workaday. The days of struggling for survival and huddling under grand pianos on the beach were over. Bacon may have been one shilling a pound and 'scarce' and claret fifty shillings the dozen, but both these commodities were obtainable. Mr Lionel Samson went from strength to strength, auctioning here, building there and continuing to wholesale liquor. Debate still raged about the harbour. A letter signed by Flumineus in *The Inquirer* demanded more buoys and permanent moorings:

> Whatever the cost I think it could be accomplished by the use of the labour of men we have recently had sent to us by the Imperial government . . . an anchorage levy might be charged. I should think the owners or captains of the ships lately driven ashore in the recent gales would have profitted paying a very heavy amount than suffer the losses they have had to submit to.

A capacity for arguing about harbours seems to flow through the blood of Perth people. In the last two years the new America's Cup marina in Fremantle provoked opposition and controversy. When work commenced on the new government-backed yacht harbour at Sorrento, fifteen miles north, protestors lay down in front of tipper trucks and the state government accused the local West Australian paper of mounting a conspiracy of opposition. Virtually every expert in the world on the subject of sand drift was consulted – by both sides. Flumineus would have been in his element.

By the end of August 1851, Stevens and his associates had returned home to New York. They took the pewter pot with them, but they could have had no idea of the obsessive hold it would exert over yachtsmen in the coming century and a quarter. The syndicate sold *America* to Sir John de Blaquiere for $25,000. He renamed her *Camilla* and began losing races. In the 1852 contest around the island she was beaten by her old rival *Arrow*. By 1862 *America* was lying sunk in the St John's River, Florida, forgotten by everybody.

The same fate almost befell the Cup. In 1857 Stevens and his syndicate gave it to the New York Yacht Club as a challenge trophy –the famous deed of gift containing the still crucial words: 'Any organised yacht club of any foreign country shall always be entitled, through any one or more of its members, to claim the right of sailing a match for this Cup.' Britain mounted a somewhat half-hearted challenge in 1871 for what the *New York Herald* then described as 'this almost forgotten trophy', but it was not until 1876 and the Canadian challenge that the America's Cup again became a major event.

The Canadian yacht, *Countess of Dufferin*, was soundly thrashed in a best-of-three series held in New York Bay. (The regatta had not yet moved to Newport.) Even the annals of the Royal Canadian Yacht Club of Toronto, the challengers on this occasion, described the attempt as 'more courageous than wise', but it was nevertheless substantial and it awakened public interest in the Cup.

The news of their fellow colonists' defeat would probably have reached Perth and Fremantle by about October, but by then they had other controversies and excitements to worry about. In a curious precursor of the 1987 contest, the seas just off Fremantle became the scene for the first international incident ever to involve West Australia.

Among the convicts in the huge Fremantle gaol, the Round House, were six Fenians, Irish patriots transported for their political activities. Then, as now, sympathy for the Hibernian cause was strong in the USA and the Clan-na-Gael society used an American whaler *Catalpa*, moored in Fremantle harbour, to spring their men. Once the escapers were aboard, the *Catalpa* stood out into Gage Roads, but could not take to the open sea because of bad weather. A police cutter ranged alongside her and saw the Fenians casually taking the air on the lee rail, but the police could do nothing. The Yankee skipper John Breslin was not a man to be trifled with, as he made clear in a note he left for the authorities:

> This is to certify that I have this day released from the clemency of her most gracious majesty Victoria, six Irishmen condemned to imprisonment for life by the enlightened and magnanimous government of Great Britain for having been guilty of the atrocious crimes known to the enlightened portion of mankind as 'love of country' and 'hatred of tyranny'; for this atrocious act of Irish assurance my birth and blood being sufficient warrant.

The next day the Perth authorities sent the old steamer *Georgette*, embarked with one old cannon and fifty 'enrolled pensioners' (the successors of the six policemen who had been hired in the week of the first America's Cup race), after the *Catalpa*. Accounts vary as to whether she fired the cannon as a warning shot. Certainly no damage was done to the *Catalpa*. Instructed by the army major on board *Georgette* that he would blow the masts out of Breslin's ship, the latter coolly hoisted the American flag and stood beneath it. England had just had to pay $3 million to the USA for a breach of international law and the outcry that would arise if the *Catalpa* were sunk would finish the colony. The authorities returned empty-handed to harbour, where virtually the whole town awaited them on the quays – a ceremony for the laying of a foundation stone for the masonic hall had been abandoned in the excitement.

The prisoners were carried safely to America where they became minor celebrities. One of them, John Boyle O'Reilly, had great literary ability and became the editor of the *Boston Pilot* newspaper, and also published several novels dealing with life in a penal colony. As he edited the America's Cup reports – on which the *Pilot* prided itself – O'Reilly could hardly have imagined that it would one day be raced for on the waters where he had stood on the *Catalpa*'s deck, a newly free man, and seen the hill-top gaol disappear beyond the horizon.

While the colony on the Swan River struggled with its growing pains and absorbed convicts among its explorers and gentry, the America's Cup settled down to become a major sporting trophy, with all the bustle, big money and ballyhoo that implied even a century ago. To a certain extent it embodied the tensions between Britain – at the height of empire but already, according to some specialist historians, past her point of greatest technological and industrial development and innovation – and America, rapidly becoming a science-led economy. The Civil War of 1860–5 had been the first 'modern' military conflict, and like many subsequent wars its catalytic effect upon industry and design (even yachts) had been enormous. Natt Herreshoff, the leading US naval architect of his day, was a graduate of the Massachusetts Institute of Technology at a time when his counterparts in Britain were still flying by the seat of their pants.

It was in 1895, when the Herreshoff-designed *Defender* sailed for America against the Earl of Dunraven's *Valkyrie III*, that the Cup next caught fire. Dunraven was an Irish peer with something of the Renaissance man about him. Besides being a brilliant sailor he was an ex-diplomat, former war correspondent and an accomplished violinist. As an amateur steeplechaser he had often ridden horses bred on his own Irish stud and won major races. His temperament was volatile and his politics radical. Had he been around Perth in 1876 he would almost certainly have been the only man cheering for the six men fleeing aboard the *Catalpa*. His first challenge for the America's Cup had been in 1893 and that had been attended by a certain amount of drama and dissent concerning the deed of gift — which had been revised in the late 1880s to give an even bigger advantage to the home boat and even greater latitude to the race committee of the NYYC.

In the weeks immediately prior to the 1895 challenge, Dunraven chiselled away at the club over such matters as boat measurements and crowd control — that is, the volume of spectator boats allowed out on the course. On some days it could reach 60,000 people aboard 200 steamers. After the first race, which he lost to the metal-hulled *Defender* by eight minutes, Dunraven wrote to the committee alleging fraud concerning the waterline measurement of *Defender*. His claim was that tons of lead had been moved into the ballast area at dead of night to make the US boat float lower than her measurement allowed. This protest was still confidential at the time of the second race when the intervention of a steam launch just after the start caused *Valkyrie III* to strike *Defender* and damage her rigging. The latter boat hoisted a protest flag and was awarded the race, despite *Valkyrie III* finishing over two minutes ahead. When the day came for the third race the Earl sailed across the start line as if in earnest and then dropped his sails and retired. This display of petulance and bad sportsmanship turned into a noisy and furious scandal when the allegations of fraud were made public. They were, in fact, absurd and impossible, but in the hothouse atmosphere of the Cup with the media following every windshift of gossip and half-truth, the Earl got carried away — as many other competitors were to do over the following century. In the aftermath of the 1895 series, relations between British and American yachting circles reached about as low an ebb as can be imagined.

It took the arrival on the scene of Sir Thomas Lipton, sporting grocer and intimate of the Prince of Wales, to smooth the Cup waters. Unlike Dunraven, Lipton had the advantage of being a natural diplomat, rather than a trained one. His royal chum had been chairman of the Squadron's Cup committee during the 1895 fiasco and was anxious that harmony should prevail across the Atlantic.

Lipton, the Ulsterman who began life in a corner shop and sailed a toy boat called *Shamrock* on a local pond before he found fame and fortune in the USA, was just the man for the task. His five challenges in *Shamrocks I–V* from 1899 to 1930 in many senses created a modern Cup. Lipton won only two races in thirty-one years, but his skill in creating a hard, competitive atmosphere that stopped short of mania and still had fun in it showed that the Prince had made a good choice. The press found him accessible and always good for a quote, and his relations with the New York Yacht Club, although sometimes sheeted right home, never came close to breaking point. After the first J-class series, fought with *Shamrock V* in 1930, Lipton went home and wrote in his autobiography:

> It [the Cup] has been my principal recreation for over thirty years. It has kept me young, eager, buoyant and hopeful. It has brought me health and splendid friends.

It also brought him election to the stuffy ranks of the Royal Yacht Squadron which, as Peter de Savary has found, does not automatically follow a distinguished and expensive challenge for the America's Cup. Lipton died, still a bachelor, in 1931, with his plans for *Shamrock VI* and the next challenge well in train. In a curious link with the modern Cup and the win by Australia, the engineer for Lipton's early attempts was Thomas Pearkes, great-grandfather of John Bertrand, who helmed the winning *Australia II*. Bertrand grew up listening to tales of the great Sir Thomas and his battle for the Auld Mug and has acknowledged how it nurtured his own love of sailing and passion for the Cup.

While New York rang with the claims and counter-claims of belted earls during the 1890s, that same period was one of intense and fevered growth in Perth and Fremantle. The investment and energy would not be matched until nearly a century later, when Alan Bond brought the America's Cup home. The reason was gold. There had already been finds and rushes in the eastern part of Australia, but nothing on the scale of what happened when gold was discovered at Coolgardie, 300 miles east of Perth, in 1892. It was comparable with the Yukon gold rush. J. K. Hitchcock, in his book *The History of Fremantle 1829–1929*, wrote of that period:

> The town was filled with people from the Eastern States and every vessel that berthed was overcrowded with men anxious to reach the find and stake out a claim. Merchants, shipowners and traders in the Eastern

States, recognising the business to be done, either appointed agents in Fremantle or established branches in the town, and business boomed. Local merchants and traders experienced great difficulty in obtaining supplies to feed and fit out newcomers clamouring for attention. The influx of the large number of people stimulated local residents towards progressive undertakings and the air of prosperity induced a companion feeling of optimism.

Most of the fine Victorian architecture in what is known as the West End of Fremantle dates from this boom, as do the town hall, municipal markets and many of the pubs. The mining equipment for the fields was shipped in through Fremantle and the precious yellow metal left West Australia by the same route. The town took its percentage on freight in each direction and grew steadily more prosperous.

After 60 years of debate and filibustering, work started that same year (1892) on creating a harbour. The need was more pressing than ever and the gold rush created the prosperity that could pay for the construction and the hugely expensive blasting programme. The Irish engineer Sir Charles Yelverton O'Conner was a polymath to match Lord Dunraven, although his accomplishments have lasted rather longer and his statue still looks out from the Fremantle Port Authority building across the smooth, sheltered basin he created. When he opened the harbour in September 1900 the West Australian premier Sir John Forrest said:

> Captain John Thomas [a founder of the colony who was still alive] can tell you that when he landed here there was only two feet and six inches of water across the bar in the entrance to the Swan. Now there is thirty-two feet of water in every part of the harbour where a steamer can or is likely to go.

Another event of 1900 is worth considering in the light of the boom and bounce that the town was undergoing. In that year a referendum of the inhabitants (in the 1891 census, the colony's first, Perth had a population of 8,447 and Fremantle one of 7,077) asked whether the bustling port should have electric light. It is a sign of the innate conservatism and streak of incipient gloom still tending to run through Fremantle that although 461 of the city's voters welcomed Mr Edison's invention, another 336 cautious souls turned their backs to the light. When one considers the resistance and opposition (much of it reasonable enough) to the America's Cup being held off Fremantle and based in the town, it is also worth bearing in mind the forty-three per cent of the townsfolk who could not see the future in a light-switch.

The transportation of convicts to Western Australia ended in 1868 with the arrival of the Fenians, later to escape, aboard the *Hougoumont*. These political prisoners were by no means desperadoes, but the government was worried enough over their presence to send for a detachment of infantry from the 14th Regiment, stationed in New Zealand, to guard them. Probably their most permanent memorial is the road bridge to north Fremantle – the approach roads being constructed on a bed of rock quarried by the chain gang. In 1888 the era of the penal colony was finally put to rest when the last transportees were released and the curiously named 'enrolled pensioner' force disbanded.

Psychologically the town had to throw off the shackles of being a penal dumping ground, just as the convicts had to lose their chains, before real and solid development as a city could begin. As late as 1876 author and traveller Henry Taunton was still able to give this description of Fremantle:

> It consists of one principal street made up of hotels and stores and a few Government buildings, including the Imperial convict depot, and a number of private dwellings all glaring in whitewash. A few churches make up an apparently sleepy but really flourishing township, which might be described as a city of public houses, flies, sand, limestone, convicts and stacks of sandalwood.

By 1901, however, the city was big and lusty enough to provide a choir of 1,700 schoolchildren to sing the National Anthem to the Duke and Duchess of Cornwall, later to become king and queen, who were on a royal visit to Fremantle. Schedules had gone awry because storms and heavy weather had forced the royal yacht, *Ophir*, to run past Fremantle and berth at the port of Albany, 300 miles to the south. The tour continued by train. Royal visits have not gone smoothly down the years. When the Queen and Duke of Edinburgh came to Perth in 1954 an epidemic of polio in the city forced them to cancel plans to stay at Government House, as would be usual, and live aboard the old royal yacht *Gothic* in Fremantle Harbour. If Prince Charles and the Princess of Wales accept the invitation of the Royal Perth Yacht Club to visit while the America's Cup is on, they might be wise to consult the royal records before making exact plans.

The success of the goldfields and the development of the railways out into the central wheat-growing belt inland from Perth all pushed the development of Fremantle onwards in the early years of the twentieth century. During the First World War it was the key port for the despatch of troops and supplies to the Anzac campaign at Gallipoli and in France. A strike by dockers in 1917 held up supplies to the soldiers and the issue became a scandal when it was realised that drugs and desperately needed hospital tents were lying on the wharf untouched. Volunteer strike-breakers came in to load ships under police protection. Ugly conflicts developed, culminating in the reading of the Riot Act by a local magistrate. In the clashes between police and strikers scores of people were injured and one docker was killed. The confidence to strike in such a way was imparted by a booming economy, but by the depression of the 1930s, which hit an agrarian and somewhat underdeveloped state like Western Australia particularly hard, the waterfront unions were forced to accept lay-offs and unemployment as problems it was impossible for them to tackle.

Yachting's most glamorous – and expensive – trophy was not immune from the effects of the depression. With the death of Sir Thomas Lipton the mantle of British challenger had fallen upon the willing shoulders of Tommy Sopwith, an engineer and entrepreneur who had made millions out of aircraft design and manufacture during the First World War. Sopwith had bought *Shamrock V* from Lipton's executors and was desperate to make a challenge through the Royal Yacht Squadron. King George V, commodore of the RYS (a position occasionally thought to carry more prestige than being merely king of England), was opposed to the challenge. Although Sopwith could well afford the cost, his sovereign was worried about the effect of such conspicuous spending on public opinion at a time when children were going hungry and men begged at factory gates for jobs. The flamboyant aircraft manufacturer prevailed over the cautious monarch by pointing out that several different yachtsmen would certainly challenge through other clubs if the squadron backed off. Reluctantly the King agreed and the fifteenth challenge for the Cup was launched.

In the USA the same factors that worried the King nagged at millionaire yachtsman Harold Vanderbilt. He decided to build just one new yacht, named *Rainbow* to signify the light at the end of the slump, to defend in 1934. Gear and rigging for her was stripped off the 1930 defender *Enterprise*, and the all-up cost of launching

Rainbow as a ready-to-sail J-class yacht probably did not exceed half a million dollars – peanuts in comparison with the huge sums spent in 1930. Though set up frugally, the series was gripping. *Endeavour* won the first two races for Sopwith and the Americans looked to be in trouble. However, with the aid of the NYYC race committee they pulled back the deficit and won four-two. The row about right of way in the fourth race rumbled on for years until well after the Second World War. Sopwith was still convinced that he had been cheated of the Cup. It was the biggest scandal since the days of Dunraven, and would not be matched until the NYYC tried to prove that a Dutchman, not Ben Lexcen, had designed *Australia II*'s keel. Sopwith vowed never to get involved with the Cup again, but he was back in 1937 with *Endeavour II*, again sailing against Vanderbilt who this time was aboard a new boat, *Ranger*. Nothing much had happened to cure the depression, and when there were plans to hold the challenge in 1936 discreet word came down from the White House that it would be an election year and that Franklin Delano Roosevelt did not relish going out on the stump to offer Americans the New Deal while plutocrats played in million-dollar boats off Newport. The hint was taken and the Cup postponed a year.

Throughout its history the Cup has had periods of lying dormant as a sporting event, but the years 1937 to 1958 were its longest sleep. Of course, the war intervened, but there was a bigger factor at work. Social change had been levelling many of the super-rich down to the standard of the well-off. Even those who had shrewdly kept their fortunes thought it less than well mannered to flaunt huge, extravagant boats, suitable only for a one-race series, off Newport. Norris Hoyt, a distinguished American yachting journalist, said this:

> J-boats were too large and too expensive and the state of the art was not far enough advanced for them to offer the possibilities of intricate development which make the closed course match race such a challenge to designer, sailor, athlete and planner. Previous America's Cup racing in mastodons under acres of canvas was spectacular and arrogantly expensive but it was bought and paid for.

What the new era called for was a class of boat that was a highly developed racing machine accessible to owners and syndicate members who wanted a direct involvement. The twelve-metre class, sailed by eleven crew and with an overall length of around sixty-five feet, answered that need. They were about half the size of the J-boats and actually handled and looked like a yacht rather than a China tea clipper. With the sophistication and fragility of a 1986 twelve-metre seems almost absurd to talk about them as if they were knockabout dinghies that could be used to go down the river to the pub, but that was how they seemed after the excesses of the 'mastodons'.

The British challenges of 1958 and 1964 were a shambles. Elderly British gentry, 'old buffers with neither teeth nor boats' as a high court judge once described the members of the Royal Yacht Squadron, seemed to think that showing the Americans we could lose decently was the prime game. Peter Scott – son of the Antarctic explorer, painter, ornithologist and excellent dinghy sailor – was chosen to stand at the helm on account of his 'leadership' qualities. Meanwhile, the Americans were running their defending syndicates with the loose-limbed democracy and can-do philosophy that characterises the best American companies. Norris Hoyt, again, offered the best indication of why the British were thrashed:

> The managers acted like lords of the manor; both crew were drilled like troops. The challenge was in the best tradition of Empire and it lost against modern management.

Australia's arrival on the Cup scene in 1962 was the most invigorating change in the trophy since the arrival of a challenge with Sir Thomas Lipton's name on the bottom of the letter. Frank Packer (later to be knighted) was a media tycoon who could have taken the last of the Tsars as his business mentor. His empire of magazines, newspapers and TV stations was known to his employees as 'Packerstan'. Packer's go at the Cup with his new twelve-metre yacht *Gretel* was run on the same rugged lines as his business. Crewmen who were stars one day would wake the next morning and find they were off the boat. Nevertheless, the Aussies enjoyed themselves and sailed well enough to worry the crew of the defender *Weatherly*. On the evening of the day they took a race off the Americans, the boys from Sydney made such a night of it in their adopted Newport bar, The Cameo, that the owners decided to sell up and retire to Florida.

Packer came back in 1970 with *Gretel II*, having had to defer in 1967 to another Sydney syndicate (stuffed with crewmen who'd had enough of Packer) sailing *Dame Pattie*. By this time the New York Yacht Club could see the writing on the wall – that if they were to lose the Auld Mug to anyone, it would most likely be carried off by the Australians. Looked at from Down Under, however, the whole business was very much an eastern states establishment game. West

Australia was an area where people raised cattle on stations the size of European kingdoms, grew wheat on slightly smaller plots, or dug nickel or other semi-precious minerals out of the ground. Andrew Spedding, operations manager of the current British challenge, last came to Perth in 1967 as a junior officer aboard a Royal Navy ship. 'It was just a country town then. A cow town. The idea that the America's Cup could be held there would have been just ridiculous.'

Fremantle's major function during the twelve-metre years after the war was to absorb the never-ending flow of migrants who came off the big liners clutching their S10 tickets. According to residents of that period it became a drab, port city of bars, brothels and heavy blue-collar industry. Employment on the wharfs dropped each year as specialised ports able to handle bigger ships opened around the West Australian coastline – iron ore at Port Hedland, oil and gas at Dampier, grain at Kwinana. The arrival of dozens of sixty-five-foot yachts would not have seemed to represent a credible new economic future for Fremantle. However, one of the migrants who trotted down the gangplank of the SS *Himalaya* was a thirteen-year-old boy from Ealing. His name was Alan Bond, and he had never heard of the America's Cup.

Chapter 4

Bond's Boys

Slightly north of Fremantle along Perth's coastal highway is an old-established flour mill. High up on the corrugated-iron walls of the mill a ferocious red dingo, the company's logo, stares out to sea over the America's Cup course. Alan Bond painted it there. When he left Fremantle Boys' High School at the age of fifteen Bond was apprenticed to a signwriter. Within a couple of years he was running his own business, by necessity and personal inclination taking on the difficult or dangerous jobs that more established firms turned down. The red dingo was one of the first.

The progress from having a paintbrush in one's hand to holding the America's Cup aloft on the manicured lawn of the White House beneath the avuncular gaze of President Reagan would be sufficient for most men. There is a good deal of evidence that it would have been enough for Alan Bond, but even tycoons can be trapped by circumstance. 'I didn't want to do it again and I think Bondy felt the same way,' says John Bertrand. 'The difference is that I can say "Been there, done that," and walk away. He can't. Perth's his own backyard. He lives there and it's almost impossible for him to turn his back on the defence of the cup.'

Despite the meticulous planning and preparation that the 1983 Bond campaign put into their effort to win four twenty-four-mile boat races, almost no one considered the implications of success. It took 101 per cent of everyone's physical and mental stamina to strive for that brief shining moment. Who had time to think about the years that were to follow? Certainly no one at the top of the organisation. Warren Jones, director of the Bond Corporation with special responsibility for mining and the television stations, and the man who has run twelve-metre campaigns back to 1975, is candid about that.

'We all said before 1983 that this is going to be our last one – win, lose or draw. And we really did mean that,' emphasises Jones. Normally he operates from a luxurious thirty-second-floor office at the top of Perth's most prestigious block. It does impress visitors to be able to see the far side of Rottnest Island, itself eleven miles offshore. When Cup time comes around, however, Jones will move to a small, sea-level office at the dockside. 'It was only after we won the Cup that we realised that we'd only done half the job. I freely admit that no thought whatsoever had been given to what we should do if we should win. Totally unprepared – no one had ever won, let alone ourselves.'

At that point a sense of being without options closed in, 'in gaol' is how Jones describes it. 'It was a matter of going on and finishing the job and the next half in front of us was going to be much harder than what we had already done. I think it will be far harder to defend than it was to win.'

The second half of the job began in November 1983, a bare six weeks after the euphoria of Newport and the triumphal homecoming to Perth. A key group set down to write a time-and-motion study that would plot a path to a successful defence of the Cup in February 1987. Bond was there, so was designer Ben Lexcen, Jones and John 'Chink' Longley, the giant former schoolteacher who began his twelve-metre career as a winch-grinder on *Southern Cross* and is now operations manager for the campaign. There was nothing as formal as a committee and the group didn't even have a name. 'Our unit never disbands – we think, eat and live twelve-metres all the time,' says Jones. 'Bennie, Chink and I would speak every day of the year on the subject, whether by phone or face to face.'

Information from the Royal Perth Yacht Club, who now held the Cup, concerning potential challengers made it plain that the forthcoming series was going to be far bigger than any America's Cup that Newport had ever seen. Countries that had never competed before such as Germany and Japan registered an intended interest. Yacht clubs that no one had ever heard of – Spider Lane of Marion, Massachusetts, the Société Nautique de Genève of landlocked Switzerland – put down a marker. The worldly wise may have seen that these scores of contenders would eventually come down to a dozen or so, but it still added up to a formidable obstacle for a syndicate intent on keeping the trophy it had so painfully won just weeks before.

'Every time you do the Cup the ante goes up,' explains veteran Chink Longley. 'Back in 1980 we did it for A$1.5 million, last time it was A$4.5 million and now we're looking at A$15 million. A year before the '83 Cup we didn't even have a boat – we borrowed two one-tonners and pretended they were twelve-metres – now we've got two twelves on line and we're about to build a third. Unbelievable.' It quickly became apparent to the Bond team that its effort was going to have to be better funded, better organised and totally dedicated over a three-year period if the Cup was to stay down under.

Yet a considerable hurdle lay ahead even before the Herculean task of keeping the foreigners at bay could be attempted. The Bond team had challenged through the Royal Perth Yacht Club and the Cup and its defence rested with the club, not the syndicate. Despite a contract between syndicate and club that nominated the former as the official defender, it quickly became apparent that other Australian yachtsmen and businessmen wanted a stab at some glory.

The tradition in America had been for the New York Yacht Club to organise a series of trials, the Observation Races, and then pick the best yacht to defend the Cup against the foreign challenger. Nothing less would be acceptable to the Australian public, among whom the phrase 'fair go' has the status of a minor but respectable religion. Bondy may have been the 'battler' who won, but now it was definitely time for others to have a fair go.

The agreement between the Royal Perth and the Bond syndicate has been the subject of some misunderstanding. It required Bond to undertake that he would defend the Cup should he have the good fortune to win it; in return the syndicate was nominated the official defender. 'Basically the club was terrified that it would end up holding the America's Cup and have to spend its own money defending it if no one else wanted to,' explained a senior, if cynical RPYC member. But the contract went on to say that Bond's team would have to beat any other Australian twelve-metre syndicates who wanted a crack at the Cup if they wished to remain official defender. A mistaken impression arose in some circles that the holders had in some way been cheated of an automatic right to defend their trophy.

While the Bond team never expected to be given a free crack at the defence, a feeling grew that to have to compete with the Royal Perth for sponsors and public attention was not quite what they had expected to be the reward of Newport. It's not a subject that is easy to discuss with the contestants. They are not given to analysing what has been and gone, and to want to have the party to yourself smacks of bad sportsmanship. Nevertheless, when talking off the record senior syndicate members reluctantly admit that it was another area they didn't plan for. To have to struggle as hard as they are doing for the chance to defend what took nine years to win might seem to be what the American legal system terms 'a cruel and unusual punishment'.

Certainly it is a situation that other challenging syndicates have thought about and dealt with in advance. David Arnold, chief executive of the British team, resolved even before the syndicate had raised money or built boats that they would reserve the contractual right to organise and market the defence off British shores in 1990, if they win off Perth. 'It's absolutely solidly written into our agreement with the Royal Thames that we have the right to organise the 1990 defence,' said Arnold. 'The location in Britain will be our choice and so will the manner the event is organised in – subject, of course, to the Deed of Gift. The situation that the Bond team find themselves in is unfair and ridiculous.'

To their great credit the team that brought the Cup back to Perth immediately devoted its energy not to moaning about the terms of the race but to winning it. The first steps involved not boats and crew, but logistics. A wealthy Fremantle fisherman Joe Rotendella, who had been at school with Warren Jones, offered a prime site on Fremantle's Fishing Boat Harbour to the syndicate. In Newport during the previous four challenges the team and its boat has squashed into a crowded dock with facilities barely adequate for maintaining dinghies, let alone the world's most sophisticated sailing machines. Other challenging yachts hung in their lifting frames almost within touching distance. There was going to be little point in entering the world of hi-tech and ultra-secret keels if the opposition could just peer over the garden fence at what they were up against.

Work commenced at the new site in mid-1984, building a complex that would include two jetties, a double lifting frame, a huge sail-loft, well-equipped machine shop, offices, and a VIP and sponsor room complete with projection facilities, hospitality area and the facilities associated with boardrooms rather than sailing club locker rooms. The latter was particularly important. Back in 1974 the *Southern Cross* campaign had been run out of Alan Bond's capacious hip-pocket. Certainly it was also a major promotional exercise for the huge housing development at Yanchep Sun City, thirty miles north of Perth, that the Bond Corporation was undertaking. *Southern Cross* and *Gretel*, her trialhorse, were kept in the new marina at Yanchep. The projected new town was referred to in all promotional material as 'Yanchep: Home of the Twelves'. The ambitious young property entrepreneur was convinced that he could ultimately stage the 1988 Olympics there. However, the property crash of '74 intervened and Bond found himself obliged to move very quickly if he was to avoid becoming a victim of it. Yanchep Sun City, complete with the flies and sand hills so detested by the twelve-metre crewmen, was sold to Japanese interests.

Despite the value, unquantifiable though it might be, of the Cup as a promotional vehicle, it was still Bond writing the cheques for everything from the winches to the crew's pocket-money. Those who were involved in that campaign love to tell the story of 'Bondy' nipping off from the dock at lunchtime to buy hamburgers for everybody at the nearby Yanchep Inn. As he queued with the holidaymakers to pay for his dozen burgers a quick-witted Aussie behind Bond remarked: 'I should put her on the Pill, mate.'

Through the 1977 and 1980 campaigns Bond remained the main paymaster, although these were burgeoning years for the Bond Corporation and there was no evidence that the proprietor's bank account suffered any lasting damage. By 1983 Bond was the owner of Western Australia's monopoly beer producer, the Swan Brewery. Twelve-metre yachts and the macho men who sailed them were an ideal vehicle for promoting beer, so sponsorship was put in train and the Swan spinnakers that became such a famous sight at Newport arrived on the yachting scene.

When the 1987 defence became a reality Bond decided that if the Australian public wanted to see the trophy stay down under then the population and the business community could play a major part in retaining it. With the budgets for each syndicate now in tens of millions of dollars it was no longer realistic to expect one man to pay for it – even with the help of his brewery. 'America's Cup Defence 1987 Ltd' was registered as a business whose sole aim was to sail twelve-metre yachts faster than anyone else in the world and keep what had become a major industry inside Australia. Companies were offered the choice of various levels of involvement. For A$1 million (plus the provision of a tender, those highly sophisticated fifty-foot workboats that service the twelves and cost around A$500,000) one could become a 'Principal Sponsor'. The first item on the package of benefits this brought was exclusive use of the Principal Sponsor logo. This variation on the well-loved boxing kangaroo showed the marsupial with the America's Cup stuffed into his pouch. Other opportunities were less comic – use of the boats and crew for TV commercials, entertaining contacts and customers on the tender vessels, priority in buying Channel Nine airtime for advertisements during the Cup series and other start-points for product promotion. Initially only Swan Brewery took the huge bait, but at Easter 1986 the Hong Kong and Shanghai Bank came to the party. The opening of Australian banking to foreign operators had led the bank to open a subsidiary down under. Bond had been a customer for years and it seemed to the bank a natural route for seeking exposure in the new country. Nevertheless, Bond could not have expected five years previously to see the chief executive of the world's fourteenth largest bank pull a boxing kangaroo rugby jersey on over his discreet grey business suit.

As in the USA, the twelve-metre community was finding that its original assumption of big business pushing its way to the gangplank waving cheque books needed a little reassessment. In America syndicates who had counted on sales of TV rights floundered as the networks ignored them. It is an indication of how seriously fund-raising was viewed by Bond's key men that, before skippers and crew were even thought of, they recruited a senior marketing figure to get out amongst the corporations. Vern Reid, a classic 'gidday' Aussie with a pungent vocabulary and boundless enthusiasm, was their choice. A former Rugby Union footballer and public-relations executive, Reid had most recently organised fund-raising telethons for charity on the national Channel Seven network. Instead of cajoling viewers at the end of a phone to part with a hundred dollars, he was now inviting himself in to the boardrooms of Sydney and Melbourne to persuade dry-footed businessmen that they should commit hundreds of thousands of dollars to a national crusade on the most exotic sailboats afloat.

'Usually when one seeks sponsorship the most difficult thing is to get ten minutes sitting down with the top guy who can make the decisions,' observed Reid. 'This is different. Because of Newport and that tidal wave of interest everyone knows who we are and what we did. It's easy to get the appointment. Everyone wants to see you. But when you get in there you find that the South Australian syndicate have already visited and the Parry people are due in tomorrow. It's very, very competitive. Australia is a small economy relatively speaking and there are only so many dollars available for sponsorship.'

Nevertheless, by the conclusion of *Australia II*'s stem-to-stern refit and subsequent relaunch in November 1984 Bond's team had assembled an impressive A$4 million worth of corporate sponsorship. At this stage no other Australian syndicate had a boat in the water. Companies such as Woolworths came in at the A$600,000 donation level, while the local offshoots of multinationals such as Mobil and Data General were keen to come in with services in kind a little further down the cash scale.

The major involvement of Data General was a logical progression from the help they had provided *Australia II* in Newport during 1983. A DG engineer named Glenn Read was loaned to the syndicate part-time for six months before the last Cup and full-time during the actual elimination series and final races. For the 1987 event the computer company have placed Read, an experienced sailor with several national and world championships on his mantelpiece, at the Bond crew's complete disposal for the entire three-year campaign. The level of hardware support was also a significant step higher. At Newport data from sensors aboard the yacht were relayed by radio telemetry to Read aboard the tender *Black Swan* with a small microcomputer. Later the results were analysed on a slightly more powerful machine kept in the dingy basement below the crew's living quarters.

By 1984 the computational side of twelve-metre racing was beginning to resemble the wilder shores of Star Wars. On board the boat the skipper and tactician would, for the first time, have portable computers that could analyse the raw data produced by the sensors mounted around the boat. But by the time it reached the screens in their laps, the information and options had already been relayed back to Read aboard *Black Swan* with a DG–30 computer, itself powerful enough to do the number-crunching for a medium-sized business.

This, of course, was just the portable and weatherproof stuff. Back at the dockside a machine known as a thirty-two-bit MV–400 was monitoring and storing all the information flying around out on the course for eventual analysis and storage each evening. In its quieter moments it was quite up to providing the word-processing power that secretaries Veronica Taveira and Shirley Grose required to keep the paper flowing in an organisation that was now not so much a sport, more big business.

The continual end in view was to assess the performance of the recommissioned *Australia II* and later *Australia III* against the six million bytes of information stored from the '83 campaign. In that Rhode Island summer *Australia II* was the fastest twelve-metre afloat and it was crucial that boat speed, wind direction, rudder angles and trim tab angles on each point of sailing, and with different sail combinations, be compared with data coming off the current boats. The history of the America's Cup is littered with owners and crews who had invested so much money and faith in a new boat that they could not bring themselves to accept the reality of a poor performance once it hit the water.

Print-outs and the cold glare of a moving cursor go some way towards removing that temptation, although they could hardly be said to add romance. 'I hope to produce a set of figures to put aboard the new boat so that when the crews feel they have it tuned up and are sailing at any given angle and wind speed, they will be able to compare figures and know how fast they should be travelling,' explained Read at the time of *Australia III*'s launch. 'From data relayed when the boat is sailing we will be able to plot any function such as true wind angle or boat speed, or look at the correlation between, say, trim tab angle and boat speed. The differences are so small they are not always perceptible to the eye, especially when the guys are concentrating on other things.'

Not every sailor of the old school, and some surprisingly young ones come into that category, accepts the word of a software program that they are not sailing the yacht as fast as they did last week or last year. Yet according to Read, who understands the breed, being one of them, once a helmsman accepts that the black box is there to help him, not replace him, things settle down. No computer is able to look at an ocean a mile ahead and pick out a catspaw of wind barely visible to the naked eye that could give a tacking twelve a vital lift if sailed for and her opponent a nasty knock. If helmsmen of ingrained skill and bone-marrow cunning are necessary for that, other crew must have muscles and stamina that don't come from programming floppy disks.

Among their other key sponsors Bond's boys picked up Australia's biggest fitness-centre chain, the eponymous Laurie Potter. Under fitness director Greg Barnes the growing numbers on the syndicate crew list found themselves working out in an ethos and environment they may previously have thought more suitable for pampered suburban housewives with a cellulite problem. However, going through a Barnes routine at 6.30 am on a chilly winter's morning with the yacht race still almost two years away cancelled the average yachtie's doubts about the seriousness of the whole exercise.

Sponsorship-seeking as practised by the Bond twelve-metre syndicate is an exercise in imagination. The dull mind may see no more than a cheque being handed over and logo appearing on company letterheads. Vern Reid thinks faster and harder than that. One of the companies to come in at the sponsor level of A$250,000 support was Tip Top Bread, one of Australia's biggest bakeries and suppliers of that ubiquitous Western scourge, the sliced white loaf. No figures have ever been available on how much of that product is eaten at the crew's quarters, but Tip Top did pay for the services of a top Sydney nutritionist, Rosemary Stanton, to direct crew diet. Her initial concern was that she would be cast as the spoilsport who told the boys to lay off bacon and eggs – which she did. 'At first I was worried that these guys would see me as some dreadful lady who wanted to feed them alfalfa sprouts and lettuce leaves,' said Rosemary, who also advises several rugby league clubs in New South Wales. 'To get the best out of them they need minimal fat and plenty of carbohydrates in their diet. My intention is to wean them on to my special breakfast muesli, a variety of wholemeal breads and plenty of water.' With flair, two initially dissimilar sponsors – Laurie Taylor and Tip Top bread – were combined into a marriage that provided both muscle-building and fuel.

Another major fund-raiser for Bond was a national supporters' club called the Defence Club, organised by the Amway Corporation, a company specialising in the neighbourhood marketing of cleaning and household products. Ordinary Aussies were asked to sign up with a ten-dollar membership fee, and although a low-key operation it had gained 100,000 members by early 1986, contributing over A$1 million to the syndicate's A$12 million target. Ironically, Amway is centred in the USA and headed by Richard De Vos, a New York millionaire best known for being chairman of the *America II* syndicate. In the boardroom power struggle that followed the on/off defection of helmsman John Kolius, De Vos was elevated from finance director to chairman of the syndicate, replacing Arthur Santry Jnr, who in turn found a niche as commodore of the New York Yacht Club. The position De Vos holds is no honorary one. Amway is a sponsor to the tune of at least US$1 million in America, but if De Vos sees any conflict of interest in backing both leading horses in the race he has never admitted to it.

What is noticeable about the pattern of commercial support for the Bond syndicate is that the really big 'blue-chip' Australian companies are absent from the list. Many of them are to be found on the sponsors' board at the Royal Perth Yacht Club. There has been a consistent feeling within the syndicate that the club 'picked the eyes out of the barrel' in terms of corporate Australia before other participants had settled down and considered their campaigns. Certainly by mid-1984 Royal Perth had Broken Hill Proprietary (Australia's biggest company), Westpac, Holden cars, Trans Australian Airways, BP and Coca-Cola signed up at A$350,000 each. There was a feeling, not confined to the Bond syndicate, that the RPYC were receiving millions of dollars for new clubhouses and administration costs while the boys on the water who made the whole thing possible were struggling for money for sails and winches.

'What the Royal Perth haven't realised is that although they've pulled a fuel company, a car maker and a bank, the corporate sector isn't very big and we're probably in with their direct rivals,' explains a syndicate figure. 'When push comes to shove down the end we're not going to give a damn about the yacht club sponsors. We're going to look after our guys.' Here the television coverage, on the commercial channels, is crucial because of the Channel Nine network's contract with Bond and Channel Seven's similar deal with the Kookaburra syndicate. 'All you have to do is sit behind a TV director at an event like this and see what he leaves out to realise that they're never in a million years going to let a competing sponsor get into shot. He's going to have someone bawling down his earpiece: "I don't care what you shoot but don't take that flag." '

Television coverage of the nightly press conference given by competing skippers was one of the earliest points of division between Bond's syndicate and the RPYC. Its initial plan was to stage the interviews in front of prominent logos featuring each of the club's major sponsors. However, not all the would-be participants were happy. 'I can't take A$250,000 worth of fuel and cash off Mobil as a sponsor and then let Alan Bond and our skipper sit underneath a BP sign at a press conference on national television,' protested Vern Reid. 'If it comes to the crunch, we simply won't be at the press conference.' In the event the compromise was that the edge of the backdrop would contain the corporate logos, visible to the media packed into the theatre each night, but not to the TV cameras which would focus on a plain central panel behind the interviewees' heads.

The question of television coverage of the Cup was already becoming an issue before Alan Bond's acquisition of Swan Television, Perth's local operator on Channel Nine and part of the national network, in late 1984. Quickly he signed agreements between the syndicate and the station (as chairman of both it wasn't the hardest thing in the world) for exclusive access to America's Cup activities and yachts. Further down the track and at a less exalted level it became clear that things were not going to be so simple. Journalists working in the Channel Nine newsroom found themselves dealing with the biggest running story in their city's history, involving not just one syndicate but dozens. Considerable commercial and sporting secrecy was involved in many of the boats and a news team regarded as in the pocket of the opposition were not always welcomed with open arms. The crunch came early and, predictably, over a keel.

In mid-1985 the Taskforce '87 Syndicate, largely financed by Perth retail millionaire and Bond rival Kevin Parry, had begun trialling its first twelve-metre, *Kookaburra*, off Fremantle. On one of the first training sessions Channel Nine put up the news helicopter to fly over the yacht and shoot some footage for the six o'clock local news show. It was as near flat calm as sea conditions ever get in Gage Roads, with only the gentlest of south-westerly breezes blowing. The sailing pictures were not too exciting, but once back in the studio editing booth producers and journalists realised that the clarity of the limpid turquoise sea had given them very clear shots of the hitherto secret *Kookaburra* keel. Only the general views went on the air in a short, routine piece – views of a twelve's keel were thought unlikely to grip the average suburban viewer. But word soon got around the twelve-metre community that the shots existed. 'We got a phone call from the Bond syndicate asking for a copy of the rushes,' said a Channel Nine executive. 'We offered them a cassette of the broadcast version but said the rest was confidential.' In the long pause that followed Channel Nine management, led by news director Terry Spence, hammered out a policy that despite being owned by Alan Bond there were to be no spy pictures handed over to any syndicate. Nor were any skippers or tacticians from Bond's camp to be taken up in the helicopter for spying rides. 'It was the integrity of the newsroom. We'd have never got in the gate of another twelve-metre compound if we were known to be doing this sort of thing,' said the executive most immediately concerned. Eventually Warren Jones agreed to television neutrality, but it was an incident that caused a lot of hard thinking to be done. The final agreement, somewhat jingoistically, admitted the possibility of Swan Television resources being used to spy on foreign twelve-metres – this being in the national interest – but not on rival Australian groups.

Conflict with Bond is most likely to occur where the rights he has acquired by virtue of owning the companies which hold them conflict with the custom and practice of the outside world. When he owns something, Bond's instinctive view is that everything to do with it should work his way, whether it is television news or the name on the stern of a yacht. When *Southern Cross* was preparing for her Newport debut in 1974 a blazing long-distance row broke out between Bond and the Royal Perth, under whose aegis he had challenged, over the lettering on the twelve-metre transom. The club were horrified to learn that it was going to read 'Yanchep Sun City: Home of the Twelves' right beneath the name *Southern Cross*. After a frantic exchange of red-hot telexes between Rhode Island and the Swan River, the rules of decorum and international yachting prevailed. 'Royal Perth Yacht Club' were the words that eventually rippled across the mustard-yellow stern of *Southern Cross*.

Bond gave in – but not gracefully. All of his experiences in Australia had taught him that what he wants to make happen he generally can. He stepped ashore in Fremantle from the passenger steamer *Himalaya* in January of 1950. Bond was thirteen. Back in the London suburb of Ealing where he had grown up doctors had told his father, Frank Bond, that the injuries he had sustained in wartime service with the Royal Air Force would kill him within two years unless he moved to a hot, dry climate. These were not poor but

optimistic immigrants clutching a £10 ticket. Frank had been a
builder in London and the family were well enough off to bring with
them to Australia a new Ford saloon and enough money to buy their
own house in Fremantle.

If his immediate family were comfortable, there was hardship in
the wider clan. Frank Bond's brothers still worked in the Mon-
mouthshire coalmine where he had once toiled underground. When
interviewers nowadays ask the Savile-Row-suited Alan Bond about
his attitude to trade unions he is fond of telling them about his visit to
a pit. 'My father worked in a coalmine from the time he was twelve.
One of my uncles took me down when I was five or six and I watched
them shovelling coal in terrible conditions. I saw the pit ponies with
pink eyes that never saw the daylight ... So I believe there are
extremes which require collective bargaining.' Until only two or
three years ago Bond kept up his membership of the Painters' Union,
a legacy of his signwriting days. But people are either collectivists or
individualists at heart. Watching coal hewn from subterranean Wales
kindled in Bond an idea that if he was tough enough, smart enough
and worked hard enough, he could be free of such human drudgery,
and perhaps even own mines rather than toil in them. There is no
evidence that he came away fired with a burning enthusiasm to build
a better and stronger National Union of Mineworkers – although he
and his British contemporary Arthur Scargill might have more in
common than either man would choose to admit.

The period of Bond's arrival at Fremantle Boys' High School was
formative. A bright scholarship winner who shone in maths, French
and Latin, his thirteen-year-old peers had already grown up together
and felt no need to open their hearts or teenage gangs to a newly
arrived Pommie swot. After school he earned pocket-money selling
newspapers and magazines on the wharves of Fremantle's booming
port. These were the years when immigration to Australia was at its
peak and hardly a day would pass without a large passenger ship
calling. Bond's entrepreneurial flair soon began to show itself. The
owner of the newsagent's wanted to close early in the evening, but
the kids wanted to work late. Bond struck a deal with the shopkeeper
to acquire his own stock for farming out once the shop had closed.
Very quickly the newcomer was employing most of his former
competitors and finding it more financially rewarding than carrying
his own satchel of newspapers.

When he reached fifteen nothing could have held Alan Bond at school. His father, bowing to a force of nature, managed to extract a promise that Alan would at least learn a trade. Having a talent at drawing, an apprenticeship to a signwriter seemed the most agreeable of the available openings. Bond finished the five-year course in just over three years and promptly left his employer to start his own business. 'It soon dawned on me,' Bond recalled when surveying his business past, 'that there were very few people who really wanted to go out and tackle the difficult work. I found there was money to be made in solving other people's problems.' High cranes, hot factory chimneys, outback mine poppets that no one else was willing to drive to – he tackled them all, including the famous red dingo on the Great Southern flour mill. At around the same time he married Eileen Theresa Hughes, a staunch Roman Catholic (like Bond) and daughter of one of Fremantle's wealthiest and most influential business families. Both bride and groom were eighteen when they married in St Patrick's church in the heart of Fremantle. The next day Bond paid a five-pound deposit on a plot of land in the nearby suburb of Melville, a little posher than Freo, and started off by building the garage which was to be Eileen and Alan's home for the next two years.

Exactly thirty years later the Bond's beautiful blonde daughter Susanne married New York radiologist Armand Leone in the same church. That was about the only thing that was the same. Eileen had the altar repainted for the grandest wedding Perth had ever seen. New green carpet covered the aisle and the confessional. Outside, the groundlings stood thirty deep to catch a glimpse through the paparrazzi and the network camera crews of Fremantle's royal family. Back at the family mansion in the elite riverside suburb of Dalkeith, a tented ballroom had been built out over the Swan River for the 400 guests invited from all over the world. The garden paths, and even the lawn, lay beneath 320 linear metres of deep red carpet, into which was woven the initials and personal monogram of Susanne and Armand. Offshore Bond's powerful and sybaritic motor yacht *Southern Cross* lay at anchor waiting to sail on the first leg of the couple's honeymoon. Guests received their wedding invitations in white leather wallets containing, besides the RSVP card, a solid gold medallion embossed with the heads of Miss Bond and Mr Leone. Upstairs in the bedrooms Bruce Oldfield, chief and most fashionable couturier to the Princess of Wales, worked on the last-minute fitting of the white silk taffeta wedding dress. It had a gold-beaded bodice and a train five yards long. Others of Oldfield's thirty new gowns were for the bride's mother, the bride's 'going-away' and the bridesmaids. In the storage space beneath the huge house cases of Krug '79 champagne were stacked higher than the windsurfers. 'Cecil B. de Mille would have given his teeth to have organised this,' said guest Dallas Dempster, millionaire promoter of Perth's casino. When they were both in their early twenties Dempster and Bond worked together in property development and have remained friends.

Although the wedding could scarcely have been a greater or more flamboyant success, in an odd way it marked the beginning of a run of bad luck for the Bond twelve-metre syndicate. On the morning he was preparing to give Susanne away Alan Bond received an urgent summons to the Fremantle dockside. Shortly after midnight the nightwatchman had discovered smoke billowing from the forty-foot container used to store sails. The fire brigade arrived to find it well ablaze following a short-circuit in the ventilation system. By the time Bond jumped out of his black Rolls-Royce, clad in shorts and tee-shirt rather than morning dress, at the twelve-metre headquarters the dockside was ankle-deep in charred Kevlar from the headsails and melted nylon from destroyed spinnakers. Tom Schnackenberg, director of sailmaking and the unsung genius behind *Australia II*'s Newport victory, was nearly in tears looking at the volume of destroyed work and experience all around him. Warren Jones estimated that the loss was about A$400,000, although that was covered by insurance. More important was the time it would take sailmakers to replace over twenty genoas and kites. With the southern summer just beginning, sail-lofts all over Australia and Schnackenberg's native New Zealand were booked out with work. No one had the capacity to take in such a large and complex job-lot and it had to be farmed out piecemeal, partly in the USA and Europe. Bond gave an impromptu news conference standing among the ashes and admitted that the fire had probably put his syndicate's campaign back six months.

The local Western Australian newspaper had managed to squeeze a couple of paragraphs about the blaze into its last edition and claimed that it had been deliberately lit. There was no hard evidence to support the theory, but it was a possibility in everyone's mind. Just five weeks earlier, after the launch of *Australia III*, Bond had faced questions concerning the level of security at the twelve-metre site.

What fuelled the queries was the mid-August bombing of a Bond Corporation development named Observation City on the coastal highway opposite the America's Cup course. It was the first high-rise block on a largely suburban shoreline where comfortable, if unspectacular, middle-class homes stretch almost down to the water's edge. In such an environment the tower was deeply unpopular with sections of the local community, and had been the subject of a planning controversy since its inception. The fourteen-storey hotel complex, incorporating bars and restaurants as well as apartments, was seen by many Perth residents as the thin end of a large wedge which could result in their beautiful oceanside city coming to resemble Miami or Queensland's Gold Coast. There were few tears but nevertheless deep shock when an unknown individual or group fixed plastic explosive to the base of the huge tower crane on the site and attempted to bring it down on top of the half-completed building. Perth had barely known ideologically divisive politics, let alone terrorism. 'If this is the America's Cup, who needs it?' was the common reaction. In this context Bond stood up and addressed the hundred or so media people who had come from the eastern states and overseas for the balloons and champagne launch of the new twelve-metre yacht.

'Without going into details the bombing has caused a tremendous upgrading of our security screen in Fremantle,' said an agitated Bond, who hates problems that remain unexplained and unsolved. 'The protection on our two twelves is very high and I'd be frightened to go down there at night on my own.' Just a few weeks later he stood among the remnants of his team's key sails, including the spinnaker that had hauled *Australia II* into the lead in the penultimate race of the final leg against *Liberty* in 1983, mulling over the knowledge that the Royal Perth had received anonymous letters threatening to sabotage the new boat, and that the Observation City bombers remained unknown and still at large.

No evidence came to light that the fire was caused by anything other than a major fault, yet the bad luck continued. In the same month of November 1985 the syndicate suffered two bad crashes while *Australia II* and *III* were sailing against one another. In the first the brand new yacht rammed the stern of her elder sister, smashing a large hole and carrying away the backstay. Two weeks later *Australia II*'s bow struck *Australia III* dead amidships, leaving a metre-long gash and several terrified crewmen. Experienced observers knew that if helmsmen are to simulate the razor-edge competition of America's Cup match racing then they have to sail almost closer than they dare to the (friendly) opposition. But to the public it looked as if the streak of bad luck was continuing – an impression that did not diminish four days before Christmas at the launch of *Kookaburra II*.

Leaving her dock to take part in the twelve-metre sailpast, an unnamed member of the *Australia II* afterguard forgot to slip the backstay, which was led over the thirty-tonne boat-hoist. With a crack like tropical lightning the mast snapped at the lower spreader – in full view of the curious dignitaries arriving for the rival's launch. 'You have to accept that human error comes into twelve-metre sailing and this could have happened to anyone,' was Alan Bond's philosophical comment – in public. Those who had to deal with him in private say they will carry the scars for a good long while. Worse was to come. Two weeks after this disaster, and each thirty-metre aluminium stick costs around A\$100,000, a brand new *Australia III* mast designed by Ben Lexcen, the first the syndicate had built in Western Australia, was badly bent in a dockside accident. The mast was largely unstayed during *Australia III*'s measurement for a twelve-metre certificate by Sydney official Ken McAlpine. A shift in the wind took the spar on the unsupported side and the bottom section was badly bent. Bondy's comments would have taken the paint off the boat said the crew later. Despite a depth of experience that went back to 1974 through four America's Cup challenges, the Bond effort was cutting new ground in running a two-boat campaign, with a third boat in the wings, over such an extended period.

'Back in 1977 we had a stab at using two boats,' recalled John Longley. 'We had *Southern Cross* as trialhorse against our new boat, *Australia*. Nothing much was done to the *Cross* except to throw the mast back in and sail her again. It was virtually useless. We'd go out and sail for an hour and everything would fall to bits.' Things were different this time. *Australia III* was a brand new yacht, the finest of the five twelves he has constructed, according to Steve Ward, the Perth family boatbuilder whose association with Bond goes back a decade. *Australia II* had undergone refits so intense as to amount almost to a rebuild. However, these were mere hardware problems. Two world-class crews had to be assembled, men willing to stay and sail for around two years. Of the eleven men who had sailed to victory aboard *Australia II* only Grant Simmer, Hugh Treharne,

Skip Lissiman, Colin Beashel, Damian Fewster and manager John Longley remained with the team. In Longley's office a wallchart contained twenty-eight spaces for crewmen's names. As the months rolled by the spaces began to fill up, but the syndicate made it clear that they did not need or want muscle-bound jocks who would have to be taught which ropes to haul on.

'We sail the boat pretty mobile. Even during the Cup you'd find the navigator up in the bow, bowman back on the handles and the trimmer up helping the mastman,' says Longley. 'It's our way of doing things, loose as a goose and use all eleven people to the maximum. That's why every one of our guys is a sailor and an athlete. They can sail anywhere. We don't go for big blobs sitting on the back of the boat.' The syndicate spent a great deal of time and effort fending off media enquiries designed to push one of its four nominated helmsmen into that sort of top-dog role occupied by John Kolius or Italy's Flavio Scala, known in the twelve-metre business as 'rock-star skippers'.

Both Longley and Jones never cease to regard it as a top priority that sailors, no matter how senior, see themselves as part of a harmonious and successful crew rather than as Grand Prix drivers with an engine-room beneath them. Colin Beashel, Hugh Treharne, Gordon Lucas, son of Bill Lucas who first took Bond sailing in the eight-metre sloop *Panamuna*, and Carl Ryves are the four 'black-coats' who alternate between helmsman and tactician at the back of each boat. Treharne was John Bertrand's tactician aboard *Australia II* during the Cup win. Beashel was mainsheet trimmer, a job calling for a unique blend of physical power to manipulate the huge winch controlling the mainsail and sensitive judgement on boat speed. Lucas was a young champion sailor and newcomer to twelves, as was Ryves, a middle-aged top amateur sailor from Sydney who had worked in the motor trade all his working life until a call from his Sydneysider friend Ben Lexcen set him heading west to Perth to drive twelve-metres. Despite the best intentions of the syndicate, as the months rolled by it became apparent the sandy-haired, shy Colin Beashel was proving himself the helmsman that other teams were going to fear when the ten-minute gun fired. He is almost Jekyll and Hyde between water and land.

In the 1985 Australia Cup held annually on the Swan River and one of the world's top six match-racing contests, Beashel was joint top scorer with Britain's Harold Cudmore when the contest reached

the last race on the last day. Cudmore, ten years older and a
formidable psychological as well as technical driver of a boat, was
taken aback by the cold ferocity of Beashel's sailing. With his sandy
hair, luxuriant ginger moustache and diffident manner, Beashel could
have been the role model for Algy, the modest sidekick of Biggles.
However, once at the helm of a boat he more closely resembles the
dreaded Red Baron von Richthofen.

'I guess I try to be the aggressor,' admitted Beashel, shortly after
winning that crucial race, 'to get the feeling going that you are the
aggressor and that the other person is trying to get away from you.'
Some skippers crank up the combativeness in the bar and locker-
room, seeking an intimidatory edge before they even get out on the
water. That manner, so definitive of Dennis Conner, is the antithesis
of the Beashel style. 'I start my psychology at the ten-minute gun. It's
the way you present yourself and your crew. You do need a lot of
confidence. If you don't feel that you're going to win I don't believe
that you will. That certainly has to go down through the crew, not
just sit in the skipper's head. They must believe that the boat is going
as fast as the opposition, that you can tack as fast as their yacht, that
you will better than match them in all aspects of sailing.' Beashel's
great mentor in the '83 campaign was helmsman John Bertrand.
Much of this psychological approach to competition is laid out for
view in his autobiography, *Born To Win*.

Probably nothing that happened in the early stages of the build-up
to the 1987 Cup did so much to upset the equilibrium of the Bond
syndicate as the publication of Bertrand's book. Although he had
always made it clear that he was not available to drive the boat again,
Bertrand was a frequent presence at the Fremantle headquarters in a
training role. His consultancy agreement with the syndicate extended
over the whole three years and was worth, according to some
reports, as much as A$250,000. Once the gripping, but highly
egocentric, account of Bertrand's life and times was published, only
the barest legal relationship remained. The Bertrand grin was no
longer seen on the dock.

Bond was outraged by the presentation of himself as a rip-roaring
land salesman, which he once was, driving around Perth in a Rolls-
Royce with a bald tyre. The description of Mr and Mrs Bertrand's
1974 ride to Yanchep in the Rolls bears repeating. 'The Corniche
turned north. The air-conditioner throbbed relentlessly against the
heat outside, which was about 110 degrees. The loudest noise in the

car was not in fact the ticking of the clock. It was Alan Bond, still pitching, still selling all the plusses and plausibilities of Western Australia.' After affluence comes a need for respectability, according to one of Perth's most respected financial journalists, John MacIlwraith, speaking of his home town.

Bond had come an awfully long way since Yanchep, and to drag up that 'Home of the Twelves' business didn't seem quite *comme il faut*. Immediately after the book appeared, becoming, incidentally, the biggest-selling hardback ever in Australian publishing, Bond declared that he had tossed the book in a bin after reading only a few pages.

'We can't let this sort of thing upset our defence campaign,' he told key personnel. 'People write stupid things about me every day of the week but I don't take any notice. I can't afford to. My advice is to forget it and get on with the job.' Barely a week after *Born To Win*'s debut, *Australia III* was launched. Bertrand was conspicuously absent from the carnival, although he had left Perth only hours before on the unpopular Saturday midnight flight back to his Melbourne home. He had an 'unbreakable' Sunday business appointment. Just a day or so before the launch of *Australia III* a lavish breakfast at the Sheraton had pushed the book on to the Western Australian market. Despite being based just a dozen miles away in Fremantle, none of the crew who, Bertrand asserts, would have given their lives for him aboard *Australia II* found time to attend the celebration.

It was an altogether messy and painful business for most people involved. Many key crewmen, such as John Longley, while unwilling to discuss Bertrand's account publicly – the syndicate imposed a pain-of-death ban on anyone speaking to the media on the subject – were known to be unhappy with often inaccurate portrayals of themselves and, occasionally, their families. Many reviewers gave the work a merciless bucketing, particularly those with a high level of involvement in Australian sport. Bertrand was felt to have committed the cardinal sin in a group effort: elevated himself above the team. He in turn was hurt by the response and lashed out at what he termed 'another example of Australia's tall poppy syndrome', where a hero is only worth creating in order to cut back down to size.

One concrete effect of the furore was to reinforce the syndicate's belief that no one could be allowed to perceive himself as being more important than the team effort. 'John Bertrand drove the boat, on average, very well. He played a major part, but only a part, in the overall effort that won the Cup,' Warren Jones told Bruce Stannard from Australia's *Bulletin* magazine at the height of the row. 'Our great disappointment is that he has chosen to boost himself and downplay the ability of *Australia II*.' It was a masterfully subtle put-down. Still angry, Bond took the Fremantle dockside boot-up-the-arse approach, and referred to the book as 'a novel'.

Bond's involvement with the defence syndicate up until now has not been huge. One of his most senior managers put his thumb and forefinger a micron apart and said: 'I'd never be quoted on this, but his presence and direct input so far has been this big.' His wedding-day arrival on the dock to inspect the fire damage was his first visit for a considerable time. The enormously ambitious purchase of the Queensland brewery Castlemaine Toohey's has been Bond's biggest immediate project during the period of the Cup build-up, and some of his sailors now suspect that they are working for a small and relatively insignificant division of the Bond Corporation. If that is true, others who know the boss better suspect he will come riding in with guns blazing if he sees the Cup slipping from his grasp – a White Knight with 101 per cent commitment. 'The point is he never, ever gives up and I respect that like crazy,' Bertrand told me shortly before the rift. 'It's the Sir Winston Churchill syndrome.'

Chapter 5

Born Out Of Victory

Britain's effort for the 1983 America's Cup was the most effective since the war. The Victory syndicate of Peter de Savary lost the right to challenge only to *Australia II*, the eventual winner. Almost all the top people in British sailing were involved in that campaign – although many of them left before the end, having reached the end of the line with de Savary's abrasive, hands-on approach to management. Aside from the feuds and personality clashes, what Victory did produce was a pool of talented British twelve-metre sailors and technicians sharing a belief that winning the Auld Mug was within the grasp of the nation that lost it in those grey seas off Cowes nearly a century and a half before. It was an extraordinary and surprising paradox, therefore, when the British entry for 1987 came not out of this Cup community, but from a retired admiral who had never been near a twelve-metre yacht in his life. It was a classic case of 'the navy's here'. The Royal Perth Yacht Club set a final deadline for entries during early 1984. Would-be competitors had to lodge A$12,000 as evidence of good faith. With only hours to the closing deadline there was still nothing from the Poms. When the cheque arrived, in the nick of time, it bore the name Admiral Sir Ian Easton, KCB, in the bottom right-hand corner.

The sixty-nine-year-old Easton retired from the Royal Navy in 1978. His career had begun flying 'stringbags' off Ark Royal and other aircraft carriers during the war, and had ended guiding the Anglo-US nuclear alliance as chief of the Washington defence staff. He now lives quietly in an Isle of Wight cottage, pottering with dinghies and a bucolic garden. An earlier resident might quite easily have seen the first America's Cup race from Causeway Cottage. Among Easton's acquaintances was a young, brilliant and somewhat eccentric designer named Warwick Collins. He had anticipated the winged keel of *Australia II* and had done further work at Southampton University on developing the concept. Collins arrived in the early spring of 1984 to see the Admiral on another matter. 'He told me something that I was unaware of – that there was no British challenge for the America's Cup,' recalled Easton, a tall urbane man with a directness of speech which belies his somewhat patrician manner. 'I said it was unthinkable that there shouldn't be a British presence in 1987.' It was then just a month from the closing date.

It took that long to persuade British Aerospace, where Easton had some influential friends, to underwrite the deposit. 'I simply wasn't in the financial bracket to write cheques for £8,000,' he explains. 'I live entirely on an admiral's pension, given to me some years ago, and I pay a significant part of my income out in alimony.' The unconventional former naval officer is no longer attached to his second wife, Margharetta Elizabeth Martinette Van Duyn de Sparwoude. An American ballet dancer named Rina now shares Causeway Cottage. The couple have a young son. On the Friday before the Monday deadline, British Aerospace agreed to underwrite the deposit. The syndicate now consisted of Collins, the admiral, and a promise. But they still lacked a club to challenge through. The deed of gift states that the Cup may only be challenged for by established yacht clubs, not individuals. Easton is a member of the small and wholly delightful Royal Solent Yacht Club at Yarmouth on the Isle of Wight. But a challenge for the Cup was never going to be within its compass. The first stop was the Royal Burnham Yacht Club, under whose aegis club member Peter de Savary had mounted the Victory challenge. The club had already declined a similar invitation from Kit Hobday, former vice-chairman of the Victory syndicate, but Easton did not know that. It also refused him. With only a day or so left the next stop was the august Royal Yacht Squadron. At least it was on the Isle of Wight and the telephone calls would not be STD. The commodore, Sir John Nicholson, held out little hope, but promised to reach every committee member he could and call back by six o'clock. When the telephone rang at Causeway Cottage the news was bad. Although it had run the original race for the 100 Guinea Cup, the squadron could not see its way clear to be the conduit for a new challenge.

Only one chance remained. Easton knew John Foote, vice-commodore of the Royal Thames Yacht Club, the Knightsbridge institution whose flagpoles overlook Harrods, and made a Saturday night call to him. He had heard that the club was not interested in the Cup, but with only thirty-six hours remaining no string was going to remain unpulled. On Sunday Foote brought his yacht *Water Music* into Yarmouth's beautiful little harbour, five miles or so from Easton's cottage. The talks were arduous, but Foote agreed that, subject to ratification by the Sailing Committee, the Royal Thames would lodge the necessary challenge before the next day's deadline. *Water Music* sailed homewards up the Solent with Easton's cheque on the chart-table.

'I take my hat off to them,' says Easton with unashamed gratitude, 'putting the challenge in for an individual who came to them with no money nor promise of it, no organisation, no experience and no connections. I salute their courage.' Eighteen months later Sir Ian stood next to the Princess of Wales on a podium in a draughty shed at Cougar Marine on the Hamble River. Her Royal Highness was engaged in smashing a bottle of champagne over the bow of *Crusader*, first of the new British twelve-metre yachts. 'This new British challenge was made on 1 April 1984, only minutes before the deadline,' Royal Thames vice-commodore Owen Aisher told the large audience – which included Alan Bond, attracting endless attention as a prominent member of twelve-metre royalty. 'That this happened at all was entirely due to the enthusiasm of Admiral Sir Ian Easton, who refused to accept that there would be no British contender for the America's Cup.' The warmth and surge of affection towards the somewhat austere figure next to the sylph-like blonde princess drove through the crowd like a breeze across a mainsail. 'The guy has standards and integrity that are very rare today,' says *Crusader*'s skipper Harold Cudmore. 'He staked his pension money to get it started,' added chief executive of the syndicate David Arnold on the day before the launch. 'It has been handed from the gallant retired officer to people like me, a medium-weight grubby businessman. Nothing I could say would adequately stress my respect for him.' The route from the meeting aboard *Water Music* to having two boats in Fremantle would be a long and bumpy one, but they got there.

Ultimately, twelve-metre campaigns always come down to money, according to John Longley, now involved in his fifth America's Cup campaign with the Bond syndicate. It can't make you win, but you're not going to go anywhere without large dollops of it. Peter de Savary never disclosed exactly what the Victory campaign did cost, but US$8 million was a widely accepted figure. In a well-reported speech at the National Sporting Club in London during late 1983, de Savary pledged to have another crack at the Cup. However, as time went by it became patently clear that his business interests in Britain and America required de Savary's presence around the Atlantic basin. He spent much of his time twelve miles above it in Concorde, commuting to Antigua where he had opened a new branch of his wildly successful St James's Club. Not even the presence of his old friend and soulmate Alan Bond could make a year's soujourn in Perth a viable and attractive proposition for de Savary. However, in the eyes of the British public he had become Mr America's Cup. If he didn't put up the money, where was it going to come from?

Only in terms of their personal energy should Graham Walker and Peter de Savary be compared. Immensely tall, reserved in manner and with a delicate pink-tinged complexion, Walker immediately reminds one in appearance of those quintessentially English army officers who reach respectable rank in a good regiment and then move discreetly into the more confidential departments of the Foreign Office. Appearances can mislead. It was Walker's money that transformed the British effort from being Admiral Easton and a promise into a full-blooded campaign. He made the money himself in the tough field of liquor retailing. Walker was born on the Wirral peninsula, Merseyside, the son of a policeman and the grandson of a miner. After a grammar-school education he was among the last national servicemen. 'I think it had quite a good effect on me,' he now observes. 'Brought some discipline into my life.' Joining Fine Fare supermarkets after the army, he worked his way up the middle-management ranks until he left to run the retailing division of the Cheshire-based Greenall Whitney brewery. When the board of directors turned down his plan to sell cut-price liquor through rented space in other people's supermarkets, Walker did it anyway – in his spare time. 'It was very successful very quickly,' he recalls. 'Quite soon I was able to resign and get on with building up a chain of off-licences and tobacco stores in an emerging chain of supermarkets. A very discount, cut-price approach to things. Nobody was into discounting at that time and it grew very quickly.' Between 1971 and 1980 it mushroomed into a business with a turnover of £100 million a year. At that point Walker merged his baby into James Gulliver's Argyll Group, taking a heap of shares and a non-executive directorship, and began to think about leisure. He had been active in rugby for much of his life, first playing for New Brighton and then running junior sides. But age catches up with rugby players and about the time Walker was thinking of retiring a friend asked him to Cowes Week 'just for a few parties and things'. He had never sailed apart from messing about with a dinghy years before. On his second Cowes visit Walker met 'some people who were talking about an event which was to take place in 1978 called the Half-Ton Cup'. Characteristically he decided to jump into yachting via one of the most competitive and unforgiving events on the nautical calendar. A designer, Stephen Jones, was appointed and mouldings acquired. 'It's funny really because we went to look at everything and I had a feeling it would turn out all right because it was the only half-tonner I could actually stand up in,' recalled Walker. On its first outing the boat won a major national title in Scotland. 'That was it, I was hooked on sailing. The whole idea was that I was just ballast, part of the crew. Phil Crebbin drove it for me with the help of a couple of New Zealanders I had got to know. In the middle of the Half-Ton Cup that year, leading the entire field, I asked some inane question about the boat and received the reasonable reply: "Bloody hell. Here we are in the middle of a world championship and Walker's having sailing lessons." '

Once he knows what he wants, Walker likes to start as near the finishing post as possible. A few years ago he suffered a nagging desire to own a vintage Bentley. Oh, and it had to be black. Driving his Range Rover through some remote Welsh hills one day he saw the car of his dreams. Flagging down the driver Walker offered to buy it on the spot. The owner, a gentleman farmer, agreed terms, but raised the question of how he was to get home? 'I'll give you the Range Rover,' announced Walker. Ten minutes later the registration documents had changed hands and each man went on his way rejoicing. 'Amazing chap, Graham, terribly persuasive,' said the former Bentley owner, Willie Gilbertson-Hart, who has subsequently become a friend of Walker. 'Once he knows what he wants, he really cracks on.'

Over the next few years Walker concentrated on building fast boats and, more importantly perhaps, finding top people to sail them. The management of the project from conception to victory was the draw. Walker knew that having started in virtual middle age he was not going to become a front-rank helmsman. 'In serious racing I'm happy to let the professionals drive the boat. I could never be as good as the standard I would wish to have achieved. It's just fascinating watching these specialists do their job,' he said. One of his favourite professionals was Harold Cudmore, for the past decade one of the world's top helmsmen and skippers. Cudmore had sailed Walker's boats in the Admiral's Cup and other events. In 1985 *Indulgence IV*, sailed by Cudmore and owned by Walker, sank after hitting an underwater obstruction in the first race of the Admiral's Cup trials off Cowes. They borrowed a standard cruiser/racer, straight off the production line, and became the top boat of the 1985 Admiral's Cup.

Before there was any real money in for the America's Cup 1987 Ian Easton had been talking to top sailors like Cudmore and Crebbin. Both men had been seriously discouraged by their experiences with de Savary in Newport, 1983. In the end they found him impossible to work with and left, having parted with years of their lives. Crebbin, in particular, was wary of any subsequent Cup involvement. But when the Admiral asked them for the name of a man who was wealthy, good to work with, and might support a research and tank-testing programme, neither had any hesitation in suggesting Walker's name.

The initial approach was a failure – Walker recoiled instinctively from the idea that the challenge might be hung around his considerable shoulders. 'I was prepared to put some funds into the development work,' he recalled, 'although at all times I've resisted the situation of allowing the challenge to become a solely personal effort financed by one individual. Apart from the danger to your wealth, it focuses too many decisions on one person – as we've seen in the past. You get yourself tied up in an ego-trip, perhaps? It may suit people who go for a particularly high personal profile, but that's not the way I want it. I was worried that any sort of personality cult would detract from the team that was here and I also sensed that industry would not support a personally led challenge. The business world would see no merit in funding somebody's personal ego-trip. I liked the idea of a wider and stronger group of people.'

In the earliest days of the campaign that had to mean designers. Easton's military experience had been largely in the running of medium-term research and development projects; Walker's competitive philosophy in yachting had been to create the best vehicles and then put top sailors on them. The two men were in accord that maximum resources should be devoted to leaving the UK with the finest twelve-metres that British ingenuity and experience could devise. Via Easton's connection with British Aerospace an aerodynamicist named Herbert Pearcey was brought into the programme to supervise the team working on tank-testing at the National Maritime Institute at Teddington, just outside London. Pearcey's 'supercritical' aerofoil suction had been the technical breakthrough that made a success of the Trident airliner and the Harrier jump-jet. Although he resembles a stereotype boffin in one of those 1950s films about test pilots (usually starring Jack Hawkins as the man with the leather flying helmet), Pearcey is no stranger to the pressures of the area where design meets multi-million dollar racing. The Marlboro Maclaren Formula One racing car was developed in the wind tunnel where Pearcey was to later work on keel configurations. 'It is a great stimulus to research, having a competitive edge to the occasion,' he observed drily of the coming America's Cup circus. Pearcey is not a sailor himself, but has written extensively about the scientific aspects of yacht design and followed the genesis of the famous winged keel with fascination. 'He brought the trained scientific mind to something that has very often been the province of flair and imagination,' says Admiral Easton. 'The developments to *Australia II* in the Netherlands showed that aerodynamics had a lot to add to what a talented designer like Lexcen came up with.'

The designer that Pearcey was 'riding shotgun' on was David Hollom. His work was brilliant. Working on a design and development project named Project Acorn (funded by Peter de Savary) prior to the '83 Cup, Hollom had anticipated the *Australia II* concept and improved upon it. Unfortunately, from the point of view of lay credibility, Hollom was a designer of 'scale yachts' – model boats to the vulgar. Easton decided that Hollom's ideas offered the best chance of a twelve-metre breakthrough, although because of his lack of 'real boat' experience it was necessary to protect the downside by combining him with International Offshore Rule designer Stephen Wallis and then having Pearcey oversee the joint effort.

'I've encountered surprisingly little prejudice about the fact that I'm a model yacht designer,' says Hollom, a forty-four-year-old merchant navy officer who left the sea to live in Yorkshire. 'I don't know why, but you do get people with the idea that model yachts are just toy boats. But then every yacht is a toy boat really, isn't it? They have no practical purpose other than to give pleasure or go fast.' Hollom is blunt and direct, the perfect antidote to the tendency towards grandeur and *haute folie* almost endemic to twelve-metre syndicates. He regards it as an ephemeral world where people are hard and projects die. Sailors and financiers pick up your ideas with enthusiasm and then drop them just as quickly – and, as far as Hollom is concerned, you still have to pay the mortgage. For a man rubbing shoulders with the top echelon of international yachting, their futures dependent upon his unproven ideas, Hollom is remarkably sanguine about his situation. 'I've always thought that in any given environment the cream will come to the top – provided there's nobody stirring too much down below,' he jokes from beneath an unruly thatch of poker-straight black hair. His belief in what the syndicate refer to as 'Hollom's grand piano' is that model yacht design has consistently been years ahead of full-scale design over recent decades. Hollom believes that if you go to any pond now and look at contemporary scale yachts, you are looking broadly at the offshore racers of twenty years hence.

His own involvement began just after the war. 'When I was around ten I can recall going into a department store and seeing a large model yacht, which I demanded and got for Christmas,' Hollom recalls. It turned out to be a model six-metre, somewhat ironic since in the modern world six-metres are increasingly being used as low-cost testbeds for twelve-metre ideas. Hollom began sailing his model on the famous pond at Clapham Common and joined the thriving club there. Before long he realised that the only certain way to sail the boat you really wanted was to design it yourself. His first effort in the Thirty-six-inch Restricted Class soared through the national championship at Wimbledon Pond and Hollom was away. 'My sport or hobby was model yachting. Designing, building and then racing them – although my real interest was only in the design,' he conceded. 'Having drawn it you are almost obliged to build it and then race it.'

1 Fremantle High Street, *c* 1902

2 Yacht racing is nothing new in Fremantle; this picture was taken *c* 1910

3   Yachts on Melville Water, with Perth in the background

4   Alan Bond and his portrait of another distinguished Australian

5   The three Fremantle harbours: *left*, Challenge Harbour; *centre*, Fishing Boat Harbour; and *right*, Success Harbour, home of the Fremantle Sailing Club

6   Not everyone in Fremantle welcomes the America's Cup

7   Colin Beashel, helmsman for *Australia IV*

8   *Australia III* in Fremantle harbour

9   *Australia II* and *Australia III* show the fleet the way home during the World
12-metre championships

10   The US yacht *Courageous*, an early casualty

11   Dennis Conner lays hands on the America's Cup for the first time since losing
it to *Australia II*

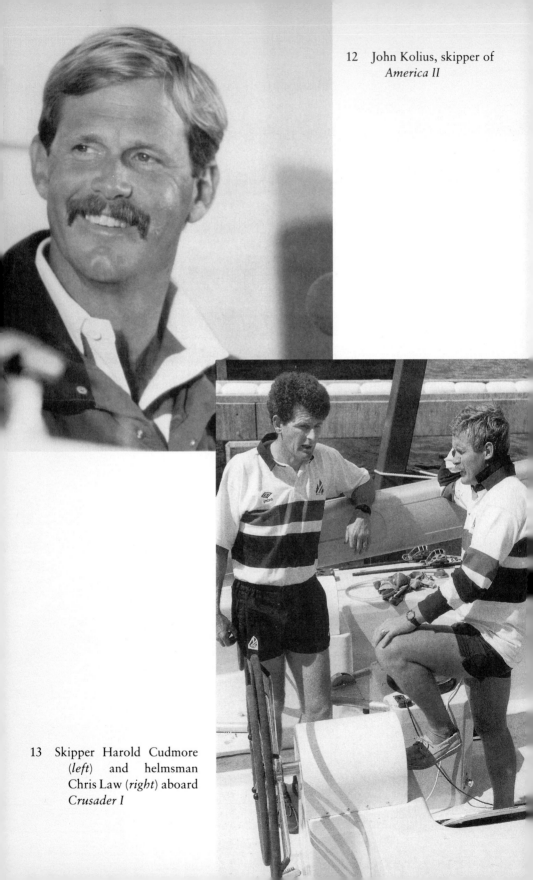

12 John Kolius, skipper of *America II*

13 Skipper Harold Cudmore (*left*) and helmsman Chris Law (*right*) aboard *Crusader I*

14　The British challenge: *Crusader I*

15 The world's first fibreglass 12-metre yacht, one of the three craft built for the New Zealand challenge for the America's Cup, being lifted from its mould

16 The Italian challenge: *Azzurra*

17 Dame Edna Everage meets the crew of the Australian yacht *Kookaburra*

18 Arthur Wullschleger of the New York Yacht Club with *US44* in the background in Fremantle

Would this also be true of a £1 million twelve-metre? Admiral Easton and the informal committee of people like Graham Walker, Phil Crebbin, Harold Cudmore (the nominated skipper) and Philip Tolhurst, the lawyer who handled much of the Victory syndicate's administration, agonised over whether it was too much of a gamble to build and then go half-way around the world to the toughest regatta on earth with a giant model yacht. They decided it was. Another ingredient was needed – Ian Howlett.

Howlett is something of a prodigy. Still only thirty-six, he designed *Lionheart* for the British challenge in 1980 and *Victory '83* three years later. Obsessed since boyhood with twelve-metre development, he had drawn yachts for 1974 and 1977 when lack of funds prevented a British presence at Newport. A cricket buff, Howlett is quite likely to pass a reporter a slightly foxed first edition of Sir Don Bradman's biography to read while he waits for the bespectacled and benign designer to finish a meeting. Despite a pixie-ish manner, Howlett has a very firm idea of how good he is. The Americans said after Newport that *Victory '83* was the best conventional boat there and would have beaten Liberty on any day of the week. With Hollom designing what looked more and more like a 'wild card', Easton and his committee began to feel the need for an insurance policy, something that would put up 'a bloody good show' if the radical boat had a fundamental flaw which had not shown up in the tanks and the computers. 'I'd wanted to get Howlett at the beginning,' said Admiral Easton. 'But I'd wanted him as part of a team and he wasn't prepared to become part of a team. Then I asked him to participate in a design competition up to one-third scale models. Howlett said he had had enough of competition designing under de Savary and wouldn't do it again. The upshot was that Howlett, with the independence of mind characteristic of Balliol men, was hired on his own terms. He would design a state-of-the-art, conventional twelve-metre. It would contain everything learned from *Australia II* but nothing unproven – a yacht that would put the crew in the front rank of any competition, yet offered no breakthrough. The downside was protected, as Harry Cudmore is fond of saying.

Away from the technical struggle to produce fast boats, the challenge was floundering. Despite hiring a succession of professional fund-raisers, the syndicate was unable to find major sponsors. One problem was the attitude of the Royal Thames in the early days. Although the club had lodged the challenge for the America's Cup, its commitment to the syndicate was less than wholehearted. For more than a year after the first contact with the Royal Perth the club insisted on the right to withdraw its imprimatur from the challenge if it was not happy with progress. Easton is convinced that such an arbitrary situation cost the syndicate its chance of substantial early funding. Certain factions within the Royal Thames let it be known to the yachting press that the commitment to the challenge was only provisional, and credibility was damaged. 'We have very direct evidence that one or two very large sponsors would have underwritten the whole thing prior to talking to the club,' said Easton. 'With one of those I have it from the horse's mouth that it had been cleared to the highest level to take a £4 million stake in the challenge. Just before the final commitment they went to the Royal Thames and were told: "We don't really know if it's going to come off. We're not sure it's going to be successful." From then on the telephones from that sponsor ran cold.'

The syndicate's relationship with the club was not helped by an ongoing problem with Warwick Collins. Since coming to Admiral Easton with some designs for a twelve-metre Collins had assumed the role of *de facto* technical director. But as the management team grew and began to include people such as Phil Crebbin and Harold Cudmore, possessing vast experience and a proven track record in big-boat racing, relations with Collins became a little tense. 'I began to feel that his attitude was not consistent with the kind of group effort we were mounting,' recalls Easton. 'He had great confidence in his own ability and it was either accept that or nothing.' Easton went ahead seeking to recruit Phil Crebbin to the campaign, not in itself the easiest of tasks since Crebbin had a thriving career in the computer industry and would not be anxious to repeat the kind of twelve-metre experience he had undergone with the Victory syndicate. Easton was successful and Crebbin became technical director. 'The next day I received a letter from Warwick Collins saying that he wished to take over the challenge or he would have nothing more to do with us,' recalled Admiral Easton. It was painful to have to part company with the man who had been the real instigator of the whole project. Easton referred Collins to the Royal Thames and a certain number of what are now referred to as 'unfortunate' letters were written. It was sheer bad luck that this distasteful process was under way at approximately the same time that the Royal Thames were receiving unofficial 'feelers' from potential backers about the soundness of the challenge. Collins resigned and became involved with a much-publicised venture to win the next-but-one America's Cup and bring it back to Torbay. One of his associates was Peter de Savary, who in discussions with Admiral Easton had not entirely ruled out involvement in the current campaign.

During an early financial crisis de Savary had sounded willing to take over the entire challenge and underwrite it. But the price was that certain people crucial to the management team would have to go. Phil Crebbin and Harry Cudmore, who had fallen out badly with de Savary during the Victory effort, were to be the prime victims, but there were others. That, and the financial aspects of any takeover, proved the stumbling block. 'I'd be delighted if he could be associated in some role or other,' says Easton of his flamboyant cigar-chewing predecessor, 'but as long as he stuck to demands of wanting key personnel changed it could never be a possibility. I suppose he might come in as patron, put up some money and enjoy the scene while it is on – be part of it.'

To anyone who has dealt with de Savary the notion of him sitting on the sidelines of an enterprise is about as likely as the arbitrary reversal of gravity. Actor Tim Pigott-Smith who is to play de Savary in a forthcoming television series on the Newport power-plays of 1983, went, by way of research, to meet the tycoon in his lair. 'The phone never stopped going. The activity in that office was just sensational,' reports Pigott-Smith. 'He told me that he has an illness producing too much adrenalin in his bloodstream, tending towards perpetual hyper-energy. When it comes on he can usually take drugs to control it, but if it is really severe he has to stick his head in a paper bag to inhibit the oxygen supply to his brain. That provides a calming effect.' It is not intended to be offensive to suggest that the only way de Savary could be involved in a twelve-metre campaign and not wish to control it completely would be to have a paper bag permanently over his head.

Despite the political problems between the syndicate and the club, many of them leaked to Fleet Street by disaffected people connected with the Royal Thames, there were companies prepared to take the long view and come in with major sponsorship. The first of these was British Airways. The airline offered the British America's Cup challenge a mixture of cash, travel to Perth for crew members, and air cargo facilities worth £250,000. BA's traffic into Perth from London was growing rapidly and an involvement with an event which promised to generate large extra volumes of business and tourism traffic seemed a sound idea. Nevertheless, a quarter of a million pounds is a large exposure and, being in the middle of a privatisation process whereby the state-owned company was sold on the share-market, BA was anxious not to encounter image problems – and there is always a risk of those with the America's Cup. Alan Beaves, marketing manager responsible for Australian routes, was very conscious of some of the negative aspects of the Cup when he decided to commit BA to one of its biggest ever sponsorships. 'It's true that in the past it has had the image of being the pinnacle of folly: yachties throwing other peoples' money – in large amounts – at an unattainable dream,' conceded Beaves. 'But the Aussies' victory at Newport somehow brought it into a different realm. Alan Bond left London as a working-class lad, made good in Australia and captivated the public imagination. Other people from that mould have since entered the Cup and it is no longer seen as solely a rich man's prerogative. The fact that somebody took it away from the Americans is good news – especially Australia because of the strength of their sporting links with Britain. If anyone is going to win this Cup other than Britain, I guarantee that nine Britons in the street would say Australia first, second and third choice.'

The airline may have begun to feel it was getting its money's worth when Cudmore and his crew of four arrived in Perth to take part in a Swan River match-racing series prior to the America's Cup. The contest is known as the Australia Cup, and most of the world's top match-racing skippers take part. BA flew the team out and, without prompting, Cudmore ensured that in defiance of all yacht-racing etiquette they wore British Airways tee-shirts virtually non-stop for the four days of the regatta. 'We've been pretty aggressive about our gear and why not?' Cudmore asks rhetorically. 'It's a little thing they've given us, maybe a thousand pounds' worth of seats since we basically came standby. My philosophy is to give them fifty thousand pounds' worth of exposure and then when it comes around next time to really paying up . . .'

Cudmore is a naturally gifted sailor who, for the past decade, has turned the running of big-boat campaigns into a management science. He tends to be a touch dismissive about being one of the three or four best helmsmen in the world. 'My principal talent is not out there on the water,' he explains with an expansive sweep across the turquoise-blue ocean off Perth. 'Steering a boat I'm as good as anybody in the world at present. Maybe the best, give or take a touch. But what I'm really good at is putting together a group, a strategy – the whole thing.' Cudmore sees himself as what he calls a new breed of sailor-managers. His approach is carefully to pick specialists for every job on the boat and, just as vitally, ashore, and then leave himself with an overall strategic brief to co-ordinate and direct their efforts. Businessmen as astute as Edmond de Rothschild, French owner of the eighty-foot maxi-yacht *Gitana*, have found his a worthwhile talent to employ.

The problem between Cudmore and de Savary in 1983 was due to the latter's unwillingness to delegate what Cudmore saw as vital matters to the people who had to sail the boats and win. He won't discuss it now. 'I don't want to be seen to criticise the previous effort, not my style. I just put things behind me, whoosh, gone,' says Cudmore dismissively. If Cudmore won't talk, former colleagues from the Victory campaign will tell you how furious he was to have to read in the *Daily Telegraph* that de Savary had commissioned a new boat for the syndicate. (That was *Victory '83*. Its predecessor, *Victory '82*, had proved, in the immortal phrase, 'a dog'.) Amid the dockside rows and management conflicts there were good things to come out of Victory. His association with de Savary taught Cudmore an assurance with the media that has grown steadily since. 'PDS was so competent at handling the journalists. I learned mountains from him,' admits the curly-haired Irishman, whose conversation is startlingly direct and contains no blarney. 'The guy is very competent at handling the media. At twelve-metre sailing? Nothing . . .'

Many crucial logistics people have been brought in by Cudmore from the previous campaign. Andrew 'Spud' Spedding will run the dock, as he did in Newport. A former naval officer, Spud now farms sheep on Dartmoor in Devon and writes humorous books on his experiences. (The day before he arrived in Perth to begin constructing the British base he had been sitting as a magistrate in Tavistock when a local came up before him. Spud was horrified to hear that the accused had admitted nearly forty counts of bestiality with sheep, and even more horrified to learn that some of the livestock probably bore the Spedding brand.) Other riggers, welders and electronics men have come back from a peaceful life away from twelve-metre boats to try once more for the big one.

'We have a carefully thought out approach and attitude based on the factors of our previous experience,' Cudmore defines their stance.

'We're a relatively older group – there won't be any young people on the programme. We have spent a great deal of time bringing in people of the very highest level of ability in sailing. The plan exists. It may not be right, but we are pursuing it and we are going to back it.'

One impressive and distinctive aspect of the British campaign is the distinction, outside sailing, of the people who have been drawn into it. Chris Law, race helmsman after Cudmore has handled the starts, gave up a directorship of Olivetti and a company Porsche to go down under and pursue the Auld Mug. Now in his early thirties, Law looks back on his twenties as a time of struggle – both financially and in reconciling the demands of a young family with the time-swallowing campaigns of an Olympic sailor. Yet, having reached the sunlit uplands, he has given it all away. 'I just believe that this is going to be the best team and hence the best chance that Britain has of getting the Cup back. Once I'd been invited I couldn't bear not to be part of it,' says Law, who was still at Millfield School when he was picked for his first Olympic sailing team.

Attracting other top-name British sailors was not a problem once the Cudmore/Law axis was firmly in place. Eddie Warden Owen and Jo Richards came in immediately beneath them in the helmsman-cum-tactician spot, and then six veterans from *Victory '83* – Andy Burnell, Richard Clampett, Chris Mason, Kevin Rawlings, John Thompson and Dave Woolner – were recruited. The contribution of sails genius Tom Schnackenberg to the triumph of *Australia II* in Newport had not gone unnoticed by the British. Angus Melrose, head of North Sails in Britain and regarded as one of the top men in the arcane field of twelve-metre sail design, was placed on contract to work exclusively for the British challenge in the year preceding the finals. The philosophy that Cudmore pioneered and nailed into place attracted those who had been through the fire of Newport and emerged feeling that it could have been so very much better. 'For better or worse it is very clear what we are doing. The sailors are running everything to do with the water,' Cudmore explains. 'Not the management side of things – I don't buy houses in Fremantle, arrange for piles to be driven at the dock, or scrounge aluminium for the boats. But the hull shapes, the equipment procurement and the selection of the crews are entirely under the control of the sailors.' Cudmore has retained to himself the contractual right of every crew appointment. He remains aware of the danger of autocracy, but in practice this can be diffused through a sailing committee. But the committee is composed of people who have stood behind the wheel of a big yacht in a gale of wind and tried to make sense of it all. People, in Cudmore's words, 'actively involved in the sport at the highest levels'.

Attracting top-level sailors might not have been a problem, but throughout 1985 funding remained a well of despair. At one stage around Easter the challenge was only days away from foundering completely. It was saved by the Royal Thames finally giving the effort its complete endorsement, and more importantly by a group of wealthier members underwriting a commitment to BACC of several million pounds. Against all his better judgement Walker got further drawn in financially. 'We had a very good reaction from the Thames,' says Walker, 'and a number of prominent members – men of greater substance than myself – agreed in principle to join the underwriting. That gave us comfort and I had said I would go in deeper if fellow members thought it a reasonable risk.' Walker's crucial involvement was becoming, against his real wishes, daily more public. Yet it was still projected in limited terms. In private and utter confidence he had told key syndicate members that, come hell or high water, there would be a challenge. If sponsors continued to stay away, Walker would make up the shortfall. That represented a possible cost of over £5 million. His remarks about 'a danger to your wealth' looked prescient.

In terms of management and administration the best thing to happen to the challenge during this lean period was the arrival, as full-time chief executive, of David Arnold – the self-proclaimed 'medium-weight, grubby businessman'. He is physically huge, finds it no problem to conduct four conversations simultaneously (two of them by transatlantic telephone) and understands commerce. In sailing terms Arnold had 'paid his dues', sailing aboard Admiral's Cup winner *Just This*, on Ted Heath's racer *Morning Cloud*, and with Graham Walker and Harold Cudmore on *Phoenix*. Having been rear-commodore of the Royal Thames prior to becoming involved, Arnold had a fairly good insight into the syndicate's problems. 'I really came into it, I suppose, because I thought the organisation was more of a pious hope than a challenge,' he said candidly on the eve of *Crusader*'s launch. 'One or two people were floating around making big noises, but there wasn't any money. Computer time from the government via British Aerospace and a DTI grant for tank-testing and that was about it, bar the odd unsigned contract.' Arnold, forty-six, had been a submariner before going into the family engineering business and building it up into a substantial concern. Having sold the company and not started another project, he was in a position to step in and help. As a full-time employee of the syndicate he is paid £18,000 a year, 'enough to keep the wife in gin' as he puts it. It was he and Walker who put in place the primary philosophical position that the syndicate should be not just a one-project charity, as it were, but an ongoing company. Its primary asset would be twelve-metre experience in design and campaigning. This had to be combined with the right to stage and market the defence of the Cup in Britain, following success in Perth. Arnold was adamant that he would not be in 'the Bondy situation' where the club through whom the challenge was mounted just said, 'Well thanks for winning it. Register here if you'd like the chance of defending.' For the company with the right to mount the defence the income potential is enormous, according to Arnold. Each challenger would pay around £30,000 in entry fees and that could be multiplied by a number in excess of twenty. 'It will be up to us where we hold it – we've got about five places in view, but the local authorities will have to cross our palms with silver. We'll take options on property, TV rights, merchandising, tourism and so forth.' Preliminary investigations have already taken place in potential venues such as Plymouth and Torbay. With the economic indicators and surveys already giving reliable information that the next America's Cup could be worth in excess of US$1 billion to a local economy, it would be a brave local council that did not fight for that opportunity. It was not easy persuading some senior figures at the Royal Thames – some of the same people who had nearly scuppered the challenge in its earliest days – that this was the future.

'We must learn the lessons that the Australians taught us,' pronounces Walker. 'But we're up against some rather diehard traditionalists among the Royal Thames. There are some of them who cannot realise that we are in a different century.' Despite the difficulty of the negotiations, when the prospectus for British America's Cup Challenges PLC went to the public, among the material contracts listed at the rear of the document was the following sentence: 'In the event that the 1987 Challenge is successful, the RTYC has agreed, on certain conditions, both to consult with and give effect to the recommendation of the Company on the location for any subsequent defence and to give the Company the right to prepare a defender on behalf of the RTYC.'

After the initial problems of financing the challenge the British syndicate consistently showed an innovative flair in its approach to money matters. For A$300,000 they bought a former nursing home in east Fremantle, a mile from the waterfront, as a crew headquarters. Crusader Castle, as it quickly became known, was a lovely old colonial building with wide verandahs and an air of tranquillity about it. At least as important, planning permission existed to build six townhouses in the grounds. The plan conceived by David Arnold was that at the end of the challenge Crusader Castle would show a profit. The idea that a syndicate might end up with an appreciating asset rather than an unusable old boat was an entirely novel concept in America's Cup racing.

The British team's most vital new idea, though, was to form a public company and invite the public to buy shares in the challenge. Through merchant bankers Guinness Mahon a prospectus was prepared offering three million one-pound shares. They were to be the equity in a company named British America's Cup Challenges PLC. The plural on the fourth word was the subtle but important indicator that depth of experience, volume of research data and competitive boats were going to be a long-term asset in the ever-expanding circus of the Cup. Sceptics were plentiful in the city. 'Gamblers or sailing freaks might splash out the minimum £1,000 stake as a patriotic gesture,' said the *Investors Chronicle* in an assessment of the offer. The formation of the company under the terms of the Business Expansion Scheme made it attractive to high-rate taxpayers, but the projected profit of £139,000 on a turnover of £2.7 million to June 1987 could only have appealed to confirmed optimists. In sailing folklore the accounts ledgers used by Cup syndicates only have a money out section. Income, other than by donation from those infected by the Cup bug, is a rare phenomenon.

Nevertheless, the cynics were confounded and the issue was over-subscribed. Small investors received their full application of shares, but quotas for some of the large institutions had to be rationed. No syndicate in history had ever raised Cup funds in such an unorthodox way, but the lesson was far from lost on other teams. The 1991 Cup is certain to see a great many public companies participating, although the mind boggles at the notion of a shareholders' meeting discussing whether the skipper should have set a number four genoa in the third race.

Aside from the incident of the keel plans for *Crusader* being stolen and offered for sale to the New York Yacht Club, the British have kept a deliberately low public profile in the two years leading up to the start of the races. In the light of the fuss and secrecy over *Australia II*'s winged keel it would not have been possible to keep our own 'keelgate' quiet. On the eve of *Crusader*'s launch by the Princess of Wales, the police in Devon and Cornwall posed as New York Yacht Club officials, even down to carrying a bank draft for US$25,000, and arrested an employee of the foundry that was to cast the yacht's twenty-five-ton lead keel.

Twenty-seven-year-old Anthony Brown had sent New York Yacht Club challenge director Tom Ehman a copy of part of the keel blueprint and offered the rest for sale. 'The New York club were kind enough and sporting enough to let us know about it,' says Spud Spedding. 'Millions are tied up in this Cup, so you can imagine the potential worth of any potentially helpful technical information.' On the other side of the Atlantic Ehman was very conscious of how the image of the club had suffered through poor sportsmanship during 1983, and wanted nothing to do with anything shady. 'I wanted to do everything I could to get the plans back to the British,' he said at the time, 'but under no circumstances did I want to see or have the documents myself.' The upshot was that a trap was laid. Brown believed that the Americans had taken the bait and turned up for a rendezvous armed with a photocopy of the plans lodged in his employer's safe. On the steps of the Mayflower Hotel in Plymouth he met the distinctly un-American Police Constable Simon Raeburn. The young constable received the plans and handed over the draft. He was wired for sound and a video camera recorded the proceedings. A squad of detectives emerged from hiding and Mr Brown's 'sting' was over. Designer Ian Howlett was not told of events until it was all over. 'I felt very sad,' he recalled. 'It's one of the human tragedies that it's almost impossible to protect against leaks from within an organisation.'

The affair had a rather curious sequel. After two months on police bail no further action was taken against Mr Brown. Even the Director of Public Prosecutions had been unable to come up with a charge that would stick. An invention can be stolen, but a keel design, however revolutionary (and this one was evolutionary), is not classed as an invention. Even an indictment on a charge of stealing the physical plans would not hold up in court because Mr Brown had photocopied the originals and returned them to the safe.

Keel espionage seemed above – or below – the law. The DPP's decision did not go unnoticed in the America's Cup world. If the law was no protection, perhaps another security guard and a taller fence would help.

A story like that was bound to attract a mountain of publicity and it did, but otherwise there was relatively little early interest in the campaign outside the yachting press. Cudmore has an explanation: 'We're a very boring story. We're boringly professional; there will be no sudden flares of genius. Our argument is that if you don't think Britain can design and race a twelve-metre to beat Australians, not Americans, sure we can't win. If you think it requires traditional aristocracy or flamboyant millionaires to help . . . Sure, that's your opinion too.

'If, on the other hand, you're someone born some time after the Second World War and you believe that things like professionalism matter, plus project management, procurement philosophy and systems to make things work every day, then of course we can do it.' Cudmore is not given to hyperbole and he seems for a decade to have been enjoying life very much as it comes. But no one close to the gifted Irishman doubts that this campaign represents some sort of culmination for him. 'The big one? Oh, yes, absolutely. I couldn't say if I'd do it again after this, but this is the end of a lot of time spent thinking. I've been enjoying life and sailing for its own sake, but there has always been a master plan of learning all the ingredients necessary to win the America's Cup. I'm sorry that John Bertrand got there before me because I was well on track – except that I ended up with de Savary and he ended up with Bond. If I'd had Bond I'd have won too.'

Chapter 6

American Efforts

Among Europeans and, to a lesser extent, Australians there is a tendency to scoff at the US reaction to losing the America's Cup. The mother-home-and-apple-pie determination to get it back – regardless of cost or sacrifice – is the source of an even greater secondary amazement. One yacht club was willing to plunge into a complex legal wrangle just for the chance to avenge national honour.

The Chicago Yacht Club, patriarch of Great Lakes sailing, had to convince the state of New York supreme court that its local aquatic playground, Lake Michigan, was an integral part of the five great oceans and not just a giant Mid-West puddle if it was to be allowed to enter the 1987 America's Cup. The deed of gift requires that a challenging club be located on the ocean or part of it, and this was Chicago's initial problem. As they were entitled to do they asked the Royal Perth Yacht Club to petition the supreme court for an interpretation of the deed. The top New York law firm of DeForest and Duer were engaged to represent the Royal Perth.

Ironically, the clause that caused Chicago their initial problems stemmed from a situation involving Canada – where two promising syndicates were already under way with no legal handicaps whatsoever. In 1876 and 1881 the third and fourth challenges respectively for the America's Cup came from clubs situated on Lake Ontario. The Royal Canadian Yacht Club entered a 107-foot centreboard sloop, *Countess of Dufferin*, and five years later Bay of Quinte turned up with *Atalanta*. Contemporary accounts make it clear that both boats were woefully inadequate for the task in hand. 'She has been constructed on principles different from those commonly received here, and as she was turned out in a hurry she is in a rough state which can hardly fail to provoke smiles from the New Yorkers . . . If the strange looking craft carries off the Cup there will be a revolution in New York yacht building,' wrote one observer who inspected her en route to New York. The *Countess* did appallingly in the racing and there was no revolution among the Hudson River shipwrights.

Atalanta was, if possible, even worse. Because of a late launch she could not be sailed to New York via the St Lawrence and the Atlantic coast. The challenger suffered the indignity of being stripped of her rig, canted over and towed through the inland fastness of the Erie canal to reach the race. On arrival one New York paper reported her to be 'rough as a hedge fence'. She lost pitifully, manned by a Canadian crew who, according to another contemporary journal, shouldn't have been allowed to navigate an anchored canal boat. The New York Yacht Club felt, perhaps understandably, that their trophy wasn't being taken seriously enough by the fur-hatted sailors from north of the forty-eighth parallel and took severe action. The deed of gift was handed back to its architect, George L. Schuyler, for re-drafting. In its new form it stipulated that a foreign yacht club eligible to challenge must 'hold an annual regatta on an open water course on the sea or on an arm of the sea'. It further quite specifically prohibited clubs along the Great Lakes from entering. For over a century the clause slept unchallenged, until Chicago got Perth in its sights.

Harman Hawkins, attorney, sailor and former president of the US Yachting Racing Union, went in to bat for the Royal Perth. He had Jordan Peters working with him and directly arguing the case for the Heart of America syndicate, which was the name of the Chicago Yacht Club's challenge. Statistics about the tonnage of freight being carried down the St Lawrence seaway, the number of fine yachts entering the annual Chicago-to-Mackinac Island race, and even the salinity of the Great Lakes themselves – all were paraded before the distinguished judges. Great play was made of the happy coincidence that in 1851, the year of America's great victory off the Isle of Wight, the US supreme court had ruled the Lakes, in an entirely unconnected case, 'in truth, inland seas'.

When the court finally answered the petition in September 1984 it decided in favour of the Chicago Yacht Club being allowed to enter the Cup, but on the narrowest of terms. No ruling was made on the general issue of whether the Great Lakes were 'an arm of the sea'. The way was clear for the Chicago Yacht Club, led by Olympic veteran Harry 'Buddy' Melges, to take a tilt at the Cup.

One club that simply had no option over whether to challenge was the New York Yacht Club. With an empty spot in the trophy room at West 44th Street it was unthinkable that the Auld Mug should languish on a foreign shore. Unfortunately, the wounds of September 1983 would need treatment from a therapist rather than a lawyer if morale was to be restored sufficiently to mount a costly and gruelling campaign on the other side of the world. Many senior members of the NYYC genuinely felt that the Bond team had won the Cup by cheating the rules concerning foriegn participation in yacht construction. Dutch scientists at the Netherlands Ship Model Basin, Wageningen, had certainly assisted Ben Lexcen with the development of *Australia II*'s radical keel. The unanswered question was: How great was involvement and contribution? In presenting this case at Newport in 1983, the club had created a public relations disaster. To the world at large the America's Cup Committee appeared as a group of sulky old men in straw hats and red trousers who couldn't take the knocks being dished out by a faster boat. Two of the most senior, Victor Romagna and Robert McCullough, decided that despite a lifetime of involvement with the Cup there would be no next time for them. McCullough was personally savaged by the press and knows he was a scapegoat. He is philosophical and would rather forget the whole thing. The sixty-seven-year-old Romagna is more forthright. 'There is a tradition in this club, and it was a great tradition,' he told the *New York Times* in 1985. 'I just did not see it being taken away by cheating. But once they took it away they can have it.'

Arthur Santry Jnr, currently commodore of the NYYC and the deposed former chairman of the America II syndicate, has thought about those grey weeks after the defeated Conner walked off the dock, weeping, ignored by his patrons. 'I think there may have been

some bitterness among members of the America's Cup Committee,'
said Santry, at sixty-eight the chairman of Combustion Engineering,
his own New England company. 'I think there was certainly
disappointment in the fact that we had not successfully defended it,
but I personally don't feel any bitterness. There were a lot of people
close enough to it to know what went on and to know that we had
been outsmarted perhaps – and I think we were. It has led to
determination and the money to get it back and put it in the middle
of the trophy room where it belongs. The way to get the Cup back is
to win it on the water.'

The club's chosen vehicle for the retrieval of the silver urn is a new
and untried syndicate called America II. Its composition reflects the
new world view of a club without the Cup. From Texas came the
sun-belt wealth of O. L. Pitts and Lee A. Smith, pillars of the
landlocked Fort Worth Boat Club. At the helm of the new boats will
be John Kolius, who did so well at the wheel of the unfancied
Courageous in the 1983 defender series. Kolius, thirty-four, a world
champion and Olympian in dinghies and smaller keel boats, is the
antithesis of Conner. Extroverted and outstandingly good-looking in
a Robert Redford fashion, he is one of the new breed of superstar
skippers. When Kolius walks down Fremantle High Street after a
training session girls stare at him. The finance director and eventual
chairman of America II is Richard De Vos, a self-made businessman
from Michigan who is not even a member of the New York Yacht
Club. Among themselves this group habitually refer to their crew and
supporters as the 'NEW New York Yacht Club'. This was not going
to be a syndicate composed of the old east coast establishment who
had fiddled around with the Cup for so many genteel Newport
summers – and then lost the darned thing. This was new America,
can-do America. The three big sponsors of America II – at a
minimum of US$1 million each – are Cadillac, *Newsweek* and the
Amway direct selling corporation, founded by Richard De Vos.
'We've taken a look at the people involved in sailing, and the
demographics are . . . upscale, very like those of *Newsweek*,' said
that magazine's Gary Gerard. The very idea that you should do a
survey to see who is who in sailing . . . Why, they were your cousins,
the children of your father's business partners, the boys you had been
at those little east coast preps with. Except that O. L. Pitts and the
good ole boys of the Fort Worth Boat Club don't belong to that
America, they don't even believe in its existence. They had seen it

shame the nation and lose the Holy Grail to a go-for-the-throat Aussie like Alan Bond.

America II was the first US syndicate to establish a Fremantle base. In October of 1984, a full two years before the first of the elimination races, the team arrived in hot, dusty Western Australia. Mentally and physically they were like men arriving on Mars. 'The approach I use is the "barren rock" approach. We're going to an area where there is no twelve-metre equipment, therefore you have to bring your own,' expounds Arthur J. Wullschleger, the syndicate's operations director. 'We're like a turtle – travel with a shell on your back. That's what makes it so darned expensive.'

Wullschleger is a crusty, ironical, tough-as-nails textile millionaire from the Carolinas. With his white hair and dapper toothbrush moustache he suits his universal nickname of Cap'n Tuna down to the ground. The soubriquet comes from his fifty-three-foot tuna fishing boat *Fire Three*, which was tender to *Courageous* and Ted Turner in 1980, Conner and *Liberty* in 1983, and now works out of Fremantle each morning shepherding the America II yachts.

In fact, after Turner was knocked out in 1980 the gregarious Wullschleger teamed up with Alan Bond's boys, who were campaigning *Australia I*. 'After Turner got beat I went over to the Aussies who were having a terrible time with their tender – called it *The Warthog* – and offered them *Fire Three* for free if they wanted it. A shake of the hand and a dollar – just for insurance purposes,' recalls Wullschleger. He has taken three years off from the family business to pursue the Cup. 'My sons are running the whole bloody show. "Do anything you want," was my advice to them. The only thing you can't do is go backwards. Fire everybody, shut the plants down, sell 'em. I couldn't care less – but don't go bankrupt.'

In the 1983 campaign Wullschleger had no management role with the *Liberty* syndicate, just a grandstand seat providing and running the tender. His now deputy, Jake Farrell, was skipper of the VIP yacht *Bravo* moored next to *Fire Three*. 'Arthur Wullschleger and I were drinking buddies,' remembers Farrell, on the frequent days when he wonders how he ended up in Western Australia running a beachhead in enemy territory. 'We would sit up on the flying bridge and have a cocktail and talk about how if we were running things this or that would happen. Six months later they called his bluff and put him in charge and the old bastard called mine and made me his deputy.'

Twelve-metre sailors are pretty heavy users of pubs, especially when away from home, but Farrell must be one of the first to actually buy one. Being virtually the first American II man into Fremantle, to establish the logistics of the dock and compound, he looked for a pleasant pub where he could get a decent hamburger. Finding neither he looked for local partners with money – he didn't have any – and then took over the Hotel Cleopatra, famous as the town's roughest, toughest licensed premises. Gallons of white emulsion, scores of America's Cup pictures and $80,000 later, Cleo's became the Auld Mug, genuinely the social centre of the twelve-metre scene. In a town where the bouncers are quick and lethal, Jake became famous for gentlemanly evictions. 'I hate to beat up on drunks because I've been there. I've been drunk and beaten up,' laughs the thirty-one-year-old physical education teacher from New York.

When the America II crew, around forty of them, are not supporting their dock boss's business and Australian breweries in general, they live in a block of apartments in East Fremantle, just down the road from the British in their elegant turn-of-the-century former nursing home. It has the air of a college fraternity house, although the presence of Cap'n Tuna lends a little restraint and the cooking of Austrian chef Erwin Pascher lifts the culinary standards far above those of the average 'frat'. He worked for the Rockefeller family in the Caribbean and trained with the CIA (the Culinary Institute of America). Add a local butcher, who was persuaded to cut Australian beef American style, and the home comforts created by America II and one sees why the syndicate is so favoured to do well. A conscious effort has been made to remove the unproductive strains of campaigning far from home while keeping the useful, adrenalin-producing tensions. The team has even appointed Jane Kent, a distinguished sailor and sports psychologist, to keep the balance in view and work on the outlook of each individual crewman.

This syndicate arrived in Perth with what might fairly be termed an image problem. After the fencing and power-politics of the 1983 Newport summer, avidly if not accurately reported in the Antipodean press, an average Australian regarded the New York Yacht Club as on a rough par with the Visigoths. When they took a lease on the modest apartment complex, local headlines had America II buying up half of East Fremantle. The compound established at Fremantle Boatlifters, on Fisherman's Harbour, had a heavy chain link fence and a permanent security guard on the gate. Later every syndicate would do the same, mostly to keep the curious public at bay rather than deter keel spies, but the NYYC suffered from being first. In the waterfront bars it was 'common knowledge' that the security guard was armed and had orders to shoot intruders. The problem wasn't all on the Australian side. The America II team admit that in their first season they were insular, slightly afraid of Australia, and relied too much on the umbilical telex and air-freight routes back to good old Rhode Island. Kathy Farrell, Jake's wife and the office supremo, had run a freight company in New York and it was the team's proud boast that they could get an item in from the US faster than the Australian teams could obtain an inferior version from Sydney.

The syndicate headquarters was always in Newport – a small cramped office off Lees Wharf containing the exuberant executive director Tom Ehman. Outside flies the same 'No Roo' flag seen above the Fremantle compound. It consists of the famous boxing kangaroo with the standard highway prohibition sign – red circle and bar – printed over it. At thirty-one Ehman is the youngest international yacht-racing judge in the world, and saw the whole of the '83 drama from the jury boat. He has won four North American yachting championships in his own right and is a firm believer in the 'NEW New York Yacht Club' idea. Thirty-three other yacht clubs within the USA have been affiliated to the challenge. When, not if, according to Ehman, the Cup comes back it will go on tour. Each of the affiliate clubs will get to keep it for a week. In return, they raise money – around US$150,000 each. But the real point is that it spreads and diffuses gut passion for the event among a much wider boating fraternity than just the traditional constituency of the NYYC. 'Plus we'll have two hundred million Americans shouting for us at home,' Ehman grins. To mobilise that mass enthusiasm for an event that has traditionally been elitist and was then tarnished by bad sportsmanship is at least as big a challenge as the technical one of building fast twelve-metres.

That particular little problem is the responsibility of Bill Langan. At just thirty Langan, a graduate of the highly prestigious Webb Institute of Naval Architecture in New York, is chief designer at Sparkman and Stephens. S & S, as they are known throughout yachting, have turned out six America's Cup defenders. It is a stable with pedigree and class, but for them, like everyone else in the 1987 Cup, a turn into the puzzling avenues of aeronautical research has been necessary. The Sparkman team sought the help of McDonald-Douglas (famous for their military and civilian aircraft), NASA (best known for putting people into space), and the Michigan Institute of Technology. Langan says that they taught him about computational hydrodynamics, an extension of the use of mathematical models on proposed aircraft designs. 'It's the technique used to calculate the lift and drag of any lifting body, be it an aircraft wing, the space shuttle, a propeller – or a twelve-metre yacht sailing upwind,' explains Langan, a handsome blond man with a lazy smile. He drew *Freedom* for Dennis Conner in 1980 and *Spirit of America* in 1983, which Conner rejected in favour of Johan Valentijn's boat *Liberty*. Explaining his prime position as sole designer to the most favoured team in the Cup competition Langan shows a nice sense of irony: 'Fortunately I did not design *Liberty*,' he drawls. In the positive sense his reputation rests very much on *Freedom*, which Harold Cudmore, among other top skippers, regards as the best conventional twelve-metre afloat.

Spirit of America, known to cynics in the Cup field as 'the ghost that didn't walk', never really had a fair outing. For the present campaign Dennis Conner and the San Diego syndicate have kept only her deck and rig, rebuilding her entire hull and re-christening the yacht *Stars and Stripes '83*.

While Bill Langan looks after the technicalities of finding that rare diamond, true boat speed, Ehman, Santry and Kolius have developed an all-singing, all-dancing routine to take across the length and breadth of the United States in the search for the dollars that will fund it. The shapely back of a Perth girl clad in a tee-shirt appears in their slide show. Detailed focusing of the projector reveals that the abstract black pattern is in fact a mass of ugly flies. 'The good news is that the lifespan of a fly is only twenty-four hours,' intones Ehman crisply. 'The bad news is that they do a lot of loving in those twenty-four hours and there are just as many the day after.' The crowd at the America's Cup evening called by the Macatawa Bay Yacht Club love it. They may not know much about Australia – next to nothing, in fact – but it is always pleasant to have one's prejudices confirmed. Next comes a slide of a large kangaroo followed by one of a large Holden stationwagon sporting a roo-bar. (On the backwoods dirt roads of rural Australia it is an essential safety precaution to have a roo-bar on the front of any vehicle. A night-time collision with a kangaroo will usually wreck the vehicle and kill the occupants.)

Ehman shakes his head. 'We have roll-bars in Newport – but roo-bars? Will we need to have them on the boats?' Flashing a picture of the lovely Perth skyline on to the screen he adds that one of the less popular twelve-metre sailors formed the view that Western Australia was nothing but flies and Aborigines. Not true, of course, he adds vehemently. It is a big cosmopolitan city, modern in every way. It all adds up to the subtle and not-so-subtle impression that maybe the Holy Grail isn't safe down there with those roo-punching fly-swatters. The most effective slide has a close-up of a Perth car registration plate proclaiming Western Australia as the 'Home of the America's Cup'. Ehman looks gleeful. 'This will become a collectors' item!' he assures the rapt audience. When the evening ends Macatawa Bay's sailors are reaching for their cheque books with something approaching religious fervour.

But not even the New York Yacht Club could make every fund-raiser a winner. Walter Cronkite, celebrated newscaster and CBS anchorman who has covered every America's Cup since 1957, put in $250,000 of his own money and became a director of America II. He also wrote a heart-wringing letter that went out to a quarter of a million comfortably off Americans. 'All my life I've loved the challenge of sailing and the loss [of the Cup] came as a real shock to me. But even to Americans who have never been on a boat before, the rallying cry is the same. WE'VE GOT TO BRING BACK THE CUP.' Unfortunately only 651 of the letter's recipients felt strongly enough to reach for their cheque books and the appeal produced a grand total of $33,079. It was a fund-raising disaster. Cronkite had said in the letter that $585,000 was needed within sixty days and the effort had produced barely five per cent of that. 'The results were . . . not spectacular,' admitted Wullschleger who, one suspects, believes more in the direct approach of hitting one's wealthy sailing friends right in the billfold. 'It was an individual fund-raising exercise for people that don't know nothing about boats. It's not mailed for free and the guy doing the mailing isn't doing it for nothing. What you evaluate is what you've got left after you've paid this jerk and the US Post Office – not a lot is the short answer.' In contrast to the short and pugnacious Cap'n Tuna, chairman De Vos is tall, elegant and upbeat on direct fund-raising.

He admits the return on the Cronkite exercise was low, minimal in fact. But De Vos, a fifty-nine-year-old self-made millionaire from Grand Rapids, Michigan, is a veteran political fund-raiser. Over a million dollars a year comes into Republican party coffers through his efforts. Some stories say that President Reagan has asked him to run for high elective office, but De Vos shrugs such suggestions off with easy good humour. 'It isn't always what you get the first time through with direct mail,' he explains. 'What you get is that one per cent return and small contributions. But they are on your list now and you can work that list, work it up from, say, thirty dollars to sixty dollars to ninety dollars, and so on. The ones that have taken the trouble to reply to the initial letter are the ones who will increase their contributions. Get them as a member of the syndicate – once they're in they are going to read more of your material and you can really zero in on them. It's a tough way to get prosperous, but that's the price you pay. In the USA that's the way the political parties run –they send millions of letters out.'

No one should doubt De Vos' expertise in this area. His Amway Corporation is now one of the biggest privately owned corporations in the world. It direct sells fairly ordinary cleaning and household products through chains of members and franchise-holders. Once someone is an Amway customer it is very rare for them to become an ex-customer and even rarer for them to slip into being a smaller customer. De Vos is also genuinely a sailing democrat. He could probably pull another couple of big corporate $1 million sponsors and save the time and trouble of winkling small dollars out of Joe Blow. It is not the road he wants the syndicate, or the America's Cup as an event, to take.

'Our goal was always to make this an all-American effort. Up until now in the United States the America's Cup has been played by a handful of bigshots with a lot of money,' says a man who would regularly slot into the upper echelons of the Forbes 400. 'But we wanted to reach out to people who could give us thirty dollars – so that it became more than a rich man's game and became a representative cause for all of America. Today we have more than five thousand people involved in this thing. It may not sound that many, and sure a lot of them are fairly rich, but you compare it with the tiny tight little syndicates of only a generation ago: all Yale and Skull and Bones.'

De Vos can be quite philosophical about the games rich men play – especially out of the office. It was he who patched together the deal that saved the syndicate after the internal storm in September 1985 when John Kolius quit. The thirty-four-year-old computer specialist and Olympic helmsman from Houston felt he was being treated like the chauffeur. Kolius wanted management of the sailing programme. If Kolius was out, it was a dollar to a frayed halyard that the big money of the Fort Worth Boat Club, O. L. Pitts and Lee Smith, would not be far behind. In a boardroom coup Arthur Santry had the good fortune to be elected commodore of the NYYC and stepped down as chairman, to be replaced by Richard De Vos. The big blond Texan helmsman had quit in tears at a Newport meeting of America's Cup challengers, saying his decision was a consequence of 'syndicate politics, which were interfering with my ability to devote my energies to the sailing effort'. As a result of changes at the top Kolius felt able to walk back through the door that had been left open for him and rejoined America II less than a month later.

'The syndicate was started by one guy, Chuck Kirsch,' explains De Vos. 'He got it off the ground, brought the first players together. Arthur Santry led the interim, sorting things out, then I came in. They asked the guy who knew least about it to do the job. The first business I ever had was running a flying school right after the war – but I didn't know how to fly. Sometimes a business is best if you don't know all those things, then you can concentrate on the team – putting the players in the right places, as opposed to the chairman having to be the guy who's supposed to know about sailboats, sail-manufacturing and all that. The chairman's real job is to co-ordinate all the experts, to get them on the team and get the money to make it happen. I know less about twelve-metres than many of the board members but that's not my job.'

De Vos is almost cynical about the problems of containing the push and drive of a group of wealthy, successful men within a group where they can't all be powerful. His formula is almost schoolmarm-ishly simple: keep them busy, idle hands and all that. 'When a group of very successful businessmen come together in a syndicate their egos are all at work, they all want a substantial role, or at the least they want to know that they are part of something and be important in the process,' explains De Vos, who still lives next door to his business partner of the past forty years, Jay Van Andel. 'As chairman I just make sure they all have important things to do – because they are big players and when they play big they want a sense of participation. It's up to me to provide that.' However, it stops well short of telling the sailors how to drive the boats and which genoas to use. That way top skippers walk out on you. 'You can't let them get in the way of the sailboat team because those guys have got work to do,' believes De Vos. Instead he charms or bamboozles some of the business community's largest-calibre bigshots into hosting guests at the compound, holding plate dinners at their yacht clubs, escorting guests down to Fremantle. You create things for them to do, says De Vos.

With his high-school and wartime friend Van Andel he has become joint owner of a billion-dollar-a-year company. De Vos would be the first to admit that you don't build up a business like that by touching projects as irrationally appealing as the America's Cup. 'You certainly cannot explain it as a logical or reasonable investment of your time or money,' he admits, while his son, a management student at Purdue University and the youngest of his four children, works stripped to the waist under the baking Fremantle sun sanding the hull of *US44*. 'There is an America's Cup bug that bites people. It must be an animal somewhat like a leech. You just get bitten by it and you just go deeper and deeper and next thing you know you're really in the middle of it. It doesn't make any sense at all, but successful people are active people. They're into things. And if they're less involved with their businesses as time goes by they need some other thing to work on.'

Leonard Greene is, in the nicest possible way, a dinosaur, a throwback to the days when one rich man bought a boat and raced it in the America's Cup. Greene is the founder and sole owner of Safe Flight, a hugely successful aircraft instrumentation company based in White Plains, New York. He is also the chairman of the Courageous syndicate, owner of the most evocative twelve-metre still afloat. She successfully defended the Cup in 1974 and 1977 and came very close to being the chosen boat of the NYYC in 1980. She is Greene's pride and joy, but when a mast breaks – as it did in only her second sail off Fremantle early in 1985 – the bills come out of his own pocket. Although the campaign is modest in some respects, the crew – almost entirely Yale graduates or undergraduates – have been sailing *Courageous* right back to the winter of 1984. There may not be money for fancy tee-shirts, according to vice-chairman Dave Vietor, but whenever it's needed for the boat Greene comes through.

'I am obsessed with the Cup but I wouldn't get a divorce for it – and plenty of men have,' observes Greene, sitting in his splendid apartment on the nineteenth floor of a block looking over the Swan

River and west to the ocean. From his bedroom window he can see the America's Cup course. His wife Joyce laughs, sitting with her elegant legs tucked beneath her on a vast sofa covered with the Courageous campaign flag. Their twentieth anniversary will be in the middle of the Cup effort. 'I'll give you a mug for a present, honey,' cracks Greene. His face is large, lumpy and likeable, very much like a character from a painting by Francis Bacon. Joyce is as body-and-soul into the effort as Leonard. 'We've been sailing together for a long time. I've made a lot of sandwiches in those years,' she laughs. 'In some ways the America's Cup just means more sandwiches.' Perhaps the Cup really has become more democratic. One can hardly imagine the wife of Harold Vanderbilt heading out in a high-speed crash boat to deliver a bundle of tuna and tomato on rye to the crew of *Ranger* the way Joyce does for the Courageous boys.

Greene issues an important, definitive warning. 'My obsession is technical. I am a scientist. Water flow, keel lift, the matching of sail forces with underwater forces are what motivate me.' He designed the highly unusual keel on *Courageous V* (with each fresh configuration the boat gets a new number) and will draw the planned *Courageous VI*, a completely new yacht, himself. But he deplores the cops-and-robbers secrecy that surrounds so much of the vastly expensive technical development of twelve-metres. At Christmas 1985 he sent an ironical season's greetings to the chairmen of all the rival syndicates – a ten by eight black and white close-up photograph of the distinctive keel of *Courageous VI*. 'I wanted to make a point. All this armed guard, barbed-wire fence and submarine pen stuff is only a fashion. But it may kill the America's Cup before it disappears,' says Greene forcibly. He believes that future events will be run on the principle of compulsory disclosure of technical details before the event. 'No sportsman wants to win by copying the work of other people. It's a ludicrous notion. If you know what the other guy has got you are going to want to do something better and faster.'

Greene's involvement in America's Cup technical advances goes back nearly a quarter of a century. The low-cut, deck-sweeping genoa grew out of one of his ideas. When he began building a keel out of spent uranium even the NYYC had to sit up and take notice. The material is non-radioactive, far denser than lead and not as expensive as gold – perfect for a high-weight, low-volume keel. Greene had a business associate at the time who was running a company involved with atomic energy and obtaining the uranium was the least of the problems. In scientific terms the idea was sound and innovative. In public relations terms it was a disaster. The cautious NYYC officials in the brownstone building on West 44th Street were not that close to the man in the street, but they knew instinctively that the idea of graceful twelve-metre yachts with a spent A-bomb just below the waterline was not going to thrill anyone except newspaper headline writers. The clause in the America's Cup racing conditions concerning 'exotic materials' was invoked and the uranium keel sank without any further fallout.

In 1982 Greene was visiting Australia and fitting instruments he had devised to measure the angle of the water flow to the keels of *Challenge 12*, then still in the Bond camp, and *Australia II*. 'To me it was just a scientific challenge, but I knew that everyone would scream the sheds down if I'd worked on the keel of *Australia II*, so I just did *Challenge 12* and told them to transfer the drawings to the other yacht. If I find it out and then someone else finds it out they're going to think Len Greene told them. It adds up to a level of tension that is not creative,' Greene recalls, revelling in the irony of the situation. He has written a political and economic primer entitled 'Free Enterprise Without Poverty' and describes himself as a conservative radical. Despite the huge sums being spent on research and development for twelve-metres, and his own admission that when it comes to Safe Flight he protects commercial secrets as zealously as any other tycoon, Greene believes that the obsessive security and paranoia among syndicates that he so much deplores is not a normal reaction to protect an investment. 'It's fashion. It's vogue. But you can go to that well too often and pretty soon the media will begin to ridicule syndicates that indulge in that behaviour,' Greene believes. 'I think if I kept my design secret it would take the fun out of it for me.

'The way you go about winning the Cup is as important as the winning of the Cup. Openness in competition will, hopefully, return the America's Cup to being a sporting event.' He has had discussions with other chairmen of syndicates and claims there is growing support for the notion that in future events a yacht would need to make full technical disclosure before being granted a twelve-metre certificate. 'We'll have our fun and games this time with concrete pens and getting your team in the newspaper by saying you've seen a trail of bubbles around the dock but, like all fashion, it goes out. The more perceptive guys can already see this. It adds considerably to the cost and, more importantly, creates antagonisms around the Cup. International competition is really the best way of promoting friendship between nations.' Walter Cronkite, besides being an America II donor, thinks in the same way as Greene. During a recent visit to Perth Cronkite announced that he believed Australia winning the Cup had caused more tangible goodwill between the two countries than the fact that they fought both world wars side by side.

Greene's syndicate takes both halves of its challenge seriously. The *Yale Corinthian* has all-American yachtsman and former Yale man Peter Isler as nominated skipper. He defected from Dennis Conner's San Diego syndicate to join the boat of his *alma mater* and has all the can't-go-back commitment of someone who has come over the wall. Even Yale's famous singing troupe, the Glee Club, is planning to come to Perth and sing such legendary ditties as the 'Wiffenpoof Refrain' at the dockside while the old lady heads out to sea and battle. 'We have fine young men on this boat. They're top sailors and they are doing it for nothing but sportsmanship. Thirty top athletes are giving away a couple of years of their lives to do this,' comments Greene, with obvious respect. 'Out of appreciation for what they are putting into it I think we should set an example of fairness on the field of play.'

As a philanthropist Greene finances the Institute for Socio-Economic Studies. He has a high level of interest in people whom he terms 'disadvantaged'. They range from employees in the company's computer factory who are deaf, mute or blind to disabled men and women who have been given the use of radio-controlled model yachts to try to make some of the fun of sailing available to them. One male quadraplegic was built a chin-control unit by IBM to enable him to sail a scale boat. 'He had been a sailor until he dove into the wrong end of a pool,' recalls Greene. 'I think he had his first good time in six years out there racing that boat.' To expand the programme some swimming pools in institutions for the totally handicapped have been fitted with huge fans to facilitate the sailing of model boats. No personal or family tragedy has projected him on to the path of helping the physically damaged – as is so often the case. 'I've been blessed, or cursed, with a very powerful imagination,' he says, the sense of power he emanates at ease with his soft, often fumbling voice. 'I can project quite easily what it must be like to be in these situations.'

It may seem a broad sweep from philanthropic millionaires who design their own yachts and have a choir to computers used to design nuclear weapons, but the America's Cup is nothing if not a broad church. On the University of California campus at Berkeley, the lead-lined, sound-proofed room belonging to the Lawrence Livermore Weapons Research Institute is the venue for regular meetings of the designers working on a new twelve-metre yacht for Dennis Conner and the San Diego syndicate. Gary Mull, a top naval architect in the field of yacht design, attended some of those meetings before he defected to join the equally high-powered but slightly less paranoid Golden Gate Challenge based in San Francisco at the St Francis Yacht Club.

'We were talking about putting scramblers on our telephones,' Mull told the *San Francisco Chronicle*. 'It was swept for electronic bugs before every meeting.' The whole business brought out a latent irreverence in Mull which did not suit the group. 'I looked down the table and said, "When are we going to hire Gordon Liddy [the Watergate burglar] for the dirty tricks department?" There wasn't a single goddamned smile. I thought to myself "Maybe they've already hired him!"' On the St Francis design group Mull has such distinguished American scientists as Albert Calderone of NASA and computer science physicist Heiner Meldner from the Livermore Institute.

Calderone, an aerodynamicist and hydrodynamicist, has views on the Cup that would probably make Leonard Greene boil in his bath. 'The America's Cup has ceased to be a sporting event. It has now become a highly technical programme. We feel the challenge of competing with the top research groups in the world. It's not only sailing that brings us into this. We are seeking the frontiers of technology,' puffed Calderon in an interview shortly after the project commenced. 'It is one of today's most important scientific challenges.' Meldner's contribution is to use computers to simulate flow over a three-dimensional body – in this case a twelve-metre yacht, but on Tuesdays and Thursdays it could as well be a killer satellite rushing through the outer ionosphere. His chosen weapon is a CRAY 2 super-computer which can handle 1.2 billion instructions per second – say a million times more powerful than the run-of-the-mill personal computer on an average desktop. 'We've already used this machine and these programmes to design aircraft, space shuttles and entire weapons systems,' says Meldner, a man who tends to find the

US Defence Department suddenly seeking him out and stamping all his research papers on neutron enhancement Top Secret.

'We consider our boat to be as highly classified as any military weapon,' said Robert D. Scott, the syndicate chairman. 'No syndicate will out-tech us this time. We have the best brains and the best computer designing in the world at our disposal.' The sailing co-ordinator for the Golden Gate Challenge is the legendary and flamboyant twelve-metre sailor Tom Blackaller. His own thoughts on high technology mirror Scott's. 'We could have the winning edge because San Francisco lies so close to Silicon Valley, the birthplace of technological breakthroughs, an area that contains arguably the single biggest concentration of scientific talent in the world. The Bay area is hometown to the nation's brain trust.' Although Blackaller, a flamboyant man with the looks of a young Charlton Heston and a great mane of greying curly hair, is prone to unverifiable statements such as: 'We are building a Twelve that will blow everyone else out of the water,' there can be no doubts of Golden Gate's sustained commitment to a highly technological approach.

Bob Cole is the major money behind the St Francis Yacht Club's challenge. A fifty-two-year-old automobile obsessive he used to race cars against Tom Blackaller at the Laguna Seca race circuit just outside San Francisco. His wealth comes from the Cole Car Company, one of the principal distributors in northern California for European marques such as Jaguar and Volvo. Cole owns around twenty classic cars, but perhaps the best known is the famous 'Blue Train' Bentley that raced the crack French express from Paris to the Mediterranean coast before the Second World War. A world-class yachtsman, Cole has managed a rare triple in west coast ocean racing: the Pan Am Clipper Cup, the City of San Francisco Cup and the Transpac. Like many of his generation who were too young for the war, Cole is fascinated by the human logistics of a project that requires participants to give an irrationally large part of themselves. But you have to have been born in the right year to become General Patton.

'I'm fascinated by people. I look at them and evaluate people in common projects,' says Cole. 'I don't mean in a critical way. I'm interested in how they behave, how well they know themselves. I'm curious as to how the credit will be distributed among the members, in seeing how accurately it correlates to the various personalities and the purity of each person's involvement. That's the exercise, and the

America's Cup represents that more so than anything else I've ever seen.'

Thinking is one of Cole's hobbies. He is fluent and analytical, if not always unbiased. Basically he feels that the west coast is now the powerhouse of America, but the east coast establishment still somehow pervades the country's psyche in an unholy and unhealthy way. 'There's an illustration of the United States that first appeared on the cover of the *New Yorker* back in the 1960s,' recalls Cole. 'In the foreground are the skyscrapers of Manhattan, with everything else panning out and becoming so distant that you can't even find San Francisco. It's a great caricature of what the east coast still practises.' Despite his affinity for British sports cars and his commercial success selling automobiles from the old world, Cole turns to the English for his critical analogies about the Atlantic seaboard mandarins. 'The English think they are so self-made that they can deny and ignore all relationship to the Almighty and divinity. East coast people seem that way to me. I absolutely revel in the notion of blowing their doors off – their money notwithstanding. And that's exactly what we are going to do on the twelve-metre.'

Leaving aside the St Francis's chances of being selected as challenger and then bringing the Cup home, no one could doubt that San Francisco Bay would be one of the finest venues in the world for such a yacht race. A course has already been drafted that has the former prison island of Alcatraz at the centre. From restaurants, houses and offices right around the Bay hundreds of thousands of people would have a grandstand view without having to set foot on a boat – which can be difficult, expensive, possibly dangerous, and restricts the live audience to just a few thousand – as it has been at Newport and will be off Perth. 'We'd love to bring back the Cup to San Francisco,' Blackaller says. 'It's really the only natural arena where so many spectators can actually watch the race.'

In Chicago they might dispute that. After its successful legal battle to have Lake Michigan ruled 'an arm of the sea' the Chicago Yacht Club is developing plans to sail the most famous regatta on one of the world's bigger inland seas. The high-rise apartment buildings and office blocks sprinkling the lake shore could provide wonderful natural grandstands for a future Cup. Even Chicago's natural epithet 'windy' could have been tailored for a city that wants to hold a yacht race.

Harry 'Buddy' Melges is the backbone of the Heart of America challenge. A world champion in the Flying Dutchman, Star and Soling classes and a winner of bronze and gold medals in the Olympics, Melges is Mr Sailing north of the Mason–Dixon Line. At fifty-six his popular nickname is the Wizard of Zenda, which is the small lakeside town in Wisconsin where Melges grew up, learned to sail a scow in summer and an iceboat in winter, and finally took over the family businesses: Melges Sails, Melges Spars and Melges Boatworks. Life on the shores of Lake Geneva (for the sake of confused yachting writers it is probably as well that the putative Swiss entry, Société Nautique de Genève, dropped out of the 1987 America's Cup), sixty miles from Chicago is quiet but comfortable. In an average year the businesses turn over around US$4 million – enough to keep Buddy, his wife Gloria and three children Laura, Harry and Hans in solid mid-west affluence.

It isn't enough for Melges. 'Zenda is not the end of the earth,' he told yachting writer Hugh Schmitt in a memorable quote, 'but you can see it from there.' John Bertrand, who describes his great friend Melges as kind, witty, and with a selfless knowledge of yachting tactics, has recalled how desperately glad he was to get to the Melges home for a short holiday in October 1974 after *Southern Cross*, Alan Bond's first twelve-metre yacht, had received a merciless four-nil drubbing from Ted Turner aboard *Courageous* at Newport. When they arrived at Lake Geneva it was midnight. Ushering the Bertrand family into his home Melges announced: 'This is the City of Zenda and I am the largest employer in Zenda.' Next morning, with the dawn, came the realisation that Zenda had slightly fewer than 500 people and that Melges was the only employer.

As sailing partner aboard the Heart of America twelve-metre Melges will have Garry Jobson, close to him but surely his antithesis. At thirty-five, almost young enough to be Buddy Jnr, Garry Jobson is a veteran of Cup campaigns in 1977, 1980 and 1983. In '77 he was tactician to the outrageously extrovert cable TV millionaire Ted Turner when he successfully defended the Cup aboard *Courageous*. His 1983 skipper, Tom Blackaller, was not so very different from the cigar-chewing, rum-sipping Turner, but Melges is a different matter altogether for Jobson. It doesn't seem to bother the Annapolis, Maryland sailor who was still in nappies when the Wizard of Zenda took his first national title. 'Melges is America's best sailor,' says Jobson warmly. 'His intuitive ability, combined with what I think are some unique design concepts, give us a very strong edge over the other contenders.' Financially it is a modest challenge. The chief executive is Bill Bentsen, formerly head fund-raiser and public liaison man for the world-renowned Art Institute of Chicago. More importantly, perhaps, he crewed for Melges in his two successful Olympic campaigns. The budget is US$6.8 million, and raising it has not been easy. Only one new twelve-metre has been built and the never very successful *Clipper* is being used as a trialhorse. Nevertheless, Chicago's campaign has consistently showed a stability, consistency and flair that some of the faster-talking US challenges may eventually come to envy. They have charmed the public with such excellent productions as the unforgettable Heart of America poster showing a close-hauled twelve-metre tacking across a Kansas wheatfield. It displays an irreverence that is characteristic of Melges. He explained recently why he had never before joined a twelve-metre campaign: 'While the Cup was in the hands of the starchy New York Yacht Club I wasn't interested. Now it's gone to Australia, I think it could be fun to win it back. It's time to join in.'

Robin Fuger is an Englishman from the yacht-infested hinterland of the Hamble River near Southampton. He is probably the most experienced twelve-metre maintenance man in the world. Beginning in the early 1960s with Baron Bich, the French aristocrat and ballpoint millionaire who caught the America's Cup bug very badly indeed, Fuger also worked for Peter de Savary's campaign and most recently for Dennis Conner. British designer Ian Howlett has known Fuger for years. 'You have to be somebody special to work for the Baron for sixteen years, run a meticulous dockside operation for that temperamental man and never learn a word of French,' says Howlett. The association with Conner ended over a lack of shared humour. Conner came back from losing against *Australia II* and said, 'Well, they had a faster boat.' Standing on the dock Fuger replied, 'They did in sixty-four and seventy, Dennis, but the Americans didn't lose.' Fuger found himself looking for another berth and came to rest with the Eagle syndicate of Newport Harbour Yacht Club, just north of San Diego in southern California.

It is an indication of the tight professionalism of that team that they were able to recruit Fuger. It is lean, formidable and with no room for amateurs. Every crew spot is going to a yachtsman of calibre – the traditional Cup policy of taking college athletes without family or job commitments has been deliberately rejected. 'I want crew who are older, more experienced,' says Eagle's nominated skipper Rod Davis, an Olympic gold medallist and, at only thirty, a veteran of three previous America's Cup campaigns. He believes that youngsters travel on too much of an emotional roller-coaster, overly reacting to each inevitable high and low of the campaign. This is a problem on the long march of a modern twelve-metre campaign.

Of course, the drawback with older men is that they frequently have families, jobs and mortgages, and need some financial security. To overcome this the Eagle syndicate has created a job-opportunity scheme where businessmen in the local Californian community employ the sailors when they are not racing and training. 'If things work out well between the employer and the employee, this crew member will have a full-time job as soon as he has finished racing the twelve-metre,' says Davis, who has himself felt this problem. He had only just re-joined North Sails to run a loft in Marina de Ray in southern California when Eagle made him an offer he couldn't refuse. 'In the past twelve-metre crews have been abandoned at the end of a campaign with no thought as to how they are going to re-enter the job market and society. This is no small problem for an individual who has spend two years messing around in boats.'

The enlightened and self-interested Eagle policy grew out of what had been done for American athletes in training prior to the 1984 Los Angeles Olympic Games. Peter Ueberroth was president of the Olympic organising committee and the first man ever to manage a games that produced a profit. He is also chairman of the Eagle syndicate's trustees. Having lodged its challenge with the Royal Perth Yacht Club in 1984 the next thing Eagle did was to spend US$10,000 at the local Chapman College. Its highly respected Centre for Economic Research was given the money to produce a survey of the predicted economic effects of Eagle winning the Cup and the 1990–1 defence taking place off southern California.

When the conclusions came through they were startling. An estimated 5.6 million American and international tourists would visit Orange County to see either the world twelve-metre championships or the America's Cup in those years. Their arrival would inject US$1,065 million into the local economy and generate 4,300 new jobs. It was enough to get Carlson Travel on board as a major corporate sponsor in the US$8 million Eagle effort. The company will market Team Eagle tours to Australia while the defence is running. Another former Olympics official who is on the syndicate board is wrestling commissioner Gary Thomson, who is unequivocal about the role of Mammon in the Cup. 'We are treating this race on a business basis,' he declares.

The syndicate began trials with *Magic*, one of the smallest twelve-metres ever built. Dennis Conner worked her up in the summer of 1982 before rejecting *Magic* in favour of a subsequent boat from her designer Johan Valentijn. The second yacht was *Liberty*. Davis and the team led by Fuger fitted *Australia II*-type wings to the keel of *Magic*. A warm friendship had come into existence between Eagle and the Consorzio Italiano syndicate during 1984. In late summer Davis acted as tactician for its helmsman Lorenzo Bertolotti when he won the world twelve-metre championships at the Aga Khan's Sardinian pleasure palace, Porto Cervo. That winter the Italians reciprocated by sending *Victory '83* to trial with *Magic* off the Californian coast. It was never intended to send *Magic* to Fremantle. All the data flooding in from her was going to Valentijn's drawing office in Newport where he was working on a new boat – to be called *Eagle*. Despite his experience with twelves, Davis resisted the temptation to 'advise' the young designer.

'I am sure that my weakest point as skipper will be that I am too conservative in how I approach hull shape,' says Davis with great candour. 'If Ben Lexcen had come to me in 1982 and shown me his design for *Australia II* with its winged keel and cutaway stern and told me the boat was going to win the America's Cup – and that he wanted to design it for me – I would have thrown him out of my office.

'In starting to organise a programme of this magnitude, you have to look within; you have to organise yourself first and understand your weak points as well as your strengths.' With that capacity for self-analysis and a sensitive, though robust, intuition, it may be not surprising that John Bertrand, himself a firm believer in the virtue of practical psychology, views the Eagle as possibly the most dangerous and underrated of the foreign challengers to Australia's hold on the Cup. 'Rod Davis is one of the hottest match-racing helmsmen in the world,' said Bertrand after Davis had won the 1985 Congressional Cup, 'and he has an excellent organisation behind him.'

Chapter 7

Conner and the Canadians

No one man epitomises the changes in the America's Cup better than Dennis Conner. A Californian with a draper's business in San Diego, the hard man of yachting insists that racing twelve-metres is his hobby. The Conner family must wish he would take up fretwork or trout fishing as a pastime. In 1980, when striving to be chosen as defender by the New York Yacht Club, he calculated that he had sailed aboard his twelve-metre *Freedom* for 340 days out of the year preceding the selection trials. Conner's rival Ted Turner — a man devoted to duck shooting, an occasional glass of rum, and his multi-million-dollar cable television network in Atlanta — sailed forty-seven days in the same period. 'I've just got other things to do,' said Turner, indicating less than total admiration for a human being who could stand behind the wheel of a twelve-metre every waking day. Yet by 1986 a situation has arisen where no syndicate will have done any less than sail continuously for a year prior to the Cup itself. It is obvious whether it is the Conner or the Turner philosophy that has prevailed.

During that year Conner has based his team in Hawaii. Originally there were plans to train in Fremantle for the southern hemisphere summer of 1985–6, but they were scrapped. The paunchy helmsman with the heavy jowls and cold eyes has always been a master of intimidatory psychology and the decision to work-up in Snug Harbour at the University of Hawaii Marine Center came right under that heading. Every rumour from Honolulu echoed around the Fremantle waterfront like a shout in a coal cellar. Teams who were well funded, with excellent sailors and who had brought highly developed yachts half-way round the world to gain experience on the actual America's Cup course trembled at the ghost of a story that one of Conner's many new twelves was one per cent faster than *Liberty*. The simple fact was that the man who broke down and wept at Newport has controlled every scrap of information coming out of his island fastness. Conner maintained a closed camp, and anyway there were next to no journalists with international links based in Hawaii. When reporters and photographers did occasionally receive invitations they were under the kind of control that would make a Pentagon press trip appear wide-ranging. In Perth the effect was devastating. With barely a scintilla of evidence as to whether Conner's boats were fast, no knowledge of crew morale, and only the wildest rumours as to the real state of his funding, he was consistently cited (off-the-record, for obvious reasons) by officials of Australian and foreign syndicates as the man most likely to win the Cup. One wondered if they could not see that they were creating a self-fulfilling prophecy. The King-over-the-Water had only to clap his hands and everyone danced to his tune.

A few months before the world twelve-metre championships in February 1986 a buzz swept through the bars and yacht compounds around Fisherman's Harbour: Conner was in town. The first confirmed sighting was at the Captain Fremantle Motel. The great man had arrived too late for lunch and couldn't get a table. No one could make contact; old friends like Jake Farrell of America II were hurt that they didn't get a phone call. Journalists rang every hotel in Perth but none had a Mr Conner staying. Yet there was no doubt that HE was here. An overweight, middle-aged yachtsman who lost his last big regatta was visiting Western Australia and it was like the Second Coming. The big question was: why was Conner in town at all? Story piled on dubious story. The front-runner was that he had reversed his previous disdainful attitude to the world championships – 'It will be a good marketing event, excellent promotion for some syndicates. From the standpoint of trying to win the America's Cup I think it could be counter-productive.'

The French yacht *Challenge 12* was up for charter, the Marseilles syndicate having returned to France with cash-flow problems. Dennis, said the know-alls, had been talking to project manager Laurent Esquier and the deal was on. A top crew would fly in from Hawaii and clean up the championship. It sounded good, but rival theories were as plentiful as cans of Fosters.

When the truth emerged it was banal enough to place the whole event in some kind of perspective. A woman who lived on her fifty-foot cruising ketch spotted Conner standing in front of a film camera on a pontoon at the Fremantle Sailing Club. 'Hi! Remember me? I'm Dennis Conner, the man who lost the America's Cup,' he was saying, with a reasonable show of good humour. 'You won't be a loser with the new five-dollar Lotto.' The ultimate professional yachtsman was making a TV commercial for the State Lotteries Commission, who run the small-time gambling game that has middle Australia totally in its grip. When the shoot was over he climbed back on his plane and flew straight home to Hawaii.

Some months later, as the world twelve-metre championships began in Fremantle, the campaign broke. So did the storm. It became clear that the Western Australian government had reneged on its initial promise to hold a lottery and give the proceeds to the defending syndicates – all of whom were still struggling for sponsorship. Instead the Lotteries Commission announced that revenue would go into the consolidated fund, the state rag-bag that absorbs everything from income tax to parking fines. Alan Crewe, commodore of the Royal Perth Yacht Club, declared himself 'astonished' at the breach of faith by the government. On their part the Lotteries Commission declared that Conner had not been paid a fee for the work. There were a great many experienced yachting journalists in town for the championships and they didn't swallow that one mast, boom and sail. 'Dennis never did anything for nothing in his life,' said Casey Baldwin of the Canadian Broadcasting Corporation, almost as much of a Cup veteran as Conner himself. But in the absence of further evidence there was no choice but to sit back and wait for the audited accounts of the Commission later in the year.

There was just as much criticism of the decision to use Dennis Conner as there was of the financial arrangements. 'The choice must have been made by someone completely lacking in taste and judgement,' says Malcolm Bailey, managing director of the Kookaburra syndicate. He found it inexplicable that a man who was dedicating his life to taking the Cup away from Australia could be selected for promoting a lottery that was – supposedly – to pay for its defence.

At Newport in 1980 and 1983 Conner had made himself psychologically impregnable with the armour of his professionalism. No gambit, however, works for ever. The Australians had matched him in professionalism and for the 1987 Cup every other serious syndicate knew that they must do the same thing to be in the big league. What the Aussies had grafted on to grit, competence and long-term effort (sailing values that hitherto practically had a Conner patent on them) at Newport was a psychological play of immense power. As Warren Jones said early in 1986 when asked whether the New York Yacht Club were going to outsmart the Bond camp on gamesmanship: 'It's pretty hard for them to psych us when we virtually taught them what the word means.' Conner knew instinctively that he had to get his hands on those levers. Moving the training camp to Hawaii, although not in the original campaign plan, was a very smart thing to do.

Deep down the Conner approach to any competition is to 'have the numbers' as the politicians put it. John Bertrand, who sailed with his America's Cup opponent several times in the Southern Ocean Racing Cup, has made the point that Conner doesn't feel happy starting a race unless he is already in front. The knowledge that he has the fastest boat, the best-trained crew and the top organisation is the catalyst that enables him to release his considerable talents behind the wheel. Bertrand's greatest achievement in 1983 was to insert into his antagonist's mind the possibility that he was on the slower yacht. When Conner began to map out his campaign for 1987 his overriding priority was to have the fastest boat – not an equal boat, not a competitive boat, but the best. He believes that the Australians came in with a new and innovative idea – the winged keel – that enabled them to win the Cup. It was a clever idea, as opposed to out-sailing the master, which had taken the Auld Mug away from Newport. Therefore the main thrust of the effort was to go into technological research. After sailing in the competition three times before, Conner doesn't feel he needs to match time sailing the boats with, as he puts it, the beginners.

The philosophy of the San Diego group was that they would not go to a particular designer or naval architect for the new yachts. Instead they set up a team which Conner has described as similar in approach to the pooled brainpower which produced the space shuttle and may yet produce the Strategic Defence Initiative – Star Wars. 'It's very competent team members all doing their part and coming up with a product as opposed to going to a single naval architect – picking one out of a hat – and saying, "Hey, draw me a boat," then saying your prayers that the yacht is the best,' Conner said in one of his rare interviews.

He actually picked three naval architects: David Pedrick, Bruce Nelson and Britton Chance. The latter is particularly interesting. Like Conner he is a 'numbers man', and like his boss he took a tumble over that belief. In the early 1970s twelve-metre yacht design in America was still dominated by Olin Stephens. He had created *Ranger*, the last of the J-boat giants and the 1937 victor, and since then the Cup had, metaphorically, stood on his drawing board. Stephens was a sociable, gregarious man with an intuitive approach to design. Chance, still only thirty, was aloof, thought by the yachting press to be arrogant, and put his faith in the numbers that came out of the tank-testing shed. In 1974 he was given the chance to draw the boat that Ted Turner, the 'Mouth of the South', would skipper in the Cup campaign of that year. The result was *Mariner*, probably the most abysmally slow twelve-metre ever constructed. She had a fat, sawn-off stern that Chance's experiments had indicated would increase her speed. It did not. On the day of the final parting of ways after a vicious summer Turner walked down to the dock, aimed a kick at the recalcitrant yacht, and said: 'Chance, even a turd is pointed at both ends.' *Mariner* postponed the dawn of the current twelve-metre era for exactly a decade. If she was the product of exhaustive tank-testing, who was going to go down that road? No one, until Ben Lexcen with his winged keel for *Australia II*.

'The long and short of it was that I was misled by the tank-test results. The tank said the boat was very good and having been exposed to years of such evidential techniques without any serious reversal, I believed the results,' explained Chance shortly afterwards. His career was very nearly ruined, and the echoes bounce on still around the yachting world. At the British tank near Teddington the hydrodynamics and aerodynamics consultant Dr Herbert Pearcey took great pains to explain why the challenge would not repeat what he calls 'the *Mariner* mistake'.

After nearly a decade in twelve-metre exile, Chance declares himself very glad to be working with Conner – whom he likes and describes as a 'very competent person'. That he is on the squad emphatically underlines the approach being taken in Hawaii. Cray Computers, manufacturers and operators of some of the Pentagon's most powerful number-crunchers, has joined the Sail America Foundation for International Understanding – as the San Diego syndicate is formally known. Access has been granted to the huge freon-cooled X–MP/48 computer from terminals located within reach of the design team. 'We lost a technology race when we lost the America's Cup in 1983,' says Dr Carlos Marino, the Cray executive in charge of the Sail America work. 'Cray is now helping to provide the intellectual tools so that the syndicate can win the technology race in 1987.'

One of the most innovative elements in the Cray support programme is the development of visual assessment of work done by designers and engineers. Previously, aerodynamic and hydrodynamic test sequences run on big computers have yielded answers in mathematical terms, but the Cray can show the impact of design changes and modifications in a visual display. According to Marino this makes the interpretation of data easier and faster and merges the pure science of computer logic with the artistic components of yacht design.

It may be unfair to call the campaign grandiose, but it has certainly been sweeping in its hardware requirements. Five twelve-metre yachts were called for. *Liberty*, loser in '83, was summoned as a trialhorse of known speed and worth. A slow boat named *Spirit of America* was completely rebuilt below the deck and renamed *Stars and Stripes '83*. Three entirely new boats were constructed over a fifteen-month period: *Stars and Stripes '85, Stars and Stripes '86*, and finally *Stars and Stripes '87*. It is an indication of the organisational intensity of the syndicate that the design group had to sign an agreement which parallels the notion of collective responsibility in a Cabinet. No matter who has designed a particular boat, they are forbidden to ever make any comment other than it was a joint effort.

This approach, particularly the intense focus on security, has not convinced everyone. Gary Mull quit after just one session with the Conner design group in the lead-lined room at Livermore. But the syndicate was never going to be a democracy. If you don't agree with Dennis, get off the boat. The paradoxical exception to this behaviour is when Conner is actually sailing rather than organising. John

Bertrand was deeply impressed when he saw how the big Californian would involve every member of the crew: asking the bowman his view of windshifts, the port grinder whether a tack was a good idea. Equally, Bertrand was puzzled that at the end of a race Conner could just hop off the boat and go and drink a few of his favourite gins with the owner or any other nearby bigshot, totally ignoring the boys he had just sailed with in such harmony – and making it clear he didn't want to see them socially.

Although he is a yachtsman of international stature, Conner does not flit easily around the world. He is as American as apple pie, and another strong reason for choosing Hawaii as a training base was that it is politically and economically part of the United States. From a logistics standpoint – sails, equipment, people – the syndicate found it much more convenient to be in the same time-zone and on quick, regular airline routes, says Conner. It was also convenient for sponsors to be able to get to the camp, and the syndicate needed a lot of money if it was going to build three new boats plus a reworked *Spirit*.

The man in charge of raising the money was Sandy Purdon, a San Diego estate agent who had grown up in the town with Conner and was willing to take two years away from his business to raise funds for the campaign. 'Everyone says that as Dennis lost the Cup while fighting on behalf of New York, he has the perfect incentive to win it back for his home town, San Diego,' says Purdon. 'That's true enough. But we have a lot more than motive. In every aspect this is the most complete challenge that has ever been put together for the America's Cup.' No other challenging or defending syndicate has thrown such an emphasis on design as San Diego. Besides the three naval architects, Conner has recruited John Marshall as design co-ordinator. Kevlar and Mylar sails revolutionised yacht racing, and Marshall was instrumental in their development during his time as president of North Sails, the world's biggest sailmaker. He already has four America's Cups under his belt.

Purdon's estimate was that by the time *Stars and Stripes '85* and *Stars and Stripes '86* were racing together off Hawaii in February 1986 the San Diego team had spent US$3 million on design and research alone. There has to be a return on that kind of investment. 'Apart from the combined brilliance of the design group, we have the advantage of Sail America foundation owning the final designs,' says Purdon, wearing his businessman's hat. 'Our designs are being developed both for this campaign and for the future. This sets us apart from some other syndicates around the world that are investing large sums of money in designs that they will never own and can never take away.' With such enormous sums being spent the group approach at the drawing board or, more accurately, at the computer video display is an insurance against the 'one designer and a slow boat' syndrome says Purdon. The risk was spread even beyond the individuals involved. Boeing of Seattle contributed work on fluid dynamics, with Grumman Aerospace also assisting in that area. Much of the co-ordinating work was done by Science Applications International Corporation, a major Pentagon defence contractor. Marshall admits that the Australians, headed by Ben Lexcen and assisted by Dutch scientists, have led the field in computer simulation of the performance of various hull designs, but he believes that Pedrick, Nelson and Chance working together will overhaul the mercurial, lone-bull approach of Lexcen. His boss's beliefs focus on patriotism.

'We're going to take the things that make America the best place in the world to live,' said Conner in an unusually relaxed interview with CBS television. 'Yankee ingenuity, the drive, leadership and motivation. We're all Americans and we'd like to restore a bit of our pride and heritage that we lost to the Australians in 1983. It's the challenge of going down there and bringing this back to America where it belongs. You don't quit just because something is hard. If it were easy I wouldn't personally be involved. The good thing about such a major event is that it will come down to good old-fashioned sailing in the end.'

It also takes good old-fashioned money to bring it off. The San Diego budget is around US$15 million and its funding programme is similar to that of the New York Yacht Club. Over thirty west coast yacht clubs have affiliated to Sail America and promised to raise money in return for a visit from Dennis and the Cup. Corporate sponsors include Merrill Lynch with $1 million and the Ford Motor Company with $500,000. In the immediate San Diego area there is huge local support. It might be a 'local boy makes good – again' syndrome, but a staggering 250,000 people turned out to watch an exhibition race in the harbour between *Stars and Stripes '83* and *Stars and Stripes '85*. One thousand spectator craft put out on to the water – as big as a final race at Newport. The effect mentioned in relation to the Golden Gate challenge should not be ignored here.

West coast America is just dying for the chance to show the east coast establishment that the golden days of summer at Martha's Vineyard with a sail or two on a classy twelve are over – for good.

'Dennis Conner is very good, but he can't sail for ever. Our Sail America Foundation is geared to ensure that we never lose the Cup again,' said Purdon.

From Conner to the Canadians. In Newport 1983, there could not have been a bigger contrast. More casual observers only really became aware that there was a maple leaf challenge when a frogman was caught lurking with an underwater camera beneath the 'secret keel' of *Australia II* as she lay moored at Newport. The spy turned out to be a Canadian, but by any stretch of the imagination it was probably already too late to help his country's effort. The Canadian syndicate had been put together by a bunch of Alberta oilmen and a Calgary lawyer named Marvin McDill. None of them had had prior involvement with twelve-metres, or even much to do with sailing, but were possessed of a vague feeling that the country lacked a rallying point. What they lacked was a yacht club to challenge from.

Established yacht clubs were not exactly falling over themselves to get involved with a challenge. The last Canadian effort had been in the late nineteenth century and had ended in ignominious failure. The country has produced fine dinghy sailors since then, Olympic medallists, but twelve-metre sailing was something else. Fortunately McDill had a friend who owned a pub on the waterfront fifty-five miles north of Vancouver, British Columbia. It was at a small and isolated harbour named Secret Cove. Late in 1981 the New York Yacht Club finally approved the Canadian challenge and by mid-1982 the clubhouse of the Secret Cove Yacht Club was under construction.

Bruce Kirby, a Canadian designer who had never done a twelve-metre before but whose Laser dinghies were raced and respected around the world, was hired to draw *Canada I*. In the meantime the syndicate acquired the American yacht *Clipper* for a lengthy winter training session in Florida. Neither the training nor the building of the new yacht progressed smoothly. Money, as is generally the case with twelve-metre campaigns, was at the root of the problem. The cause had been conceived as a 'people's effort', but the Canadian populace had obviously been away from the America's Cup scene too long and were not particularly keen to go back there. The attempts to raise a C\$5 million budget through raffles and buy-a-ticket barbecues were not a success. In the interim, business interests had to step in and underwrite the construction of *Canada I*, although in the end it was largely funded by small contributions.

Once at the battleground the Canadians seemed out of their depth. They had mast problems, an inadequate sail inventory and inexperienced crew. Compared to challengers like the Bond syndicate, or even Peter de Savary's extravagant, if splinter-prone, British effort, the men from Secret Cove looked like kindergarten refugees. *Canada I* scraped through the elimination series into the last four, but failed to win a single race in the semi-finals.

By the time thoughts turned to 1987 it was obvious that it had to be done differently and better. The nucleus of the Canadian I syndicate kept going, centred around Kirby and McDill. But on the Eastern seaboard the proud seafarers of chilly Nova Scotia were mobilising. Their challenge was to be called True North and had Ontario businessman Don Green as its chairman. Green had taken over a C\$500,000-a-year automotive parts company founded by his father, and in fifteen years had transformed it into a manufacturing group called Tridon which exports to seventy countries and has local plants in many others, including one in Australia. It now has a C\$150-a-year turnover and Green owns it all. He is a rich man and a contented one – but for the Cup.

'I have a beautiful ski chalet in the mountains, a lovely home in Hamilton, Ontario, and a summer house in Florida. Why do I need the America's Cup?' Green poses the rhetorical question in True North's headquarters on the new twelve-metre harbour in Fremantle. He sits perched at the desk normally used by his meteorologist. Why does an otherwise quite sane auto parts tycoon need to employ a highly qualified weather person? 'It is a crazy business. You try to rationalise what you are doing and you have to be very honest with yourself. All I've got – and fingers are permanently crossed here – is a dream that this will catch on in Canada as a very worthwhile Canadian project. If that doesn't come through I'll feel that I've failed – even if the boat does very well or wins.

'Many times you wonder if anybody is going to support you. Are you going to have to run the whole bloody thing yourself without anyone really coming on board to help?' The budget for True North is C\$16.3. So far about half that has come in from outside sources, including C\$1.5 million from the Nova Scotian provincial govern-

ment. According to Canadian yachting journalist and broadcaster
Casey Baldwin, who lives in Halifax and can see *True North* trialling
from his study window, the decision was politically very unpopular.
'We have a lot of unemployment and social problems,' says Baldwin.
'The town's not unlike Fremantle before it won the America's Cup.
For the government to give money, and quite a lot of it, to something
that has a low public image and smacks of elitism, like the America's
Cup does to most ordinary Canadians, went down real bad.' To put
taxpayers' money into a syndicate is not unique in the world. The
Elysée gave a donation in goods, services and technology to the two
French syndicates that amounted to around ten per cent of their final
budgets. In Adelaide the state government made a flat donation of
A$1 million to the South Australia syndicate. It was done for the
same reason that they backed the 1985 Grand Prix – to increase
public awareness of their state, which was faring poorly compared to
boom-town Perth and the power and money of the Sydney/
Melbourne axis. The rationale was that since Newport 1983 the
America's Cup had become an event held in high esteem by
Australians and there was little downside in backing it. Good ole
Bondy could hardly be elitist, could he now? Yet in Western
Australia, new home of the Cup, the Labour government of the
pragmatic Brian Burke had decided there was too much political risk
in supporting any would-be defender with money from the public
purse. Let them raise their money in the market place. As one
syndicate fund-raiser said unabashedly: 'None of this is money that
was earmarked for Ethiopia. It was all budgeted out in the corporate
advertising accounts. We're just siphoning a little of it off for yacht
racing.'

Perhaps for reasons that date back to the debacles of the last
century (and maybe 1983 didn't help too much), the Cup has an
ambivalent image in Canada. By Easter 1986 True North had a
plethora of sponsors, over 200, but that brought its own problems.
Seeing him wrestle with the needs of one sponsor against another and
how it was taking momentum out of the boat campaign, Green's wife
said to him: 'Next time you do one of these things I want it to be your
money. All of it! So that you can call all of the shots and do
everything the way you want to do it.' He tells the story in a way that
suggests he doesn't find the idea altogether unappealing.

Green was with the Canada I challenge in the early stages of its
development prior to going to Newport in 1983. As an experienced

competitive yachtsman whose two-tonner *Evergreen* won the Canada Cup, he was in charge of initiating the sail programme. The work was done, but he left the team. His public explanation has always been that the needs of his own business forced him to withdraw, but those close to him are certain that he could see disaster looming and did not want the Green name on a failure. 'There were aspects of that campaign I didn't agree with, and the way they were running it. But even so I really don't think I had the time,' is as far as he will go now. The True North organisation has made repeated overtures to their west coast rivals for an amalgamation, but the crusty and combative Marvin McDill will not agree. 'If they can't do it properly, a weak campaign . . . that's what really worries me. It would damage the image of Canada as a whole,' says Green, whose first major experience under sail was as a student between high school and college. He went round the world with explorer Irving Johnson aboard his private yacht and, as a precocious eighteen-year-old author, wrote a bestselling book about it called *White Wings Around the World*. He became a sailing buff, some competitive, some cruising.

True North, the syndicate's first twelve-metre, was launched in early August 1985. Mrs Sandy Green, Don's wife, threw the ritual bottle of Bollinger at the razor-edge bow (protected by a specially constructed 'champagne shield') and the boat was in business. She was only the second twelve-metre ever to be built in Canada. Construction took place at the small yard of Crockett McConnell in Bridgwater, just outside Halifax. While officials of the Nova Scotian government stood on the dockside next to *Bluenose*, the legendary Canadian schooner, watching the ceremony and continuing to worry about whether public money should have gone into such a project at all, the men at Crockett McConnell were in no doubt. The yard began to experience what other organisations in other countries have felt as the 'Cup effect'. Orders increased throughout the building period as articles and TV items about *True North* reached the public. Once she began sea trials and training off Halifax the surge became a flood. '*True North* increased our rate of growth substantially and we're already working on getting other yacht contracts,' says the chief executive officer of the two-year-old company, Robert Crockett.

The yacht, her dark-blue hull and red coachlines making her probably the most beautiful of all twelve-metres, was designed by Stephen Killing. Like most of his rivals in the field of yachting naval architecture, Killing drew the boat on a computer system. The thirty-three-year-old Killing created a software package called 'Fast Yacht' with a colleague named George Hazen. It enabled the designer to programme a hull shape and various other specifications, such as sail plan and total displacement, to determine how fast the twelve-metre would go under varying sea and wind conditions. The designer had been a junior member of the team that created *Canada I*. In fact many of the collar-and-tie men on the syndicate had the look of being refugees from that earlier effort. Skipper Geoff Boyd was tactician aboard that challenge. The title of the book he wrote about that experience was virtually self-explanatory. It was called *Trials*. Terry McLaughlin, now a True North helmsman, was the skipper at Newport in 1983.

The third member of a triumvirate, literally a steering committee, on the back of the boat was Hans Fogh. Danish by birth but Canadian by choice, Fogh, forty-seven, won Olympic medals in Flying Dutchmen and Solings and has been world champion in both classes. He is also a successful businessman – his North Sails loft in Toronto is the company's largest such franchise in the world. Fogh is a competitor, a hard man in a hard world. As early as the world twelve-metre championships in February 1986 outsiders were warning Green that three superstar skippers on the back of any twelve-metre was a recipe for trouble. So it proved. Before the races both McLaughlin and Fogh sailed on *True North*. That didn't work. At the start of the regatta McLaughlin was driving. After five races he wasn't winning. Green and his operations director Peter Farlinger took the decision to move the mast forwards and throw McLaughlin off the back. Of course it was put more discreetly in the official statements and at the press conferences, but that was what it amounted to. Fogh began helming and the boat moved up the fleet. Rumours were all around Fremantle that the rested driver wanted his ticket home. No one's going home, barked Green when the subject was raised. He conceded that McLaughlin and Fogh would, from then on, be sailing the boat on alternate days – never together. Were they happy with that? persisted a journalist. No, conceded Green, in a tone that implied they would have to damned well lump it. In the end Fogh didn't, and quit.

Green is fascinated by the human dynamics of putting together an America's Cup team. 'When I had the opportunity to talk to John Bertrand about all this he was saying that it's not going to be the fastest boat at all – just put a good yacht in there and make sure your crew are very cohesive, good communications and everybody's working together.' Green pauses, his genial features in one sense opaque. If he sees the contrast between Bertrand's words and the mayhem on the back of his own twelve-metre he is not about to acknowledge it. 'There are syndicates who have only been sailing in Fremantle a month and they are falling apart at the seams. So many stresses and strains for just a few races. What are they going to do over Christmas and New Year when they've been here for months and there are ten races in ten days and everything to play for?

'It's going to be fun, believe me, an endurance test, a demolition derby. That's why we have a sports psychologist with us – sits next to the meteorologist. You know these fellows that sail these boats, a lot of them have super egos. They're world champions in small boats, dinghies. They're their own boss; and then we throw them into a situation where they have to be part of a team. Then you've got the defeats. So much is subjective – the keel's not right, the mast isn't raked enough. Everybody has got a bitch or points the finger at somebody else. The worst of people's personalities comes out in contests like these.' Green may be a newcomer to the volatile world of twelve-metres and the America's Cup, but his words have an uncanny echo of that veteran English designer, Ian Howlett. Earlier in this book he made the point that when the going gets rough in a contest with enormous stakes, not many of the guilty are willing to put their hands up and say, 'My fault.'

Honesty or perception is a fundamental point with Green. But he also applies it to nationality and patriotism. In recent decades the Canadian record of innovation, wealth creation and formation of employment has been almost as good as that of any country in the developed world. No Third World peoples have been killed by Canadian bullets, nor maimed or blinded by pollution from industrial plants that Ottawa considers too dangerous for home soil. Yet, like most post-colonial populations, the Canadians see themselves as losers, also-rans. It is a failure of perception, not achievement, says Green and those who think like him.

In a mid-1985 issue of the magazine *Canadian Business* a writer named Alexander Ross said: 'Until quite recently Australia was regarded as an Antipodean clone of Canada, with the same tendency to import almost everything and pay for it with a dwindling store of natural resources. The same post-colonial clipping, Ascot-attending

Establishment; the same bland willingness to let outsiders take most of the risks. All it took was an America's Cup victory and a few superb films to demonstrate to the world, and even to Australians, that the place is a gold mine of overlooked virtues and underexploited opportunities.' Green may not have a finger in movies, but he can do something about the Cup.

'I realised that Australia was going to make this next America's Cup a world-focus event – like no other event in the world. And they were cleverly using this opportunity to focus attention on their country and particularly a slightly neglected part of it – Western Australia. To attract money here, investments, tourists, to sell Australia to the world export markets, to give the people pride and self-confidence, to wave the flag,' Green pauses for breath and glances out of his first-floor window which overlooks the yacht hoist in one direction and the harbour road in the other. Outside in the lane a small huddle of expatriate Canadians stand beneath the True North sign, resplendent with a huge maple leaf, and one of their number takes a group photograph. The same scene has happened dozens of times every day since the syndicate arrived in Fremantle and set up camp. 'It did a lot for Australia to win the Cup, but the defence is going to do even more. So it's a marvellous opportunity for any country participating to tag along with all this, just to be there.

'Then we look at our country. Canada is a very conservative nation, but I feel one of the finest countries in the world. Twenty-five and a half million people, widely divided because it's a spread-out land – in politics and ways of life too – needs some unity. But it has to fit in with a very careful, cautious way of living. We are a seafaring nation surrounded by three oceans, famous for shipbuilding. *Bluenose*, the Nova Scotia sailboat, is on the back of every Canadian ten-cent piece. What could be a better project for Canada to be involved in than the America's Cup?' Green recognises only too well that the stolidity of the very people he hoped to mobilise precluded a sudden wave of enthusiasm and financial support based on the mere announcement that there was to be an America's Cup campaign. There had to be a boat, at the very least. But that meant setting up most of the design, logistics and maintenance team in advance – twelve-metres do not exist in a vacuum. The seed money for the challenge came from Canadian National Sportsmen's Shows, a non-profit-making organisation that promotes boat shows and the like across the country from St John to Vancouver. It paid for a feasibility study in which Green, already on the board of CNSS as one of his charitable activities, participated. What it showed him was how big and tough a game the next Cup was going to be, how Corinthian idealism alone would be swamped by dollars and hired expertise. 'We realised that to win the America's Cup it had to be run as a business,' says Green, gesturing around the Fremantle operations room that could easily pass as the open-plan office of a medium-sized insurance company – bar the hunched, intent form of Geoff Boyd watching a video tape shot from a helicopter of *True North*'s performance the previous day. 'It's not a weekend regatta. We had to treat it as a real big business without losing the entrepreneurial feeling of such a venture. But it's a crazy business because you have to get a hugely expensive project going without having the funds in place.' This has largely been the experience of other new syndicates. The public, private and corporate, likes to see something tangible before parting with serious money. To raise funds to build a boat you need to have a boat.

Yet the spirit of innovation that Green speaks of, and its awakening, is not illusory. On their first visit to Fremantle among True North's impedimenta was a unique floating boat hoist. It looked like the framework of a child's swing mounted on a pair of floating pontoons. On the central girder was an electric winch that could lift a thirty-ton twelve-metre yacht out of the water in minutes – with the crew still on board if necessary. Yet the whole apparatus could be dismantled in a day or so and packed into two standard forty-foot containers for shipment overseas. Bryan Gooderham, an engineer by training and a full-time sailor by choice, joined True North at its inception. When he looked at the cost of building a conventional boat hoist – two deep-piled finger jetties with the crane erected on them – at each of the team's three training locations, Gooderham knew there had to be a better way.

He collaborated on the construction of the new hoist with Marine Travel-lift, the company which makes the wheeled boat hoists now familiar in every shipyard. The design was patented and enquiries began to trickle in. Some came from rival twelve-metre syndicates anxious to save a dollar. Others made it clear that there could be a useful application for such a hoist among small island communities, particularly in the South Pacific, where there were neither the funds nor the logistical support to build complex jetties or conventional slips. Such people still live off the sea and the floating hoist could transform the maintenance of their boats.

Rivalry between east and west has managed to replicate itself on three continents during the build-up to the current America's Cup. In the USA, in Australia itself, and in Canada the dislike and antagonism between syndicates who look to different oceans seems almost to surpass their ambition to take the trophy away from Perth. 'East is east, west is west and always the twain shall rubbish one another,' Kipling might have written had he been covering the 1987 America's Cup. True North and Canada II do not speak well of one another.

'All of the spite emanates from their end,' expostulates Perry Connolly, the Vancouver project director in late 1985. 'Donald Green is always saying how he's going to take Marvin McDill out of the America's Cup, and how last time it was a shambles, and how this time he's going to run it real well. Well it's going to be fun to whip his ass, I tell you.' The Canada II programme called for major modifications to be made to *Canada I*, the Newport 1983 boat, while design and tank-testing of a second yacht proceeded. The team's trialhorse, *Clipper*, was sold to Buddy Melges and the Heart of America syndicate with the proviso that they bring her north for one month to trial against the revamped *Canada I*.

The work on that boat involved adding about a metre in length, one-third of that at the stern and two-thirds at the bow. She had always had a rather fine entry and designer Kirby believed that in the heavier conditions off Fremantle the bowman would need a great deal more space in order to work safely. The stern modifications were of a more technical nature – designed to change the quarter wave and produce more boat speed. Also for reasons of safety, the hatches and deck-openings were made smaller and more watertight – 'in case she is the boat chosen to go to Perth,' as the syndicate put it.

Bruce Kirby puts his own hopes succinctly: 'What we are looking for with the *Canada I* and *II* testing are little improvements – the keel to which disturbed flow re-attaches faster, the skeg-rudder flow pattern that allows straighter steering, a hull/rig combination that will withstand thirty knots of wind and punishing seas but not give anything away in ten knots of breeze and smooth water. The boat that wins at Perth will have been built light enough to hold together, but only just, in the toughest conditions, so that she will be able to win in the medium stuff. If she is designed perfectly everything on her will disintegrate as she crosses the line to win the final race.'

As the months rolled by it became increasingly apparent that the syndicate was struggling to find the money to build a new twelve-metre. Effort and thought put into the rebuilt hull and newly created winged keel of *Canada I* (or 'One and Three Quarters' as she was beginning to be dubbed in the sceptical international yachting press) began to look as if it might have to carry the team through the most competitive regatta in history. However, when Melges and Jobson came north to British Columbia with *Clipper* they found a powerful opponent. The four-race series, christened the Maple Leaf Cup, was sailed in snow and sub-zero temperatures. Melges, who sails ice-yachts on the frozen lakes of Wisconsin at 150 kilometres per hour, must have felt at home, but he still couldn't make *Clipper* win. The Dave Pedrick design had been built for the 1980 Cup and campaigned without great success then and in 1983. Yet she had always been sailed below her true potential – either as a second-string yacht or with a poor crew. *Canada I* took the series three–one. The only loss happened when she tore a headsail while well in front of *Clipper*. Melges and Jobson were impressed enough to warn people in Fremantle during the world twelve-metre championships that it was a shame *Canada I* wasn't there – she'd be showing them things. 'She's a very fast boat indeed,' says Jobson, who worked during the championships as a commentator for Channel 9 television – Alan Bond's station in Perth. Melges had a good look around the fourteen-strong fleet during his visit and still rates *Canada I* – the revamped version – as among 'the fastest twelve-metres in the world'.

In the early stages of the Secret Cove campaign Terry McLaughlin, who had skippered the boat at Newport, was still favourite to be helmsman; but after his defection to True North (another event that did nothing to help the syndicate's credibility in the public's eyes) another Terry, Terry Neilson, a 1984 Olympic gold medallist, began to figure on the back of the boat. Despite having a twelve-metre that now looked fairly quick and was highly rated by someone as experienced as Jobson, McDill and his team were as sensitive and prickly as ever, firing off telexes and telegrams to anyone who publicly doubted their Cup chances.

John Longley, manager of the Bond syndicate and grinder aboard *Australia II*, attracted his anger by suggesting in the 'America's Cup Intelligence Report' that the syndicate were thirty-three-to-one outsiders in the Cup stakes. McDill claimed that just because his outfit had adopted a softly-softly approach it did not mean they were to be discounted. 'Any prognosis at this time by odds-makers is rather meaningless,' he sniffed. 'There has never been any suggestion by us that we were proceeding with a breakthrough boat. We believe the evolution of our current design programme as well as the sail programme will make us a very serious contender come 1987.' McDill has a theory that taking a modest and unpublicised approach to the Cup unfairly consigns one to the backburner before the boat is even in the water. 'It is probably through lack of information, perhaps attributable to our quiet approach, that comments attributed to Mr Longley have been made,' he continued. 'Many comments have been made concerning our activities by Canadians who hope to gain by attempting to discredit our efforts.' Some observers of the present Cup would argue, and not without evidence, that attempting to win the Auld Mug in a quiet, unpublicised way is about as likely as Madonna entering a convent unphotographed. It is a contradiction in terms.

Whether or not both Canadian challengers turn up on the starting line – and in April 1986 True North hit a funding crisis that caused it to suspend operations for thirty days – it can only, *pace* Don Green, have energised a talented if under-confident nation to regard itself as capable of performing on a world stage previously reserved for the major-league players.

Chapter 8

New Zealand, France and Italy

Sleek twelve-metre yachts dangling from the end of a crane have become a familiar sight in Fremantle in the summer prior to the Cup itself. It sometimes seemed that every tide had brought in a freighter from somewhere in the world carrying a twelve or two as deck cargo. Most have been unloaded with their elegant underbodies and highly secret keels shrouded in tarpaulins. When the two New Zealand boats were unloaded, however, they were as naked as the day they were moulded. 'Where we come from only girls wear skirts,' shouted Michael Fay above the noise of the crane. Fay, thirty-six, is syndicate chairman and an Auckland merchant banker. It was the type of chic yet provocative remark or gesture that has come to characterise the New Zealand effort.

Only an hour or so later as the boats were towed into the dock compound the Kiwis were able to surprise once again. Perth's local Maori community had arranged a Powhiri (traditional welcoming ceremony) for the two *Wakka Taua*, or war canoes. 'You are our warriors in your boats for war,' Maori leader Shalima Fryda told skippers Chris Dickson and Graeme Woodroffe. 'We are proud of your courage. This land is no longer strange because we have cleared it of evil spirits for yourselves and the *Wakka Taua*.' Amid the soft, swaying chant of Maori battle hymns, punctuated by long passionate orations from the elders, the entire crew lined up for the ritual of rubbing noses with the welcoming committee. Mammon is normally the most visible god in the twelve-metre heaven. An event of such genuine spirituality had a powerful, invigorating (and intimidating) effect upon those who saw it.

New Zealand's challenge for the America's Cup has curious origins. When Bond won New Zealanders celebrated nearly as much as the Australians. The island country of three million people is yachting mad. Auckland is known as the 'City of Sails' from the way the harbour packs with pleasure boats each weekend. The Kiwi reputation in ocean racing is unsurpassed. For such a small community to manage two competitive entries in the recently completed Whitbread Round The World race is astonishing. So the knowledge that the Cup was going to be in Perth and could be won by non-Americans was kindling wood to an already sparked national imagination. Yet when the Royal Perth's closing date for entries approached in early 1984 there was still no New Zealand nomination. Then, literally at the eleventh hour and fifty-ninth minute, a Sydney-based futures broker named Marcel Fachler put up the A$12,000 deposit in the name of the Royal New Zealand Yacht Squadron. It was a puzzle in Auckland. No one there had ever heard of Fachler. It emerged that he wanted to open an office in New Zealand, was keen on yachting, and felt that such a public-spirited action might promote goodwill. For a week or two it did. Then headlines of a different sort began to appear. Fachler's companies were in trouble to the tune of millions of dollars; investigations were under way. To the relief of the RNZYS he withdrew voluntarily. However, the Kiwis still had nothing more towards a campaign than a legitimate entry financed by a vanished fairy godmother.

In its earliest days the campaign seemed to lurch from chaos to disaster. New Zealand agreed to buy the former American twelve-metre *Enterprise* from the Azzurra syndicate for A$350,000. Chris Dickson, the twenty-four-year-old *wunderkind* Kiwi helmsman and his crew, were to sail it in the 1984 world championships before shipping it home as a trialhorse. She was so neglected as to be barely seaworthy. 'The gear kept failing and there was constant tension on board as to what was going to break next,' recalls Aussie Malcolm, then project director. 'All we knew was that we weren't going to pay four hundred grand for that heap of crap.' They didn't and the lawyers were busy for months.

The syndicate's saviour was another lawyer, although rather a *manqué* one. Michael Fay was twenty-four when Security Bank fired him for being 'too disruptive'. The next day he started the fund-raising operation that was to grow into Fay Richwhite merchant bank, a company which is now capable of generating billions of dollars for New Zealand's largest companies – most of whom are clients. Fay is not a yachtsman. He rarely goes out on boats and is fairly often sick when he does. What he does love is a challenge, the harder the better. Fay also knows what the America's Cup as an event could do for an economy the size of New Zealand's if the next one were to be held in Auckland. Only a generation ago New Zealand had very nearly the highest standard of living in the world; now it wallows way down the table, next to Greece and Libya. The potential is still there, Fay believes, if the right catalyst arrives.

Fay Richwhite agreed to fund three months' worth of design and development work on hulls. No twelve-metre had ever been built in New Zealand, but top yacht designers abounded. Unfortunately, like many Kiwis, they had sought fame and fortune overseas. Of the triumvirate that was eventually formed, Ron Holland lived in Cork, southern Ireland, Bruce Farr in the USA, while only Laurie Davidson has clung to the land of his fathers. Computer spoke unto computer on satellite links between the three countries and hull shapes began to emerge. It was announced that the first boat would be a conventional development from *Australia II*, with a refined winged keel. A further boat would be the imaginative gamble. Almost every syndicate had said much the same thing, so little notice was taken beyond the Tasman Sea.

In October 1985 the New Zealand challenge became news. At a minor Perth business luncheon Michael Fay dropped into his speech the fact that there were two Kiwi boats not one – and they would be made of glass-reinforced plastic (GRP), commonly known as fibreglass. Twelve-metre syndicates around the world shook. Since the mid-1960s every twelve had been built of aluminium. Meanwhile the whole world of racing yachts other than twelves had moved over to light, strong and cheap GRP. The problem was that twelve-metre class rules require that each boat be built to Lloyds 'scantlings', a quaint nautical word meaning design specifications. For a twelve, these are complex, and very, very strong. Many syndicates had researched the notion of building in GRP over twenty years, but had always put it in the 'too hard' drawer. Steve Ward, the Perth boatbuilder who has constructed every one of Alan Bond's boats except *Southern Cross*, says *Australia II* was a whisker away from being built in GRP. 'We did all the design work to the same point. We could have gone with plastic. I think it was just too much of a gamble, in the end,' says Ward – who has subsequently built *Australia III*, *IV* and *South Australia*, all in aluminium.

The reasons for the New Zealanders taking such a punt were clear. The design trio, particularly Ron Holland, are world leaders in the design of GRP racing yachts. Holland yachts have won every classic ocean race, from the Fastnet to the Sydney–Hobart. If that talent and experience could be moulded into a twelve-metre, the challenge would be going somewhere. The second reason was a chronic shortage of time. The months and weeks it takes to build two aluminium yachts were simply not available. The beauty of GRP is that once the mould is created hulls can be turned out of it very quickly indeed. Having two identical boats has been an enormous help to the New Zealand team in tuning and development – a process known as 'leapfrogging'. If boat A and boat B are identical in terms of hull, sails and rig, but you change one item on B making it faster than A, then there has clearly been an advance. By changing A to the specification of B, one has moved to a higher level of performance and the sequence can begin again. If the yachts are not identical, then because of hull differences or whatever, the change that made B faster may not work on A. For a challenge syndicate that has no background data from previous Cups (as do Bond, Conner and *Courageous*, for instance) it was a boldly innovative yet logical route to take. Secrecy about the project was maintained not just for the tactical reason of surprising the opposition; it was also to avoid the syndicate getting egg on its face if the gamble failed. Fay and his team made the commitment to GRP at Easter 1985, but it wasn't until late that October that Lloyds – whose surveyor had been at the boatyard since day one, paid for by the syndicate – announced that they were satisfied with the work and the hulls. 'It was far more difficult than we expected and took far longer than we had anticipated,' said Fay, once he'd landed the 'plastic fantastics' in Fremantle. 'If any other syndicate wanted to follow the route we'd be delighted – if they started now they should miss the Cup.' Such was the interest from other syndicates and the media in the space-age hulls that Fay joked about getting the mould set up in Marten Marine's yard on Auckland's Tamaki River and turning out production-line twelves for sale by auction. (Later the same day he learned that the mould had been left out in the sun, warping the lines dreadfully. There would be no more boats from it – ever.)

John Bertrand has stressed that the one thing you can never get enough of in a twelve-metre campaign is not money (although that can be a problem), but time. 'Sitting in that boatyard surrounded by a mountain of crap and unfinished boats at Christmas I did not believe we were going to get here,' said Fay in early February 1985. He was speaking after *KZ5*, the second Kiwi twelve, had just amazed the sailing world by winning the first heat of the world championships. Her skipper, Chris Dickson, revealed that the three-and-a-half-hour race had virtually doubled the yacht's total hours spent on the water.

As a sailor Dickson was virtually a child prodigy. He won the keenly contested world youth championship three times as a teenager. His father, Roy Dickson, is one of New Zealand's top international yachtsmen. While Colin Beashel may telephone his father for advice, Chris Dickson goes one better and has his standing next to him. During the major part of the world championships Roy Dickson was sailing aboard *KZ5* as tactician, with his son Chris at the wheel. It seemed to be the perfect partnership. The traditional problems of the helmsman/tactician relationship are probably half-way solved if they have already lived in the same family for twenty-four years. In the end, though, the problem was a physical one. Aboard a twelve the tactician has the secondary job of setting up the backstays after each gybe or tack. These are the guyropes which lead from near the stern to half-way up the mast. Only the one on the side the wind is coming from needs to be tight, but the work of changing them is demanding and gruellingly repetitive. Physically it is too much for a man of fifty-five, especially in the big seas and stiff breezes off Fremantle, so Dickson senior retired from his post.

New Zealand's other skipper is Graeme 'Woody' Woodroffe. At forty he is a veteran of countless ocean races and of a different generation to Dickson. His consummate seamanship in picking up his bowman (who had fallen overboard) on the first pass in mountainous seas during the fifth world championships heat was admired by all who saw the manoeuvre. In contrast, John Kolius aboard *US42* took three attempts to retrieve his man overboard, while the two men swept off the elegant grey *Italia* were left for the Royal Perth's safety boat to recover while the yacht headed home.

Despite his lack of years Dickson is an accomplished performer at press conferences, always providing laughs and the ready-made quote. Woodroffe is the reverse. Although a jolly and companionable man in private, 'Woody' clearly does not relish time in front of the microphones. On the water the rivalry between the skippers became a problem for a campaign which required close co-operation in boat evaluation. Although it was largely kept out of the newspapers, the problem did not go away. Many in the Kiwi administration have wondered if it wouldn't have been feasible to produce skippers, as well as twelve-metres, from identical moulds.

Probably the greatest coup for Fay and his team did not come on the water at all. Almost all the initial funding had come from Fay Richwhite, but Fay knew instinctively that if the campaign did not become a national effort with broad-based support it would quickly come to be seen as a rich man's whim and fade for that very reason. In December 1985 the syndicate became the Bank of New Zealand Challenge for the America's Cup. *KZ3* and *KZ5* were painted in the bank's livery, as were all the syndicate's vehicles. Besides its own financial sponsorship, the bank announced that it would set up a New Zealand Supporters Club, using as its logistical base the 385 branches and 7,000 staff spread across a geographically troublesome country. The aim was to raise NZ$3 million, a dollar for every New Zealander. Before committing itself, the Bank of New Zealand did a great deal of research. The professionalism of the syndicate was quickly established, but in the final analysis intangibles carried more weight. 'The attention that a strong challenge, let alone a successful one, will attract for New Zealand abroad makes this Cup a unique opportunity to promote the country,' said the bank's chief executive, Robert McCay, on announcing the support. 'Secondly, we have determined that the trade and promotional benefits to New Zealand of a successful challenge are considerable.' The Australian predilection for cutting 'the tall poppy' down to size is well known. Consistently people refer to the America's Cup as hyped, over-rated and essentially unimportant. The extent to which the winning of it has helped Australia to create an image for itself in the world is perhaps only measurable by looking at the importance that Canada and New Zealand, similar post-colonial nations, now attach to pulling off the same feat.

Fay is nothing if not a 'doer'. The eighty staff at Fay Richwhite work under wall-hung exhortations as various as WORK SMARTER and MAKE MONEY. On the evening in January when the Royal Perth Yacht held its stuffily smart cocktail party as a prelude to the world championships, one of the New Zealand yachts, *KZ3*, lost its entire mast, boom and mainsail overboard in a sudden squall off Fremantle. With the championship only days away and two new masts weeks away from completion, the situation looked critical. While the Kiwis fretted on the dock, 1,600 Perth socialites, twelve-metre syndicate members and crew promenaded on the razored lawns in front of the Matilda Bay clubhouse. The Perth social scene adores to dress up and anyone – bar the extravagantly clad ladies – not in immaculate blazer and pristine white ducks would have felt distinctly uneasy; assuming, that is, they managed to slip past disapproving matrons on the specially installed iron gates. Into this mêlée of sartorial snobbery strode Fay wearing grubby old shorts and a disreputable tee-shirt. He was looking for a mast. It took just a few minutes to find Flavio Scala, reserve skipper and executive boss of the Italia syndicate. Sure, they had a mast. Fay and Scala shook hands on the price and the scruffy merchant banker headed back to the dock without even having a drink.

The New Zealand syndicate spent a lot of money before a major sponsor came aboard, and all of it was Fay's. His own finances are kept decently private, but he owns exactly fifty per cent of Fay Richwhite, a company which now owns quite sizeable chunks of New Zealand corporate life. A month after arriving in Fremantle he realised that there were just over eighty people on the Kiwi workforce. Even crewmen, who are on allowances not salaries, have considerable and expensive appetites. 'This is getting out of hand,' he joked. 'I think I'll let it get to one more than de Savary had at Newport, just to have a record, and then send half of them home.' He hasn't yet. One of Fay's prime principles from the day of the team's arrival in Western Australia was the need for openness and for a move away from the kind of obsessional secrecy that characterises the New York Yacht Club syndicate. In the first few weeks the Kiwi compound was open house. Press and public wandered in and out, chatting to crew and shore teams. It was unworkable from the team's viewpoint, although very pleasant for the media. Very soon the big gates closed and the New Zealand challenge hired a security guard – just like everyone else. At the same time a security screen, of the type used to hide secret keels, went up around the boat hoist. 'I always said that when we had a state secret we'd hide it,' explained Fay, somewhat abashed by the volte face. 'I suppose that we have now.' The secret was a new keel shipped over from Auckland to be fitted to one of the two yachts.

At about this time a curious incident occurred at the New Zealand compound. The night security guard spotted the shapes of two divers and tell-tale air bubbles beneath the hull of the second twelve-metre. It was only mid-evening and normally the dock would have been crowded with maintenance men and crew. However, this was the final evening of a short series of match races against *True North*, the twelve-metre from Halifax, Nova Scotia. *True North* lost every race and the Canadian syndicate had to pay out on a side-bet – the losing team treated the victors to dinner. It was a barbecue at the True North compound, with every Kiwi invited. Their suspicions were obvious if only circumstantial, but sufficient for the New Zealanders to send True North a telex suggesting that underwater movements by night be notified to avoid accidents. The Canadians denied any involvement. Probably it was just a case of 'give a dog a bad name'. After all, it was a Canadian frogman who was apprehended beneath the winged keel of *Australia II* at Newport in 1983.

While work proceeded back home on a third yacht, also in GRP, Fay decided that the crews and boats would stay in Fremantle throughout the southern winter and continue training. This was not the easiest decision to explain to the major sponsor, the Bank of New Zealand. The bank had counted on the two boats being back in New Zealand, and with a high public profile, for sponsorship purposes. Fay had to battle for his own way on this issue, but he felt it essential if the campaign was to have maximum chances of success. It also appeared, like the security changes, to be a change of tack. But one always has the feeling with Fay that much of this had been planned a long time back – the public would know when he was good and ready. This approach goes right back to the decision to build in GRP – and not one boat but two. Whatever the Kiwis do in the Cup itself, it will be different from the announced plans. All sorts of people involved in the twelve-metre world have now begun to look at the facilities in Auckland. With the kind of flair that created the country's biggest merchant bank from nothing in just over a decade, Fay has now started a subsidiary named Cup Challenge Limited. It owns complete and exclusive rights to a New Zealand defence.

Despite the continuing French passion for '*patrie et gloire*' there is nothing of the obsessed patriot about Serge Crasnianski. His company, KIS Française, wholly owned by Crasnianski and with a turnover of around A$300 million a year, is the sole commercial sponsor of *French Kiss*. This pearl-grey twelve-metre is one of two French entries in the 1986–7 America's Cup. Uninterested in sailing, Crasnianski was looking for a promotional vehicle that would provide a sponsorship outlet for his group and a high international profile. 'We hoped to do Formula One, then soccer – a lot of things,' explains the forty-three-year-old engineer from Grenoble, where the company now has seven factories and a huge research and development facility. 'The most difficult competition to do was the America's Cup, so we thought it was a good idea.' KIS was formed out of a misfortune that Crasnianski suffered a decade ago. He lost his car keys. Appalled at how long it took to obtain a replacement set, he researched the market for instant keys. From that acorn grew heel-bars, mini photo-labs that could be installed in corner shops and provide family snaps in one hour, and then colour copiers. Although Crasnianski is no aristocrat, the business that supports his Cup bid is not so different from that of Baron Bich and his ballpoint pens. In every other way the two men are at opposite poles. Bich lived for the Cup and squandered a fortune on *France I, II and III*; in Newport his entourage included Cordon Bleu chefs and the finest cellar west of Bordeaux. 'When I sail a twelve-metre I am 'alf-fish, 'alf-bird,' exclaimed Monsieur le Baron from the wheel of *France I* on a memorable day in Rhode Island Sound. Crasnianski does not sail. 'I will not become hooked on the America's Cup. It is not a passion. This is absolutely an occupation,' he declares. 'The Cup is business for me.' His aim is to make KIS a huge international company, and having seen the business doors that opened to Alan Bond after Newport Crasnianski knows that his instincts in choosing the event are right. A French business magazine runs an annual review of millionaires, somewhat akin to the Fortune 500. The table is based not so much on cash worth as on visibility, drive and 'national importance'. In 1984 Crasnianski did not appear in the list; in 1985 he was sixth. The only difference between the two years was the involvement with *French Kiss*. The publicity has sat well on his broad shoulders. Like Fay, he is a natural for the media.

If ever a boat was designed for publicity it was *French Kiss*. Her skipper, and the originator of the project, is Marc Pajot. In his teens

Pajot sailed into the national consciousness by winning world championships in the Flying Dutchman class with his older brother Yves. In his twenties he won fame sailing in transatlantic and round-the-world races, and also from a much-reported split and then feud with Yves. Since the older Pajor is now the nominated skipper for the second French challenge for the America's Cup, the gap between the siblings has been artificially reinforced. But it nevertheless exists. 'He is my brother first,' said Marc on the day that Yves left Perth after the temporary collapse of his syndicate due to money problems. 'But we have not been on a boat together for fifteen years. We have no sailing relationship except to be rivals.' Devastatingly good-looking and with an easy charm, Pajot is one of the syndicate's biggest assets. The other is designer Phillipe Briand. Almost as good a helmsman as naval architect, Briand has been world one-ton and half-ton champion. He also assisted in the design of *Severige*, the 1977 Swedish challenger for the America's Cup. In the world twelve-metre championship *French Kiss* showed great speed, especially upwind. Her design is not like that of other twelves. The high, flared bow both keeps the foredeck safe to work on in high seas and seems to maintain higher boat speed.

Her curved and somewhat truncated stern is also quite unlike any other twelve seen in Fremantle for the championships. What the close-guarded keel is like no one can yet say for sure, but well-informed rumour and the odd glimpse from a helicopter while *French Kiss* was tacked over suggest only tiny, deltoid wings towards the rear of the keel. Pajot, speaking at a post-race press conference, showed the gamesmanship endlessly surrounding keels when he complained that his boat's race position had suffered after heavy weed fouled the keel. A guffaw went round the press hall, since one thing that was well known was that *French Kiss* has a fin with the leading edge swept aft – impossible to catch seaweed on. Still, if Pajot wanted to throw the hounds off the scent, why not? Probably the most remarkable aspect of Briand's achievement with the hull design is that it went straight off a computer screen to the shipyard. The now conventional and hallowed process of spending hundreds of hours towing vastly expensive one-third scale models up and down huge tanks was completely bypassed. Nor were the keel models tested in a wind-tunnel – another process that has become a standard technique. Briand believes that the sophistication of computer design models and the volume of data now accumulated around twelve-metre performance renders such lengthy and costly empirical research obsolete. The performance of *French Kiss* off Fremantle during the southern summer in conditions ranging from five-knot calms to three-metre seas has not proved Briand or his yacht wrong.

Although the world championships demonstrated the worth of *French Kiss*, she nearly did not get a chance to compete. The Royal Perth took the view that her name contravened Rule 26 of the International Yacht Racing Union, under whose regulations the regatta is being sailed. This forbids racing yachts to be named after commercial products or the business interests of a sponsor. The Frenchmen argued that their name was spelled differently to the company's name and was simply a rather good joke – at least, it is in English-speaking countries; in France the term has no meaning. In Australia not everyone seemed to be clear on what exactly a French kiss was. One flag officer of the Royal Perth thought it a bodily interaction of a much more louche kind. This kind of misunderstanding added to the French conviction that opposition to the name was simply prudery. 'This is a problem of Anglo-Saxon attitudes,' stormed Paul-Armand Blouzet, managing director of KIS Australia, at a summit meeting with RPYC. 'No it isn't,' replied America's Cup director Noel Robins somewhat wearily. 'This is a problem of the rules.'

For the Royal Perth it was the sharp end of the America's Cup. With so much at stake and a dozen other syndicates, who had not dared to name their yachts after sponsors, ready to reach for injunctions, the club ruled *French Kiss* ineligible to compete under that name in the world championships. The syndicate refused to back down. The boat's name was not printed in the first version of the official programme. After a French complaint she was reinstated, but with an asterisk and a footnote explaining the situation. Royal Perth's ruling affected only the first two invitation races; for the seven-race series proper an IYRU jury had been convened. *French Kiss* showed up at the start line for the first invitation race to cheers from the spectator fleet. There was no doubt whose side the public were on. The controversial twelve-metre led the fleet for much of the twenty-four-mile race. On the final leg, with around one kilometre to the finish line, she was engaged in a bitter tacking duel by John Kolius sailing *America II*, which was just astern of her. Straining every aspect of the ninety-two-foot rig to the limit, the French mast suddenly snapped and fell overboard. Royal Perth were spared the embarrassment of a disqualified yacht winning the first race. During the week prior to the second race a stand-off developed. The Royal Perth played what local media commentator Howard Sattler called 'dirty pool' and declared that if *French Kiss* started in the second invitation the race would be abandoned. This had the effect of pitting other syndicates, hitherto supportive of the Pajot team, against *French Kiss*. Knowing that the jury decision was only days away the French raced with great broad strips of white tape masking the blue and red lettering below the cockpit. Aboard the press boat half of the journalists seemed to be wearing *French Kiss* sweatshirts, a silent but highly visible protest.

When the jury met it took them less than two hours to decide in favour of *French Kiss* keeping her name. It was probably the most significant thing to come out of the world championships. 'We realised that for the America's Cup to survive we have to keep money in it and that means sponsors,' said one of the six-man jury, who has asked not to be named. 'This is not dinghy-racing on some little lake with a boat costing three thousand dollars. There was no way in the world we were going to throw the name out. It was just a question of finding a way through the rules.' The impact on future yachting sponsorship will be enormous. Alan Bond, then about to build *Australia IV* with his A$15 million budget still incomplete, immediately joked, 'I'm going to call the new boat *Fourex*.' The name is the premier beer produced by Bond's newly acquired Castlemaine Brewery in Queensland.

For Marc Pajot's older brother Yves the Cup began to turn into a nightmare that contrasted sharply with the fairytale beginning for *French Kiss*. In the early days Challenge Française, based in Marseilles and backed financially by that city, looked the more solid and experienced of the two syndicates. They acquired two twelve-metres very quickly: *France III*, which had campaigned at Newport in 1983, and the Ben-Lexcen-designed *Challenge 12*, bought from the Australian state of Victoria. The syndicate were the first of the French teams to arrive in Australia for training, bringing both boats and moving into a former hospital for alcoholics, in the Perth suburb of Applecross, that they had leased as a crew base. Yves Pajot's team arrived just a week or two after the bombing by French intelligence agents of the Greenpeace vessel *Rainbow Warrior* in Auckland, New Zealand. Fearful of any local anti-French demonstrations, the syndicate threw out a spray of disinformation about which day the yachts were arriving and on what ship. They were, of course, found out, and a large posse of photographers and TV cameramen produced more publicity than the event would normally have warranted. There were no demonstrators.

The denouement came when *France III* and *Challenge 12* were towed round to the Challenge Française dock in the new twelve-metre harbour. An Australian civic administrator with a sense of irony had allocated Pajot's men the compound immediately adjoining the New Zealanders'. 'All will be civilised,' pronounced Michael Fay. 'This is yachting, not a branch of government.'

With their chic scarlet one-piece oilskins the French crew were undoubtedly the best-dressed yachtsmen off Fremantle, but it became increasingly apparent that the two old twelve-metres were not competitive against the new generation of yachts. The decision to ship both of them, plus two crews and all the necessary logistical support, to Australia began to look both eccentric and expensive. Meanwhile, back in France, designer Daniel Andrieu was running into money problems with the new yacht he was creating for Challenge Française. In mid-January 1986, after nearly three months in Australia, the team flew back to France in disarray. *Challenge 12* was chartered to British businessman and yachtsman Chris Griffiths to use in the world championships and *France III* was laid up in a Fremantle boatyard. Once Baron Bich's pride and hope, she lay ignored among old prawn trawlers and neglected powerboats. Even plans to paint *France III* red and use her to double for *Liberty* in a TV mini-series about the 1983 Newport Cup fell down after problems about the payment of waived import duty if the syndicate were to earn money rather than merely spend it.

Ironically Yves Pajot and the last of his unhappy crew were leaving Perth at the same time as Marc and *French Kiss*, buoyant with Crasnianski's money and their new boat, were arriving. The two brothers, who earned Olympic silver medals aboard the same Flying Dutchman, must have passed one another flying in opposite directions somewhere over the Java Sea. It was a dramatic illustration of the point that while it is absurdly easy to waste huge sums of money in the twelve-metre racing, there is no way forward without it, no matter how talented the sailors.

Neither of the two Italian syndicates contesting the Cup are remotely short of money. Together or singly they are probably the best-funded of any campaigns, including front-rank US outfits like Conner's and the NYYC's. At the launch of *Azzurra II* in Venice the Aga Khan, president of the syndicate, sat next to Gianni Agnelli, one of his committee members. Agnelli's family company, Fiat, are a major sponsor. So are Cinzano, producers of probably Italy's best-known liquid export. San Pellegrino, the company that sold over one billion bottles of mineral water around the world last year, are on the Azzurra masthead. Anyone who savours fine hotels will have heard of the Gritti Palace in Venice. Its owners, Cigahotels, are also backing the Azzurra syndicate. Barilla, Europe's biggest pasta producer and operator of the largest spaghetti factory in the world, are in there too. The involvement of these blue-chip companies, twenty-three in all, flows from the extraordinary surge of interest from the Italian media in the America's Cup. The skippers of the twelve-metres are super-stars at home. In Rome and Milan they are mobbed in the street as top soccer players might be.

Italy's first involvement in the Cup came only five years ago. In March 1981 the Aga Khan telexed the New York Yacht Club laying an official challenge for the 1983 Cup in Newport. It came through the Costa Smeralda Yacht Club, based at Porto Cervo on the north-eastern tip of Sardinia. For twenty years a consortium headed by the Aga Khan has been engaged in creating and promoting a resort coast to rival anything that the Côte d'Azur might offer the seriously rich. The fine natural harbour at Porto Cervo has been developed into a base for some of the largest and most opulent craft afloat. The Yacht Club, while young in years, yields to no institution in grandeur of membership. The promotion of international sailing events such as the Sardinia Cup is part of the high profile of the resort. Participation in the America's Cup is a logical extension of the process.

In Newport the Italians enjoyed themselves; and Rhode Island enjoyed Azzurra. The syndicate's parties became legendary for their style and high fun-ratio. *Azzurra '83* did well, although as first-time challengers they found the British and Australians a little too experienced and well-prepared. There was never any doubt after Alan Bond had cradled the Cup in his arms that the Azzurra team would come back for a second shot.

The America II syndicate, Cup arm of the NYYC, were the first challenging syndicate to set up a Perth beachhead. That was in November 1984, just one year after the Bond's audacious victory. Almost simultaneously *Azzurra* arrived. Soon the two foreign twelve-metres were trialling in lonely formation through the big waves off Fremantle. Their presence put down a marker of serious intent. The Royal Perth were impressed enough to appoint the Yacht Club Costa Smeralda as 'Challenger of Record'. Commodore Gianfranco Alberini and his flag officers became responsible for organising the entire 600-race elimination series that would result in one foreign boat coming forward in February 1987 as the challenger. It was a formidable responsibility and one that the club took exremely seriously – possibly too much so. Men like Alberini and Riccardo Bonadeo, president of the executive committee, who learned so much about twelve-metre campaigns at Newport, began to divert their considerable talents away from the yacht and into organising this huge regatta. Although the Royal Perth were happy to see the task being done so fluently and competently, more than one senior figure expressed the fear that the drive within Azzurra to put a fast, well-sailed yacht on the water was being dissipated.

Certainly there was evidence of that possibility. In January 1986 a new *Azzurra* arrived in Fremantle with a new skipper. Mauro Pelaschier, who sailed Finn class dinghies against John Bertrand in the Olympics and is immensely popular with the Italian public, had been replaced by Lorenzo Bertolotti, a defector from the rival Italia syndicate. Internal politics had bedevilled the Azzurra campaign and this move did not look like helping. A feeling grew up that Pelaschier had been sacrificed for the opportunity to strike a public relations blow against the opposition. Bertolotti left Italia because he wanted more policy input but was being told to drive the boat and keep quiet. After a few weeks trialling off Fremantle followed by competition in the world championships it became apparent that neither was the new yacht fast, nor were the crew gelling around Bertolotti.

The linchpin of the Azzurra campaign is Cino Ricci. The fifty-two-year-old sports director is a veteran of numerous Admiral's Cups and skipper of *Azzurra* in Newport. A philosophical man by nature, he thought hard about the problems of harmony between the tactician and helmsman – the two most important people on the boat. Bertolotti and Stefano Roberto, just a year younger than his skipper, were not a happy afterguard. 'It is an impossible relation-ship,' mused Ricci in the cavernous Azzurra sail-loft after a race. 'The tactician is making the important decisions, he must win the race. But it is necessary to be subordinate to another man who has the boat in his hands. The press want only to make a star of the helmsman and the tactician must put himself aside. But probably he has a big ego himself.' On both the Bond yachts the skipper/tactician teams of Colin Beashel/Carl Ryves and Gordon Lucas/Hugh Treharne have paired men almost a generation apart. The idea of a father-and-son relationship being a solution to the psychological battle was perhaps taken to its logical conclusion by the New Zealand syndicate when they put Roy Dickson aboard *KZ5* as tactician to his son Chris.

Ashore Azzurra moved steadily forwards, always with flair. A grand, porticoed Victorian building at the west end of the High Street was acquired as syndicate headquarters. Officially it was the 'Azzurra Pavilion', but to locals it was never anything but the Pink Palace, because of the salmon-pink paint applied to the whole edifice. Inside it oozed style. Most twelve-metre teams are run from poorly air-conditioned Portacabin offices with not enough phones, bits of boat underfoot and half-read telex messages littering every desk – if there should chance to be more than one. The Pavilion has elegant dark-blue sofas straight from a Milan design studio, good paintings on the walls, computers that looked fashionably hi-tech but are powerful enough to put a twelve-metre on the moon, and its own bar stocked with the sponsors' products. At the rear a brilliant green astroturf lawn has been laid, reached by a charming little path through a bower of rose bushes. Meanwhile the crew were squabbling and the boat was slow.

Media attention concerning the Azzurra syndicate inevitably tended to focus on the Aga Khan. The yacht capsizing off Fremantle would have received less attention than the titbit that His Royal Highness had booked two entire floors of Perth's five-star Merlin Hotel for himself and his entourage during the later part of the Cup racing. *Shergar*, his sumptuous white motor yacht that shares a name with the unfortunate racehorse kidnapped and murdered by the IRA, will also be in Perth during the event to provide a floating grandstand for the Aga Khan and the syndicate committee. But in the evening a chap needs a bit of comfort.

The same philosophy led the syndicate to purchase one of Fremantle's best-known buildings, the old Trades Hall, to create a restaurant and hospitality centre. The imposing two-storey house, overlooking Esplanade Park, had most recently been used as the base and commune for Fremantle's large Rajneeshi community – prior to the Bagwhan's spot of bother with the US authorities. The Orange people had run a simple but successful vegetarian restaurant there for some years, but the Azzurra representatives had something a little grander in mind. The best Italian restaurant in Australia was their modest aim. With nearly half of Fremantle's population having roots in the *Republica*, it may not have been tactful to announce that Freo possessed nowhere which served decent Italian food, but if the America's Cup has one unifying effect it is to encourage people to go completely over the top.

The notion would horrify Azzurra's national rivals. Consorzio Italia is based around the Yacht Club Italiano in Genoa. Founded in 1879 this club is the oldest in the country and is very much the equivalent of the Royal Yacht Squadron – old money and old boats. In the days before the Republic membership was very much based around the Italian royal family and nobility. HRH the Aga Khan and his internationalist associates across the Tyrrhenian Sea in Sardinia are seen very much as yachting's nouveau riche.

Yet America's Cup racing has room for every sort of excess. When Consorzio Italia arrived in Fremantle for a season of training and the world championships, the crew resembled a daily fashion parade. One of the syndicate's fourteen major sponsors is the Gucci fashion firm, and it has a responsibility for outfitting the fifty-strong team. Each crewman arrived with a 290-piece wardrobe of Gucci items, ranging from shorts, through dock-shoes, to one-piece storm suits. Their appearance was superb. Around the pavement cafés of Fremantle or at sea, no one looked as good as the Italia boys. The only slight drawback was that the crew were accommodated in student housing at Murdoch University, several miles out of Fremantle. No architect designing rooms for a student would provide hanging space for a 290-piece wardrobe, so the crew's rooms came to resemble a fashion warehouse with clothes stacked everywhere.

Other backers of the syndicate are as blue-chip as those of Azzurra. Foremost in the field is Montedison, the chemicals giant; but others range from Aeromacchi, the aerospace contractor responsible for the world-selling Macchi jet, to the Buitoni food company – Italy's answer to Heinz. With A$14 million in the bank before the campaign rolled, Italia lacked only experience. To a large extent they were willing to buy that in wherever possible. Immediately after Newport the syndicate bought *Victory '83* from Peter de Savary for use as a training boat and trialhorse. It went on to win the world championships at Sardinia in 1984, with Lorenzo Bertolotti at the helm. However, the vastly experienced US sailor Rod Davis (busy putting together his own Eagle syndicate at Newport Beach) was brought over to stand beside Bertolotti as tactician. When the time came to build the first new twelve-metre, christened *Italia* and easily the most beautiful boat to be launched in 1985, the syndicate chose naval architects Franco Giorgetti and Giorgio Magrini to design her. To some observers it was a puzzling choice, since the team had hitherto been responsible for powerful motor cruisers and large luxury cruising yachts rather than racing classes. However, British designer Ian Howlett, who created *Victory '83* and went on to draw *Crusader* for the British syndicate, was brought in as a consultant to Giorgetti and Magrini. The testing facilities and technology of Aeromacchi were used to develop the hull and keel – which came out with deltoid wings uncannily like those of a Macchi jet fighter. With its gunmetal-grey hull and its livery in the red, white and green familiar from a million Gucci bags, *Italia* looked a stunning boat. Unfortunately, during her first Fremantle season she had problems beating her older stablemate *Victory '83* – to the embarrassment of the syndicate.

The central pivot of the Italia effort is Flavio Scala, reserve skipper and day-to-day executive boss. A champion sailor in various classes who still runs his family hotel on the shores of Lake Garda near Verona, the distinguished and heavily moustached Scala is able to articulate the ethos of the syndicate concisely: 'We want only quality, no commercialism,' he says, before reeling off a list of the sponsors' names. What they indicate is that Consorzio is just as commercial as any other twelve-metre syndicate; it just prefers the carriage-trade end of the market place. 'There will be no salami or milk on our sails. It is a hi-tech challenge,' he adds, in an obvious jibe at the opposition.

Nevertheless, in some worlds style is all. When the three-masted schooner *Creole*, once the property of Stavros Niarchos and reputedly the most beautiful craft afloat, glides into Fremantle harbour as the headquarters of the syndicate, no one will doubt where Italia is coming from. The yacht now belongs to the Gucci family and has undergone a A$6 million refit to equip her for the arduous social trials of an America's Cup summer.

Chapter 9

The Commercial Cup

In remote areas of Papua New Guinea there exists a phenomenon known as 'Cargo Cult'. Tribesmen believe that at some unspecified time in the future (a notion somewhat akin to the Second Coming) white people from sophisticated, faraway countries will arrive laden with wealth and goods. This will be distributed to the tribe, who will then grow rich without effort. Cynics say that Alan Bond's victory in the America's Cup was the beginning of Cargo Cult in Western Australia.

As usual, the cynics are misguided. They have glimpsed the outline of a truth but then projected it on to the big screen, with consequent distortion. Western Australians are notable entrepreneurs. Out of a tiny population they have produced such major players in world business as Robert Holmes à Court, Alan Bond and Lang Hancock, plus scores of others who are front-rank in Pacific and South-East Asian terms. What the people of Perth foresaw was the descent of the globally rich and famous on their isolated home town. In Alan Bond's memorable sentence about the America's Cup: 'It's where very successful men come to be with other very successful men – and where men who would like to be successful gather on the periphery.'

Western Australia is full of people who would like to be successful, and they don't even have to travel to be on the periphery of this event.

Travel is to be at the heart of how Western Australia is exploiting the commercial possibilities of the Cup. In a decade of falling prices for resources (and Western Australia is primarily a state where things are grown in, or dug out of, the ground) and rising unemployment, tourism offers fast, high-volume job creation and the opportunity to earn large amounts of foreign exchange. The state government was quick to seize on the strategy, and appointed local travel industry entrepreneur Warren Pateman to spearhead an America's Cup tourist drive. Statistics, slogans and projections began to pour out of the Cup unit within the Western Australia Tourist Commission. 'America's Cup – What the World's Coming To' runs the masthead on hundreds of thousands of glossy brochures.Of course, evidence was needed that the world would be coming, and it was a very solid relief when market research firm McNair Anderson produced the golden figure, late in 1985, that over one million visitors would be coming to the 'State of Excitement', as car numberplates proclaim Western Australia, during the period 1986/7. And these were not just to be any old visitors.

Pateman's America's Cup unit has a marketing plan that describes them:

> It has been stated that as much as $200 million will be spent by foreign challengers in their attempts to take the America's Cup, yachting's most sought-after prize, much of this contributed by major multi-national corporations. It is reasonable to expect that a very high proportion of the international visitors expected in Perth during the Cup elimination and finals series will be corporate-sponsored guests with substantial financial commitments to accommodation, transportation, boat-charter and hospitality. *It is expected that an abnormally high visitor spending rate will apply during the period October '86 through February '87.*

Figures from the Bureau of Industry Economics show that the average visitor to Western Australia stays ten days and spends A$976. Such sums could be tossed out of the window when one began talking America's Cup. 'For the Cup there will be a high proportion of big-spenders,' says Pateman. 'The Aga Khan, for example, is not going to stop at nine hundred and seventy dollars.' It doesn't seem likely that such a sum would even pay for a day's room

service on the two floors of the five-star Merlin Hotel that the leader
of fourteen million Moslems has booked for the exclusive use of his
entourage. According to Pateman – whose speed of travel, speed of
thought and general gung-ho approach to everything from boat
shows in Hawaii to departmental budgets has left some of his
essentially civil service colleagues a little bruised – by mid-1986 Perth
will have more five-star hotel rooms than Sydney. Indeed, with the
casino as the jewel in the crown – 'Las Vegas in Thongs', as one
irreverent overseas visitor dubbed it – Pateman feels able to describe
the city as the best-equipped hospitality venue in the southern
hemisphere. 'Tourism is our number three industry,' he affirmed
when his work began. 'But it will be number two next year and
number one very soon after that.'

There is a certain articulate but minority opposition to such a huge
planned growth in tourism; it does not go without sympathy on the
part of state premier Brian Burke: 'Disadvantages to tourism?
There's a symmetry to everything and all economic activities tend to
have a downside. If you have a resource-based economy you dig
bloody big holes in the ground and pull down whole forests.
Environmentalists who say let's stop mining or forestry and replace it
with tourism don't seem to realise how destructive tourism can be.
It's pretty environmentally destructive to have gaudy signs everywhere and big queues of people pushing for the instant development
of the film they have just taken. You have to prepare, and if you
don't, you destroy those things that tourists come to see.'

Estimates of what such a volume of visitors will spend, assuming
they materialise, vary considerably. The most used figure is around
A$2 billion. But the anxiety that lurks never far from the minds of
the government and the tourist industry is the 'Los Angeles
syndrome'. When the 1984 Olympics was held in LA the period
immediately beforehand saw a spate of media stories, both within the
USA and internationally, warning of fifty-mile traffic jams, astrono-
mically inflated prices for accommodation, and the near-impossibil-
ity of securing seats for the events. Visitors stayed away in droves –
and none of the evil things came to pass. The lesson has been taken
on board with a vengeance in Perth. Any journalist who has the
temerity to ask a question or produce a story that questions the
veracity or likelihood of the tourist scenario as envisaged by the
WATC is firmly squashed. One story – that a projection of visitor
numbers from Italy had been reduced by nearly eighty per cent

following detailed research by a civil servant – resulted in the man being demoted and lengthy calls from Zurich, where the relevant minister was on a trip, to the newspaper concerned. Some months later in the federal parliament, the matter became a national controversy threatening the career of America's Cup minister John Dawkins.

In some respects it was an unwholesome scene for the media. The use of propaganda and the holding of an unwavering line seemed more appropriate to times of war. Syndicate heads had said often enough that the America's Cup was war; perhaps it was true for governments too.

Having decided that it would be state policy to bring the world to see the America's Cup, the Western Australian government's big problem was how, physically, to get the visitors over the threshold. Perth is served by relatively few scheduled flights and almost no charters. When travellers do secure a seat on one of the heavily booked jets, they arrive at an airport which could barely cope with the traffic of twenty years ago. It was not unusual for the 450 passengers of a jumbo to take three hours to clear baggage and customs. Since the vagaries of airline schedules used to produce two choke points – when a group of international arrivals met another group of domestic arrivals – each day at noon and in mid-evening the single terminal resembled the streets of Calcutta. In the heady, expansionist mood immediately after the Cup victory, the government of premier Brian Burke decided to tackle both problems in a big way. They hired American Ron Smith, a former vice-president of United Airlines, the biggest non-national carrier in the world, as a consultant with a brief to (i) assist with the promotion of the America's Cup, (ii) get more airlines into Perth, (iii) look at de-regulation of the domestic industry. Secondly, Burke decided to rebuild the airport. In December 1983 the go-ahead was given for the construction of a new A$60 million international terminal on the opposite side of the airfield from the present facility. Capacity was to be great enough to cope with five jumbos and 6,000 people an hour. The new white control tower, an elegant 220-foot spindle with a bobbin at the top, is visible from all over Perth. It seems to symbolise the can-do determination of a city that could use the catalyst of a yacht race to build what is virtually a new airport. For some worried administrators, however, the situation has garnered all the attributes of a kidnap and a ransom. Australia's unions are powerful and embedded into the polity – none more so than the Builders Labourers Federation.

It was clear to all that if the new facility was not operating in time for the Cup then the event would be a shambles, with spectators and participants queueing clear back to Singapore. The administration would not so much have egg on its face as be buried in the yolk. By mid-1985 the control tower alone was running six months behind schedule as a result of strikes, stoppages and demands for bonus payments. Officials began to count off the months to September 1986, when the first wave of tourists was expected. So too did the union. They were looking at it through a different pair of binoculars. One group felt embarrassment and shame at the prospect of an unfinished showpiece, the other did not. 'On the project being completed in time for the America's Cup, to be honest we couldn't care less about it,' said Kevin Reynolds, forthright secretary of the BLF in Western Australia. 'I don't believe the average person is going to benefit by the Cup and, as a whole, most people would wish that Alan Bond hadn't even won the bloody thing.'

Whether the entire membership of the BLF would go along with that position is a good question. In the year or eighteen months prior to the beginning of the Cup defence it seemed as if the metropolitan area, and particularly downtown Perth and Fremantle, had been turned into a gigantic building site. Labour became the ultimate seller's market. The award rate for a plasterer was around eleven dollars an hour; in reality a customer could not get a tradesman to come to the phone for that sort of money. At the unfinished casino, cost over-runs and the need to get the roulette ball rolling – and revenue coming in – led to work going on twenty-four hours a day, and the kind of hourly rates that might have tempted Alan Bond to get his tradesman's paintbrush out again. It was a labour market where the builders working on the airport control tower felt confident enough to stage a one-day strike demanding full pay for attending a nuclear disarmament meeting. On the Fremantle wharf militant waterfront workers went on strike over the need to have a man employed to hold an umbrella over fork-lift drivers while they moved from truck to minibus during rainy weather.

Even the confident and aggressive Bond fell victim to the market forces his Newport win had unleashed. Just along the Fremantle waterfront from the Australia II dock and compound he bought a plot of prime land. The concept was to build forty-five villas of considerable style and luxury, use some of them for crew accommodation, and sell the bulk of them on the open market. The profit, which was anticipated to be close to A$1 million, would go into the syndicate war chest. Called 'Fremantle Waterfront' the development, according to the glossy brochure which was produced to sell the villas, was 'simply, like the rest of Fremantle, a charming, stimulating and intelligent environment. If the water, sun, yachting or relaxation are important in your life, then the "Fremantle Waterfront" is almost certainly for you.' In the artist's drawings it looks a charming arrangement of sophisticated city houses with ocean views and plenty of trees and shrubs surrounding the subtly coloured houses. Unfortunately it was never built. Drains and services were put into the plot, but the scheme never reached a firm foundation. Building unions talked of 'Cup bonuses', two building firms, including the giant Multiplex construction company, failed to produce tenders that made the project remotely viable for the syndicate. As they say in Australia, Bondy 'pulled the pin' on the entire project. It was a hectare of open, sandy embarrassment. To compound the angst, just two hundred yards down Marine Terrace the Kookaburra syndicate, bankrolled by Bond's great rival Kevin Parry, had managed to build twenty or so superb townhouses as crew accommodation with a view to ultimate resale at a profit. They were a little less grandiose than 'Fremantle Waterfront', but real enough and situated bang opposite the Australia II headquarters. It was a provocation that Bond was powerless to react to. Back in the 1970s he might have taken on the unions over such a thwarting of his plans. Now Bond Corporation was involved in too many big construction projects all over Australia to rock the BLF boat – even a twelve-metre – over crew houses for the syndicate. It was an indication of how, intentionally or not, the Cup had diminished within Bond's scheme of things.

This has not been the case, however, in every area of the tycoon's business interests. Bond's ownership of Swan Television, the operator of Channel 9 in Perth, placed him in the forefront of the plans to televise the America's Cup. Commercial television is very big business in Australia and it relies heavily on sport to generate big audiences, especially at weekends. With the Cup being the largest sporting event of truly international interest that has been held in Australia since the pre-television days of the Melbourne Olympics, it was obvious that a huge effort was going to be made by the commercial networks – 9, 7 and 10 – to take as large an involvement as possible in broadcasting it.

Twelve-metre racing could not have come in front of better cameras. Australian television has pioneered the coverage of cricket, golf, tennis and particularly motor-racing in new and exciting ways. Channel 7 pioneered the development of 'Race-Cam' – a tiny, lightweight camera weighing around two kilos that is mounted in the cockpit of a Formula One car and gives the viewer a driver's-eye view of the race-track. The Formula One Constructors Association awarded Australia the TV Trophy for best 1985 coverage in respect of the Adelaide Grand Prix, beating forty-five countries where motor-racing is better established.

Channel Seven has plans to mount several of these lightweight automatic cameras aboard the Kookaburra yachts. Powered by the onboard computer the signal will be bounced up to a helicopter or an airship overhead. Should that fail, skipper Iain Murray – who will be wired for sound and will provide occasional commentary – once worked as an assistant cameraman at Channel Seven in Sydney and should be able to direct the pictures himself. Channel Nine are planning much the same sort of effort with cameras aboard *Australia I* and *II*, and with both the airships above the course belonging to Bond's UK-based company Airship Industries, he may have surveillance and graphics facilities not widely available to competitor channels.

Such is the rivalry and tension between the channels that almost the only time they co-operate is when the joint lifeblood – money – is threatened. A remarkable example came in late 1985 when Robert Holmes à Court, owner of Channel 7 in Perth, was accused of having considered the removal of the state government over the granting of a new television licence. In a hearing of the Australian Broadcasting Tribunal investigating the desirability of a third commercial station in Perth, it was alleged that Holmes à Court had discussed a small coup with Bond who, as owner of Channel 9, was equally threatened by the possibility of a new rival. Bond, it was said, went to premier Burke with details of the conversation. Writs flew from Holmes à Court and the other parties, but no court case ensued, all agreeing that the dust should be allowed to settle. Different aspects of various conversations were disputed, but to an outside observer the startling aspect was that ownership and revenues of TV stations were seen in such a light. In capital terms the channels were worth about A$50 million to each man – not huge in terms of their overall portfolios.

Immediately after Newport 1983 it was apparent that the

televising of the next Cup was going to be a major issue. In the light of the current plans the coverage that historic day off Rhode Island looks prehistoric. There were just two camera positions, one afloat and one in a helicopter. Considering that Channel 9 routinely uses thirteen cameras to cover a Test match, puts microphones in the stumps and will field thirty-eight cameras at the Australian Open golf classic, one doesn't need to be psychic to predict a bigger effort. The interaction between sponsors and television has made it certain. Companies who have put perhaps A$1 million into a boat – and there is no shortage of those – want to buy air-time and segments of high-quality coverage in order to make the most of their investment. In early 1986, when the world championship was under way, it was belatedly realised by many people that Channel 9 was providing live coverage. The next day the sparse spectator fleet was augmented by a large ketch sporting a huge banner bearing the words 'Jones, Lang and Wootton', strung between the two masts.

The problem for the Royal Perth Yacht Club when the question of televising the five-month event arose was who to give, or rather sell, rights to. Both Channel 7 and Channel 9 would have paid large sums for exclusive rights, but the problem for the club was that these stations reached only urban Australia. 'We felt very strongly that the winning of the Cup was a victory for all of the country,' says Noel Robins, executive director of the RPYC's America's Cup committee. 'It followed from that that the maximum number of people out in the bush and up north ought to be able to see the defence, not just the people in the big cities.' From that position the only logical answer was to negotiate coverage and transmission rights with the Australian Broadcasting Commission. Via the newly launched satellite Aussat, the ABC is the only broadcaster to cover the whole of the vast Australian continent. Unfortunately the ABC has a poor reputation for covering sport. It is an expensive business requiring massive amounts of equipment and manpower. No organisation had ever covered a yacht race in this sort of depth and breadth before, and it was certain to cost huge sums (current estimates put it at around A$3 million) for waterproof cameras, helicopters, boats and the like. The solution was to form a pool. The three major commercial networks plus the ABC would form a common unit to provide raw picture coverage of the entire 1986/7 America's Cup. Their fee for an input of manpower and hardware would be a signal to which they could then add commentary, graphics, interviews and so on in order to make it distinctively their own programme. For instance, although Channel 7 is a major participant in the pool there is no agreement that the pictures from on board *Kookaburra*, or the sound of Iain Murray's muffled oaths as another wave hits him in the face, will be fed into the pool mix. It is these ingredients that will make Channel 7's coverage different from Channel 9's.

There were understandable fears that the pool would have all the worst attributes of a committee and none of the inherent dynamism of a live sports programme. In addition, the Royal Perth, needing to raise around A\$5 million just to meet the cost of running the America's Cup, were a little sad that the chance to make a big sale of TV rights (and the sums paid for cricket and golf in Australia run into millions) had disappeared – although, as it turned out, the disappearance was only temporary.

When Mark MacCormack arrived in Perth to assess the commercial possibilities of the America's Cup as an event, he brought with him the knowledge that it had to be television which would generate big bucks. However, according to IMG's man in Perth and longtime RPYC member Ernie Taylor, it was not quite the mega-dollars that some club officials saw dancing before their eyes. 'Originally there were Australians who thought it [the race] was worth ten million dollars to TV,' says Taylor. 'That's dreamtime. The real figures are probably between one and two million.' That sum has to be seen in the context of the first rung of a ladder. Yachting of this sort – indeed any sort – has never been televised in a highly organised, multi-camera way before now. When IMG first acquired the TV rights to Wimbledon it was a gentle game of lawn tennis discreetly covered by the BBC, not the annual ratings blockbuster that it is now. Many tennis fans and ordinary Wimbledon buffs (a large proportion of the English population) preferred it the old way. It may turn out to be the same with America's Cup. However, in yachting there are no clocks to be turned back.

One of the flashpoints of the present Cup is certain to be sparked off over the right to go out and film the yachts racing. Most English-speaking people have grown up with half-digested notions about the freedom of the high seas. Seen through twentieth-century spectacles that is also assumed to include the right to hire helicopters, fly over an event, and point a camera at whatsoever moves. That philosophy, however loosely woven, cannot accommodate a situation where broadcasting organisations have paid for something their rivals will not have.

'The organiser doesn't have an event if you can't protect it,' explains Jim Bukata, vice-president of IMG's television arm, Trans World International, 'especially from a television standpoint. If a television company in a particular area of the world has purchased the rights, it is beholden upon the organiser to protect the exclusivity of those rights in that particular territory.' In plain terms, since the cable sport network ESPN and the broadcast network ABC have acquired the America's Cup in the USA, it is the Royal Perth's job to ensure there are no CBS or NBC crews out on the oceanic racecourse making bootleg documentaries.

It would be fair to say that this is an area of activity new to yacht clubs. The exclusivity even extends to news access, an area which always invites vigorous debate in the press and other media. Within America, for instance, ESPN and ABC will be granted what the organisers call 'protection against news access from outside sources'. In return for this monopoly they have to grant reasonably free access to news material, say two minutes a day, to other channels and networks within that country. 'As a result you get the exposure that you are looking for but, to the extent that the exposure is there, the organisation that bought the rights is in control of it,' explains Bukata, a bulky former accountant from New York. He is not a sailor.

A partnership like the Royal Perth Yacht Club and IMG has to be careful that the granting of broadcasting exclusivity does not diminish or restrict the potential audience too much, since the team is also hoping to sell sponsorships, licensing agreements for everything from sweatshirts to coffe-mugs, and support agreements. These all depend, at the end of the day, on the aggregate number of people who are going to follow and take an interest in the event. 'I think you walk a line between the credos of maximum revenue and maximum exposure,' says Bukata. He has enormous experience with the televising of tennis, particularly Wimbledon, and big boxing matches. 'The problem is that you wish to expose the event to the greatest possible extent but you also want to generate as much revenue as possible. Sometimes there are conflicts that occur.'

Early in the world championships, during February 1986, a small but illustrative clash of interests, and cultures, did occur. Some months earlier the BBC had decided that it would make a documentary series on the build-up to the America's Cup and then on the event itself. It is to be a programme made up of three one-hour films. A crew were despatched to Fremantle to secure coverage of the syndicates taking part in the world championships and film some of the fleet races themselves. Among the three to four hundred journalists and media people present it was considered no honour or treat to be on the 'press boat'. The *Captain Cook* is a grubby, cramped riverboat dating from the 1940s. However, the six-man BBC team were denied even that privilege after the first day.

The producer was astonished to receive a telex from his London department head saying that IMG had asked US$10,000 as a fee for limited filming rights during the world championships. He was to take no further action until the corporation had made a response, and in the interim the crew were not allowed to work from the *Captain Cook*. When producer Bob Saunders suggested that the seas were open to all and that, provided he did not infringe racecourse navigation limits, his crew might film from their own chartered lobster boat, the reply was unequivocal: Royal Perth, advised by IMG, made it clear that if this happened media accreditation would be withdrawn from the BBC. At such an event as the America's Cup, controlled by security that is tight and will only get tighter, this is the ultimate sanction. It worked and the Beeb withdrew, leaving for Hawaii and Dennis Conner. 'Despite everything I've heard about Conner, it can't be harder than this,' said Saunders as he left Perth.

After explaining how IMG always hoped that the organisation which had bought national TV rights would control news access in a reasonably free way, Bukata says: 'It's the perfect marriage, although obviously there will be people who object.' The logic of the position is impeccable. Within the electronic media no experienced person would any longer anticipate unrestricted access to Wimbledon or the US Masters golf tournament. But two factors in the America's Cup seem to make conflicts inevitable. First, the nature of the arena: rightly or wrongly (with the exception of military installations) people do expect to be able to take boats anywhere they will float. The concept of part of the ocean several nautical miles off Perth having a legal and commercial 'fence' around it is one that is likely to take some time to absorb; second, this is still such a new event in media terms that most of the personnel covering it are still feeling their way, and it would not be unfair to say that, in organisational terms, so too are the Royal Perth. Because of its huge experience IMG appears to be closing off areas before some people have even realised they exist. 'There's nothing new in any of this,' expounds

Bukata in the Perth office IMG opened specifically to deal with the Cup. 'It's just the first time it's been applied to yachting and that seems to be a major headache. It's not a headache for me personally, but I think there will be a knee-jerk reaction from some people. The biggest aspect of difficulty is that in many sports the ground rules have been established over the years – like Wimbledon. In yachting there hasn't been any significant interest before.

'If you look at the numbers of media attending the sailing events at the LA Olympics there were probably ten people on Newport Beach. Fantastic sailors performing – but they were the numbers on the buoy. This twelve-metre class has something about it that makes it an international event.' Bukata, with his lack of interest in boats, complete lack of social pretension, and self-confessed absorption in 'the numbers' of any IMG project, is a good yardstick for the changes in the America's Cup.

'I think what happened in 1983 and what happened here in Australia in terms of enthusiasm has done more for yacht racing than anything else in the history of the sport,' Bukata believes. 'I live in New York. Nobody talked about Newport before Newport – if you know what I mean? I guess a select few people sat around and said, "Gee, the America's Cup is here again." The *New York Times* reported it, and maybe the *Washington Post* plus a few sailing magazines. But now, leading into this, you have people talking about it in the street. Taxi drivers in New York, for God's sake, ask you how you'd rate Dennis Conner against the NYYC.' He gives much of the credit in the States to the cable network ESPN. It has done a lot of hard work educating people and exposing the sport to a public who had no existing knowledge of its techniques or technology. 'They did one show where they basically took apart a twelve-metre and showed what each crewman's job was and how he did it on the boat – highlighted it, did slow motions – and I'm sure that for ninety-nine per cent of the Americans that watched that it's the first time they've ever understood what twelve-metres are all about.'

For the first time in yacht-racing history a radio commentary has been arranged, again with the help of IMG. Macquarie, one of the biggest commercial networks in Australia, has signed an exclusive agreement with the Royal Perth Yacht Club to be the 'host broadcaster' for the challenger and defender elimination series plus the finals. It will cost Macquarie around A$1 million for the entire operation, but that covers equipment, personnel, and operating costs besides the royalty payment to the RPYC – which is probably in the order of A$250,000, although neither side will confirm this. The ABC radio network, by far the most extensive in Australia and the only broadcaster in most outback areas, was offered the radio deal but could not afford it. Presumably, having conceded the pool arrangement for television, the yacht club felt that altruism had gone far enough. IMG have the right to market the broadcast commentary overseas, but it remains to be seen how well it will compete commercially against television. At previous Newport Cups radio has been a vital and authoritative medium, in the absence of other than sporadic TV coverage, for taking the Cup off the racecourse. Since the action happens at a fairly leisurely tempo in twelve-metre races, the scene rather lends itself to the painting of a skilful word-picture. During the world championships the Macquarie network ran a commentary service which was largely a 'shakedown' for the Cup itself. Unfortunately, the sports reporters assigned to it took horse-racing as the pattern for the broadcast. At each rounding of a buoy a list of the yachts, in position and with the time gaps between them, would be gabbled down the microphone, sounding for all the world like a 'blower' in a betting shop.

In some respects the commercial relationship between the Royal Perth and the media has been smoother than that between the club and its domestic sponsors – the professionalism and experience of IMG may well have been a major factor in that. Early in 1984 the RPYC signed up six major Australian companies as key sponsors. It cost Broken Hill Proprietary (the biggest company in Australia and the subject of Robert Holmes à Court's recent controversial bid), BP, General Motors Holden, Westpac, Coca-Cola and the government-owned airline TAA A$350,000 each to buy into the event. Later Alan Bond's Swan Brewery came in as an 'international' sponsor for a reported but never confirmed fee of A$1 million. This caused some uneasiness among the original sponsors, most of whom have operations overseas. It had always been assumed that a Cup sponsor could promote its involvement wherever it traded. Such confusion is to be symptomatic of the relations between the club and the companies. 'In the euphoria after the Newport win, perhaps people bought into the mood of the affair without knowing precisely what they were expecting to get out of their buy,' says a senior club official who has been responsible for clearing up some of the misunderstandings. The problem over the backdrop for the televised press conferences was a typical case. The six big sponsors believed that their corporate logos would be on a backdrop behind the winning skippers and other interviewees. As already described, the Bond team objected, and so did almost every other syndicate. It also turned out to be against broadcasting practice within Australia to hold a news event in front of what is virtually a free advertisement. The logos were relegated to the very edge of the backdrop; they would be included in only the widest of shots, when the whole panel was on screen, where they would be indistinguishable on the average television screen. Ernie Taylor, now the Perth representative for IMG, was in at the ground floor in bringing sponsors to the yacht club. He was a director of Marketforce, a Western Australian advertising agency that acts as the commercial face of ADAC (more properly, Australia's Defence of the America's Cup 1987 Pty Ltd, a trust that was set up to deal with all commercial aspects of the Cup and raise the money necessary to organise the defence). Taylor knows as much about the financing of the 1987 Cup, from the Royal Perth point of view, as anyone. 'There has been confusion in the market place as to what locations and opportunities are available,' he says. 'It will be the smart people who take advantage of what they have bought.'

One sceptical school of thought says that the club sponsors have purchased nothing – they are associated with an event, but the public associates with boats and teams. The other viewpoint is that the event itself is bound to be a success – and all sponsors want to be linked with success. Only one twelve-metre yacht can win the Cup (and perhaps a certain glory will accrue to the beaten finalist), and the other sixteen or so will be losers. 'The people that have backed the boat that comes through to be the actual challenger or defender are going to be fine,' continues Taylor, 'but I don't know about the other dozen and what they've been promised.'

Of more direct concern to RPYC has been a certain disillusionment among its own sponsors. Little things can mean a lot in this area. Although sponsorship is a commercial decision, hard-headed directors of multinational concerns often act more like donors than investors. Just as parents require children to be adequately grateful for a birthday toy, so sponsors have needs which are not entirely rational. Small mistakes, such as when Holden delivered a dozen Commodores to the club as courtesy cars and no one remembered to tell the local press of the presentation, rankled a touch. A company that gives away A$120,000 worth of cars needs its ego rubbed occasionally.

Several of the sponsors have begun to feel the need to compare notes and establish an ad hoc committee to deal with the Royal Perth. It is here that a certain paranoia has crept into the relationship. The contract with each of the six contains a 'confidentiality clause'. Not every agreement is identical and the club does not want its partners comparing notes. 'Sponsors are supposed to meet with us, not with each other,' says an RPYC official. Needless to say the sponsors have gone ahead and met together. According to one person present lawyers outnumbered sponsors by a considerable factor. Grumbles ranged from trivial doubts about whether there would be free tickets to the America's Cup Ball to serious worries about the use of the official logo. This design, with the silhouette of two mainsails and a spinnaker, plus the Cup itself inset, has already become famous across Australia. Sponsors have the right to use it – but only on prestige items that are given away to customers, not those that are bought. Thus TAA were entitled to put the striking blue and silver design on a flight bag it wished to give away to first-class passengers, but not on a larger holdall to be sold in its ticket offices. Even more absurdly, Westpac (which is Australia's biggest and best-known bank) has found that it is entitled to put the logo on cheque book covers but not on the face of each cheque – which is what the bank wanted to do. The rationale is that cheque book covers are 'given away' but, because of tax, each cheque is regarded as having been sold. Despite the club's initial opposition to sponsors meeting together, it was only after this began to happen that some of the problems were ironed out and the relationship started to proceed more smoothly.

In some respects the America's Cup has begun to resemble a battle between logos more than a contest between yachts. Some of the warfare can get pretty savage. One US syndicate, based around the Blue Dolphin Yacht Club at Newport Beach, California, fell apart in mid-1985 after spending most of the campaign funds it had raised in a courtroom struggle against American Express. At stake was the use of a logo showing a twelve-metre silhouette above the words: 'America's Cup – Don't Leave Perth Without It'. It was, of course, a gentle parody on the well-known advertising slogan used by American Express in newspapers and television around the world for its credit card. Leonard 'Skip' Riley, chief executive of the Blue

Dolphin team (more properly called the Return America's Cup syndicate), thought the joke should be carried to its logical conclusion and wrote to Amex, on writing paper headed with the logo, suggesting that it might care to contribute to campaign funds or become a sponsor. The corporation sent not a cheque but a process-server, who handed Mr Riley a writ seeking to debar Blue Dolphin from using the slogan – despite the fact that he had applied for a California trademark.

Over a period of four months Mr Riley fought Amex in the state courts. Finally he decided that the contest was detracting from the yachting effort and might jeopardise the chances of ever getting to Perth; he signed a consent decree to stop using the slogan. Unfortunately it did not cover the six licencees who were producing clothing, posters and knick-knacks containing the offending phrase. When this came to the attention of Amex the company pounced like a hawk – suing for contempt of court, perjury and triple damages. It was the end of the line for Riley – who had sailed as a crewman aboard the 1964 Cup defender *Columbia* – and the syndicate folded.

'We were up and running until this came along,' he said at the time, 'but so much time and money has now been spent fighting American Express that we will have to finish or look to combine with another syndicate.' No merger occurred and that was the last to be heard of Blue Dolphin. In New York the giant American Express professed slight regret, but maintained that it had no option but to defend its trademark. 'The whole thing is rather unfortunate,' said spokeswoman Sarah Mullen. 'The America's Cup is a good event. We may end up supporting it.' Unless one counts the number of people who made the journey to Perth courtesy of their plastic passport, there has been no sign of Amex backing the Cup.

It would be unfair to pillory Amex too much. Its intensity in defending a slogan is easily matched by the Bond syndicate's care of its famous boxing kangaroo, first seen at Newport in 1983 as a battle flag flying from the forestay of *Australia II*. 'What we're selling and what ultimately holds us together commercially is the boxing kangaroo,' says marketing manager Vern Reid. Licensing the logo should bring the syndicate around A$500,000 during the course of the campaign. But it isn't all jam. 'We spent about A$30,000 on lawyers' fees fighting one guy who was pirating the design. They all argue that it's got a different head or the tail is a different angle. Mostly a few stiff letters fix it. Often they then come on board as official licencees.' The greatest logo of all is, of course, the Cup itself. It was also the subject of one of the most bizarre disputes imaginable. In the middle of 1985 the Western Australian Tourist Commission commissioned a young Perth artist named Mark Sofilas to produce a poster that combined the Cup with a distinctive Australian theme. He came up with a print that showed the gleaming Auld Mug with a grinning koala clinging to it as if it were the trunk of a eucalyptus gum. The prurient claimed that the expression on the bear's face suggested that it was mounting the silver ewer. Certainly neither the design, nor a caption that read 'What's the difference between the America's Cup and a boomerang? The boomerang comes back' showed any great reverence for the trophy. An embarrassed Royal Perth asked the Tourist Commission to withdraw the thousands of copies of the poster already printed. 'We thought it was in bad taste and, as the club virtually represents the state, we asked that the poster be withdrawn,' said Peter Dalziell, who was commodore at the time. 'We believe the posters are demeaning to the Cup itself.' The Tourist Commission caved in and the koala and the Cup became a *cause célèbre* throughout Western Australia. The artist was furious and so were many ordinary Aussies. The strong suspicion was that the Royal Perth had given in to the stuffed shirts of the New York Yacht Club, although that body never made a formal complaint. We didn't win the Cup by Bondy giving in to them over the winged keel, ran the argument. How will we keep it if we surrender over a small joke with a koala?

The reality of the situation was more interesting. The Royal Perth was involved in delicate negotiations with the New York club to take over the copyright of the America's Cup as a name and a symbol. The talks were, in fact, to take eighteen months and the koala row occurred right in the middle of them. The NYYC had held the copyright for 132 years and were not about to pass it on lightly. Yet the force of the Royal Perth's argument – that no defending club could afford to organise the regatta without those marketing rights – was undeniable. In more practical terms, the club had already sold 'exclusive' licences to use the America's Cup logo to twenty-four supporting Australian organisations, ranging from garden furniture manufacturers, through the inevitable tee-shirt makers, to a Melbourne paper plate factory. Until the Royal Perth obtained the copyright from Manhattan, these licencees could not be effectively protected from 'pirates' – as some of them were finding out.

Eventually, in February 1986, the two clubs signed an agreement passing the commercial rights in the Cup as a name and emblem to the Royal Perth. In the event of the Auld Mug moving, the rights will pass smoothly to the new holder. It also provides for the 'Challenger of Record' and bona fide defender and challenger syndicates to use the emblem to support their efforts. Predictably with the NYYC, there was hesitation over the question of proper veneration and respect for the pot that had stood on its sideboard for 132 years. In the end the contract was signed, between commodores Alan Crewe and Arthur Santry, with no money changing hands. But a cuddly koala nearly undid the deal that will make future America's Cup races financially possible.

In some respects, the sums handled by the yacht clubs and the syndicates are beginning to look like small beer in comparison with the money being spent globally by companies wishing to be associated with the Cup. Westpac, for instance, a major RPYC sponsor at a cost of A$350,000, have looked carefully at the possibility of sponsoring the Bond syndicate. This would have cost a further A$500,000. But the bank's really big money is being spent on chartering *Sea Goddess*, a 4,000-tonne, 300-foot liner that normally cruises routes in the Mediterranean and West Indies. The cost is around A$10 million for the period 1 October to 27 February. It may seem a huge sum for what will largely be corporate entertaining, but at the 1983 Cup Westpac chartered a much smaller yacht for just three weeks and managed to arrange loans and facilities worth A$13 million in that period. On the Fremantle dockside behind the *Sea Goddess* mooring an old warehouse will be converted into a convention and conference centre for Westpac clients – actual and potential. No wonder a director of the bank felt able to say rather patronisingly, apropos the RPYC sponsorship, that he felt it becomes a large organisation to help a small one trying to organise a large event. In other words, it's small change to us, cobbers. *Sea Goddess*, with her Swedish crew serving nearly sixty double suites, may be among the most luxurious passenger ships in the harbour, but she is far from the biggest. *Achille Lauro*, the liner which shot to prominence after being hijacked by the Palestine Liberation Organisation, will spend the Cup in Western Australia. Its passengers will probably do little more than lift a glass and gaze at the yachts. Aboard yet another liner, the 15,000-tonne *Mediterranean Sky*, eyes will be fixed to the green baize and the roulette wheel. Perth property tycoon Stephen Chew decided shortly after Alan Bond won the Cup that a floating casino was needed in Fremantle. By going out to watch the twelve-metre races each day and proceeding just beyond territorial waters, the *Sky*'s casino will skirt the Western Australian monopoly granted to Dallas Dempster and his A$200-million gaming house on the Swan River.

Whatever the spectators are drinking – and Alan Bond's Swan Brewery is building more capacity – they surely won't ignore the America's Cup official whisky. 'You can take a White Horse anywhere' said the memorable advertisements of a year or two ago – even aboard a twelve-metre yacht, it seems. The fifth biggest-selling whisky in the world has paid the Royal Perth, via IMG who negotiated the deal, around A$500,000 for the right to be the official America's Cup scotch. With the special product and promotions involved – including 200 couples coming to Perth from all over the world as prize-winners – the company will spend around A$4 million on its sponsorship. It will be the largest such deal ever undertaken in the spirit world – and it has raised the hair on a few necks within the company. 'We wouldn't normally touch yachting as a promotion,' says marketing director Paul Antrobus. 'It's a minority sport with overtones of exclusiveness for most people. Our product is mass market, so we can't go down that elite road.' His initial reasoning seems sound and the Board of Distillers, who make White Horse, were initially unwilling to overturn it. However, Antrobus (who once marketed Levi jeans and knows a mass market when he sees one) showed the board the ten-point test he applies to all sponsorship proposals. The Cup passed every one.

'The America's Cup has become a huge event, not just a regatta. It is now also perceived as a national contest, whereas it was once just a few rich old men getting rich young men to sail their boats off Newport,' concludes Antrobus. The potential for national fervour; the tangible aura of glamour that always surrounds big boats; huge worldwide television coverage: all this has brought the board on board.

One point more than any other illustrates the growing commercial importance of the Cup. It is not the most obvious. Not everyone knows about it and those that do quite often fail to appreciate its significance. But the fact is that syndicates as diverse as Dennis Conner's Sail America, French Kiss, the New Zealand challenge and the British effort have all retained for themselves the marketing and commercial rights relating to a defence if they succeed in winning the Cup. No yacht club is ever again going to find itself in the fortunate position of the Royal Perth. Syndicates will be putting up A$15 million for a crack at the Cup, which might seem a lot of money. But viewed as a lottery ticket that could win a country in excess of US$2 billion, it looks worth the punt.

Chapter 10

Other Australian Efforts

Other Australian twelve-metre syndicates eager to defend the newly won Cup began to emerge within hours of Alan Bond's victory at Newport. Or, to be more accurate, dreams were formed, speeches made and ideal crew lists drawn up in those heady months before real money had to be spent and sheet aluminium stitched into graceful racing yachts. In the event, only three other syndicates managed to put boats on the water: Taskforce '87 in Perth, South Australian from Adelaide and, belatedly, Sydney yachtsman Syd Fischer's Eastern Defence Syndicate.

Of these it was Taskforce and the Kookaburra yachts that quickly showed they were playing to win. At fifty-three, Kevin Parry is a year or two younger than Alan Bond. In some respects they are rival Perth tycoons, although the Parry Corporation is nothing like the size of the Bond empire. Since Kevin took to the twelve-metre game the two men have been deadly rivals in everything. Rubber chase boats have been rammed, libel cases threatened and A\$250,000 wagers offered and rejected. Parry is short, pugnacious and has a cheeky-chappie grin that sits uneasily beneath one of the worst hair transplants in the southern hemisphere. He is the complete local boy, an alumnus of the famous Perth Modern School that produced Bob Hawke among a heap of other distinguished Australians, and in many ways embodies the best and worst of Western Australia. Parry is gutsy and has boundless imagination. His business empire began with department stores – which still exist although they only represent around twenty per cent of the corporation – and goes through to complex underwater vehicles for the oil and defence industries. Yet he is parochial to the nth degree. A reporter from eastern Australia or overseas can ask him a perfectly intelligent question and be answered scathingly: 'If you were from Perth . . .' A senior stockbroker visiting Perth from London was lunching at Lombardo's waterfront restaurant in Fremantle just prior to the Cup. Kevin Parry was pointed out to him at the next table. The stockbroker declined the offer of a third party to make an introduction and went across with his hand outstretched. He had the misfortune to be wearing casual trousers of a light black and white checked pattern. 'The fish is off,' growled Parry, before the hellos were uttered. 'I'm sorry . . .?' stammered the visitor. 'You're the chef, aren't you?' answered Parry. 'The fish is off.'

Although personally extremely wealthy he chooses to spend his holidays on Rottnest Island, the small holiday idyll just off Perth and to the west of the America's Cup course. He will load his sixty-foot launch *Sutherland* with food, Swan lager, plus his wife Helen and five children and head off from Fremantle. Most times he won't be on the island more than a day or two before boredom sets in and he decides to have a Parry Corporation board meeting. Directors have to come across by boat or plane and most likely end up in the back bar of the Quokker Arms toasting the afternoon away with the boss.

Despite, or perhaps because of, such capricious behaviour, Parry inspires great loyalty in those who work for him. He is said to reward them phenomenally well and people like his right-hand man Laurie Humphry, regarded as outstandingly able, stick with him for years in spite of offers from more glamorous or prestigious organisations. In his country there is a well-used and loved expression: 'dinky-di Aussie'. Parry is it. Patriotism of a deep and profoundly old-fashioned kind is the fount of much of his business drive. He loves Australian bluntness, deplores the clamour for sophistication, and believes that simple teamwork is the key to much achievement. Describing his young skipper and project director Iain Murray, for whom he has the highest respect, Parry could find no greater praise than to say: 'Iain Murray is a professional person who understands what it takes to mould a team, to be a team person. He understands the stresses and he knows what he has to do to combine them to produce the result.'

Unlike Alan Bond, Parry has played competitive sport at a high level – baseball, paradoxically enough. At the age of fifteen he left 'Mod', as the school was always known, and went to work in his father's struggling furniture factory just outside Perth city centre. He had been a promising rugby winger at school, but work at a lathe six days a week ruled that out. Kevin Parry turned to baseball, the only competitive sport played on Sundays. He was good enough to represent Western Australia several times between 1959 and 1969, and he went on to become a state selector. At a Saturday morning interview in his luxurious Dalkeith home, half a mile or so up-river from Bond, his two youngest sons, Scott and Cameron, come in clad in baseball gear and looking for a lift to the game. Parry Fields, out towards Perth's airport, is the finest baseball stadium in Australia. In nearly thirty years of involvement he has taken the game from being an eccentricity to a major national sport. When Parry talks of the achievement it is cast in terms of the good of the country. His patriotism is so direct and traditional that it puts non-Australians off balance and confuses Sydney sophisticates. He uses it to explain his Cup involvement. 'The sense of pride, the wonderful euphoria around Australia was really something. You had to be moving around to actually witness and feel it,' he explains. 'That's my prime motivation. To maintain Australian national will and pride.' He goes on to add, with characteristically brutal honesty, that if it hadn't fitted in with the Parry Corporation's diversification into marine engineering and underwater technology he wouldn't have done a thing.

It is likely to cost him A$20 million before the Cup is over. The initial budget was A$4 million, and according to top Parry management he has never once wavered in moving the project forwards. Sponsorship has been slow to come. 'There have only been a few people in the east that have responded. Channel 7 finally got behind us. Digital and Slumberland have been excellent but really speaking I'd say that sponsors are only giving us around two million dollars,' says Parry, who can oscillate between financial candour and total secrecy with bewildering speed. 'We are going it alone, really. We always set out to underwrite it totally if nobody came in and helped.'

Kookaburra, the laughing, slightly grotesque bird of the Australian bush, was a name that Parry chose instinctively for his boats. The first was launched in early 1984. Built in Fremantle by a team headed by world-renowned boatbuilder Toby Richardson, creator of *Condor of Bermuda* and other famed maxi-yachts, the gold-hulled boat is distinctively different in appearance from anything previously seen in local waters. She was designed by young local naval architect John Swarbrick and nominated skipper Iain Murray. Neither knew a damned thing about building twelve-metres, although one might conjecture that Murray knew a slow one when it was under his feet.

The young Sydney yachtsman was the helmsman aboard *Advance*, the twelve-metre entered by the Sydney syndicate of veteran sailor Syd Fischer in the 1983 America's Cup. It was a baptism of fire for Murray. *Advance* sailed with all the grace and speed of a railway sleeper and Fischer is known as one of the hardest and most cantankerous men afloat. At the end of that campaign Murray, six times world champion in the extraordinarily fast eighteen-foot skiff class, knew everything that a twelve-metre campaign didn't need.

John Bertrand rates Murray very highly indeed. 'He is such a naturally gifted sailor,' says the man who won the Cup for Australia. 'He has excellent leadership qualities and people enjoy working with him – not for him. That's very important over a long campaign.' At only twenty-seven Murray is very much the glamour boy of Australian yachting. He drives a petrol-blue Porsche 911 with the registration plate IM 911. He used to race it in Sydney club competitions and motor sport observers say he could as easily have gone into Formula One as yacht racing. On the dock road from east Fremantle to the waterfront twelve-metre compound it is not uncommon to see a dawn tussle between the Porsche and the powerful Moto Guzzi motorcycle of the New York Yacht Club's operations manager Jake Farrell. 'He's a top driver, but I have to say the bike had him,' laughs Farrell. Invariably Murray's mongrel dog Cliff would be in the passenger seat beside him. Those who are out on the water watching the *Kookaburra*'s trialling will swear that they occasionally see a canine nose poking over the yacht's side, next to the bulky figure of Murray at the wheel. His crew invariably refer to the somewhat overweight skipper as 'Lard'. It is ironic that a non-drinker and small eater should have a weight problem. According to Murray's petite wife, Alex, when he began sailing skiffs in Sydney Harbour Iain was so skinny that he had to sail the unstable craft wearing a diver's lead weight belt in order to hold his share of the balance. It was with the skiffs that Murray taught himself boat design. He was the first to use carbon fibre and to go for the esoteric technique of baking the entire boat in a giant oven. The skiffs attract enough attention and cash for him to have become familiar with the interaction between business sponsorship and yachting. All Murray's boats were called *Color 7*, sponsored by the commercial TV network of that name. Part of the Channel 7 sponsorship deal is to put mini-cams, of the type used to cover grand prix races from the cockpit of a Formula One car, aboard *Kookaburra*. They are remotely controlled by computer. However, the joke aboard the yachts is that the skipper will end up behind them directing his movie. The multi-talented Murray also trained as a television cameraman during his association with Channel 7.

From the outset Parry realised that his philosophy of paying top people high rates was going to have to extend into the traditionally amateur world of yachting. Murray's salary has never been disclosed officially, but reliable sources put it at about A$100,000 a year, with a substantial bonus if *Kookaburra* becomes the defender of the America's Cup. 'We recognise the traditional problems of America's Cup challenges have been unrealistically low budgets and lack of imaginative fund-raising initiatives,' comments Parry. Certainly no expense has been spared in getting the right people into the team – even if only for short terms. English sailor Lawrie Smith, who was the principal helmsman aboard the British boat *Victory '83* at the last Newport Cup, was paid A$45,000 to come to Perth for three months early in 1986 to provide Murray with match-racing practice. Straight off the aeroplane he beat Murray six out of six in the first races. To avoid tension between helmsmen and tacticians, who are competing amongst themselves for just two top jobs, it became syndicate policy from an early stage to bring in outside 'consultants', who for reasons of nationality or other commitments were not struggling for a permanent place on the yacht. 'We need people that are smart and are good sailors to race against us,' explains Murray. 'Guys that know from the start that they can't be on the boat and are employed to do a job.' Other Englishmen were brought in on a permanent basis early in the Kookaburra action (crew have to be resident in a country for two years before they qualify for America's Cup competition). Derek Clark, who was navigator on *Victory '83*, was hired as a new kind of sailing animal – a performance specialist. *Kookaburra* is probably the most highly computerised twelve-metre ever built.

Digital have packed every conceivable kind of sensor into the boat, feeding data to a display screen that Clark can read from. His role is to interpret to Murray and his deputy, Peter Gilmour, the information coming in.

'On *Victory '83* we experimented by covering up all the instruments and allowing the crew to sail it by the seat of their pants,' recalls Clark, who is a long way from anybody's idea of a boffin. 'They were all hot sailors who were sure they could sail a twelve-metre to within one-tenth of a knot of its optimum. In fact, they were out by a full knot, and that's a twelve to fifteen per cent error.

'Interfacing the instruments with the computer we've found that we can lift the element of "feel" way beyond what's been done before.' Dinghy sailors have this intangible relationship with the boat beneath them quite naturally, but with a twenty-eight-ton, sixty-five-foot beast of a twelve-metre, it takes electronics to put the guys on deck fully in touch with the yacht. That said, one has to cope with the contradiction of Marc Pajot winning a bitterly contested heat in the world championships with complete electronics failure and not an instrument aboard *French Kiss* working.

The key computer person ashore is another foreigner, Chris Todter, an American who has worked on computer guidance mechanisms for airborne vehicles as diverse as the Boeing 767 and laser-targeted guided missiles. Todter worked with a team of local programmers and analysts under him, many of them trained at the highly regarded Western Australia Institute of Technology. Parry decided early in the campaign that his two boats would be given to the institute at the end of the Cup; it was his equivalent to *Australia II* going into Canberra's National Museum. But being Parry he would rather die than see his boats go east of the Nullarbor.

It was listening to Alan Bond give a speech at a post-Newport business luncheon that launched Parry into twelve-metres. From the day the idea took root relations between the two camps deteriorated. When the first *Kookaburra* was launched Bond was quick to brand it a 'dog' – the worst conceivable insult in Cup circles. It was this that led to the famous quarter-million-dollar wager offered by Parry. Bond and Parry were sitting opposite one another at a black-tie dinner at the Parmelia Hilton, Perth's top hotel. According to Parry, in order to make conversation he asked Bond why he wouldn't race *Kookaburra*. Bond replied, 'You put up two hundred and fifty thousand dollars and I'll race any time, anywhere.' Confusion comes in here. Parry was totally serious about accepting the bet and wrote it down on a piece of paper. Bond treated it more as a joke and backed off – which Parry took as an insult. 'I felt really ashamed for Alan Bond,' Parry told the local *West Australian*, which splashed the story across page one. From that point on the gloves were off between the two syndicates.

When the Kookaburra team made arrangements to sail a series of trial races against the New York Yacht Club's *US42*, the Bond camp were quick to accuse them of aiding and abetting the enemy. 'If the Kookaburra syndicate go ahead with this then I don't think they understand twelve-metre racing at all. It would be naivety in its worst form,' commented Warren Jones, chief executive of the Bond syndicate. He added that if the Parry outfit sailed against any foreign challenger then they would never race a Bond boat. If this was a war of words then the conflict came very close to shooting a few months later, when a high-speed chase boat nearly sank after a 'spying' incident. Iain Murray was driving a forty-five-knot 'rubber duckie' of the type syndicates use for transferring sails and personnel between boats, and taking a close look at a race between *Australia II* and *Australia III*. The skippers thought he was too close by far and the fifty-five-foot tender *Black Swan* began barging the tiny inflatable aside. Certainly the boat was swamped and there were later claims from Murray that his craft was rammed twice. Tempers flared and it could easily have ended in tragedy – no one is in any doubt about that. Taskforce fired off an angry complaint to the Royal Perth Yacht Club, while Alan Bond, caught outside a Sydney board meeting, was unrepentant. Sounding like a Victorian squire referring to poachers he said: 'My boatmen have orders to sink them if it happens again. We'll cut their boat in half.'

Despite continuing announcements from the Bond camp that *South Australia* is the boat to fear in the defender series (cynics point out that they trained the Adelaide crew and Ben Lexcen designed the boat), there has never been much doubt among knowledgeable observers that the final battle to be defender of the Cup would be slugged out between Bond and Parry. In terms of professionalism of approach, commitment, skill of the personnel and willingness to spend the necessary money the newcomers have matched and, in some areas, outreached the old hands. All they lack is experience, and the next few months will show whether that is too big a handicap.

Third in what one might term the Australian twelve-metre pecking order comes South Australia. The syndicate had a slightly curious genesis. Sir James Hardy, probably the best-known sailor down under prior to the ascendancy of John Bertrand, is a South Australian. Hardy had been involved in so many unsuccessful Cup attempts, with Bond and Sir Frank Packer, that the Newport win fired him up to go back to Adelaide, the state capital, and look at creating a syndicate for Perth in 1987. He found a ready-made partner in Roger Lloyd, managing director of the local offshoot of multinational advertising agency Leo Burnett. The project appealed to a new breed of younger businessmen in the city that Lloyd describes succinctly: 'Five years ago this challenge would have had no chance of getting off the ground because for generations Adelaide has been controlled by a handful of men who sat on the same boards and did it all their way. Since the late 1970s this has changed dramatically.' He pauses. Like all advertising men Lloyd believes implicitly in the future. 'Those old warhorses have gone. A new breed of aggressive young businessmen and women are taking over Adelaide.'

An agreement was reached between the new syndicate – which had raised around A$4 million from such sponsors as Mitsubishi, the South Australia Brewery, and the state government – and the Bond team. Ben Lexcen would design the new yacht. Steve Ward would build her. The crew would work within and be trained by the Bond boys. For the period between the launch of the deep-blue *South Australia* in April 1985 and *Australia III* six months later, the two syndicates worked *Australia II* and *South Australia* as sister ships. The poor performance of *South Australia* was at first ascribed to crew inexperience. In races off Port Adelaide and then back in Fremantle the lovely-looking twelve that Lexcen had said was the next step on from *Australia II* kept failing to win. A new keel, grafted on shortly before the world championships, was an admission that something was wrong and did provide an improvement. Yet on the whole the boat's performance in the world championships was dismal. In the way that cruel nicknames so quickly spring up in twelve-metre racing, the Bond camp took to referring to the whole South Australia camp as 'fantasyland'. 'They think they are in the Cup,' was the brutal explanation.

The partnership between the old hands and the rookies was always an unequal one. A crucial example is in the field of computers. No one could expect to go into the Cup as a serious competitor without onboard electronics and data processing. The Bond team's experience in this area went back to 1974, when a crude black box named Fred was installed aboard *Southern Cross*. With the aid of Data General they have come a long way since then. However, it was part of the A$600,000 development contract with South Australia that there would be no transfer of computer know-how. The Adelaide men hired their own programmer and obtained two Hewlett-Packards to start from scratch. Alan Bond did not reach his current position in the business world by going into deals with people and coming out on the downside. The Adelaide syndicate proved no exception to the rule.

After a summer of disappointing trialling, bad results and unimpressive participation in the world championships, the final indignity for *South Australia* came via a film. The producers of *The Challenge*, a six-hour mini-series for television, needed a yacht to play *Liberty* for two weeks while they recreated the Newport races. The Adelaide syndicate badly needed money. The dark-blue boat was trucked back to Steve Ward's shed south of Fremantle and painted a dull cherry-red. The words *Liberty* were inscribed on her stern and actor Nicholas Hammond, playing Dennis Conner, took the wheel. Eighty thousand dollars was said, around the bars, to have been the fee for using *South Australia*. A lot of money, but the two weeks of filming did not help Sir James and his men look like serious contenders when they were clearly not as race-tuned as they should have been.

In the last ten years the growth of Australia in the eyes of the world has focused on the increasingly sophisticated Sydney/Melbourne axis – providing everything from award-winning films to gay areas that rival those of San Francisco – and on the brash west. Here, millionaire entrepreneurs who would be at home in Dallas seem to spring out of the sandy soil, and such outrageous japes as winning the America's Cup are possible. Adelaide, sandwiched in between, has felt compelled to strike out and show she has more than churches and a festival. The Adelaide Grand Prix is a strikingly successful example of that urge. The America's Cup defence syndicate is another example. Neill Kerley, a legendary tough man from Aussie Rules football management brought in to co-ordinate the challenge, said in the early days, 'I told an eastern states radio announcer that he should remember Australia does not finish at the Blue Mountains.'

In similar vein, the syndicate started out determined that the crew should all be South Australians – an understandable idea, but geography has seldom been a powerful enough motivation to win the America's Cup.

In the east of Australia, where the money and the people are, it is a curious phenomenon that even into early 1986 the emergence of an eastern states defence syndicate has been problematical. Syd Fischer is the chairman of the group. A veteran Sydney yachtsman with numerous Admiral's Cups and big international victories behind him, Fischer has a reputation for being pugnacious and granite-hard to sail with. 'I learnt a hell of a lot from him,' Iain Murray says of his ill-fated time as helmsman of *Advance*, 'but I never want to get back on Syd's boat.' Of course, there were as many yachties who loved Fischer as felt the other way, but before the Sydney and Melbourne establishment parted with big bucks they wanted two things: first, that it wasn't going to be a repeat of the *Advance* fiasco; second, that it would not turn out to be just a one-man band. Despite having what tank-tests had shown to be an excellent design from Sydney naval architect Peter Cole, sponsors were slow in coming forward. As a major-league businessman, Fischer could have afforded to fund the challenge himself – but that would have run up against the second objection. His former skipper on *Advance* once described him as having 'moths in his wallet', but that is just one man's view. Finally enough money (around A$5 million) was raised from a consortium of over thirty varied businesses to construct the new yacht, and she was launched in Sydney shortly after Easter of 1986. The consensus in the twelve-metre world was that without even an experienced twelve-metre skipper in place – the pool of Cup sailors in Australia having already been raided by three preceding syndicates – Fischer's bid was a case of too little too late. On the plus side he did have *Australia I*, the Bond boat from the 1977 and 1980 Cups, as a trialhorse. However, as the French Kiss syndicate had found out with *Enterprise*, having a pacing boat two generations slower than the current benchmark is not in itself wildly helpful. With the boat now a solid reality, the participation of the eastern states in the Cup looks settled, but there has to be a large question mark against their hopes.

One man who tried long and hard to get a syndicate formed and a boat in the water was Rolly Tasker, a Western Australian sailing legend. When a visitor leaves Perth and enters Fremantle via the road bridge across the Swan River he cannot help but be aware of Mr Tasker. His name looms down in bright red letters a metre high from a boatyard and sail-loft next to the Stirling Highway. Winner of a record eleven Australian national sailing titles, the sixty-year-old Tasker designed his own twelve-metre and spent a great deal of his own money tank-testing final options in Holland. By building the boat in his own workshops, Tasker believed he could create a viable campaign for A$2 million. Robert Hemery, a Perth public relations consultant who had been vital to the early Bond efforts at Newport, resigned from the board of trustees with Australia III in order to raise funds for Tasker – an indication of considerable credibility. 'Rolly's capacity to design and build maxi-yachts of international repute, his sailing record over the past two decades, and his keenness to play a part in the defence of the Cup all make him a worthy contender,' said Hemery at the time. Yet the support was not forthcoming. In any location other than Perth a man of Tasker's stature could probably have found the backing for his effort. But with Bond and Parry both running big, impressive campaigns and fighting for every available sponsorship dollar, it was not feasible. Tasker's involvement with the Cup turned out to be limited to setting up a showpiece America's Cup museum on the ground floor of his main building. It contains a detailed model of every America's Cup-holding yacht ever built. It seems a shame that his own will never stand a chance of being there.

Easily the most fun Australian syndicate never to build a twelve-metre were the Pilbara Pink team. The Pilbara is a vast, empty land of dust, sheep and iron-ore mines about a thousand miles to the north of Perth. The area is roughly the size of Texas, and is distinctive for the red dust that turns everything – people, vehicles and animals – a deep shade of pink in the harsh sunlight. It is a land where men drive 200-ton dump trucks at the iron-ore mines and midday temperatures reach 120° Fahrenheit. The pioneering spirit is strong and the soft city people of Perth are invariably regarded as incapable of doing anything for themselves. This dubious view of city competence even extends to defending the America's Cup. A pharmacist named Vince Cooper from the dusty iron-ore-exporting harbour of Port Hedland designed a boat and created a fund-raising drive. In every mining camp and sun-blasted village store in the Pilbara, people bought 'Defence Bonds', as Cooper christened them.

The plan was modelled on the War Loan and certainly caught the region's imagination. Unfortunately, there were just not enough people out there to fund a top Flying Dutchman, let alone a twelve-metre. It seemed a shame to most observers. Fast or slow, everyone was dying to see the world's first pink twelve-metre.

Chapter 11

The Common and the Goose

> The fault is great in man or woman
> Who steals a goose from off a common.
> But what can plead that man's excuse,
> Who steals a common from a goose?

Graffiti like this have become the headlines of those dispossessed by the America's Cup. All around Fremantle any blank factory wall or iron security fence is a canvas for the spray-gun protestors. 'The Cup runneth over with despair', howls another. 'Keel over Bondy', makes a more personal attack than the starkly political 'Fuck the Cup – Eat the Rich'. Of course, only a tiny minority have been out painting their feelings on walls. Most of the people in the town have gone on quietly proceeding with lives that do not involve the Cup. They see glamour, they see colour, film crews working in the streets every day of every week, and it is only when they can't park the family car near the town centre or when another favourite little shop disappears that ambivalence has crept into their attitudes. Most Fremantle people love the Cup, as long as it doesn't inconvenience them.

Australia as a whole was overjoyed by the winning of the Cup. It gave the nation a collective charge of adrenalin like nothing in its history had ever done. As the defence of the Auld Mug grew closer, distance from the action was the key component in measuring enthusiasm. In Sydney, Melbourne and the other eastern population centres the Cup was still the biggest thing since sliced bread. Huge numbers of people proposed to make long-deferred trips west to see a part of Australia that is still a foreign country to most of them. In Western Australia itself, mixed feelings have emerged as 1987 looms closer. In Perth, and particularly Fremantle, the population divides itself into 'for' and 'agin'. An opinion poll in early 1986 showed that nearly half the population were totally indifferent to the impending Cup circus. A tiny proportion of those were out on the streets painting eighteenth-century protest poems on factory walls. 'The results of the survey staggered us,' says Chris Conway, managing director of the market research firm that did the work. 'At best seventy per cent of the people surveyed are not interested at all, or only very slightly interested. A big majority of the people we approached had a "So What?" attitude.' In Fremantle many of the survey clerks found that respondents were hostile and refused to talk about the Cup.

John Cattalini is mayor of Fremantle. He came to Australia from Italy as a three-year-old. Now the proprietor of a thriving modern pharmacy on the High Street, he became interested in the council while doing his first job – working for Sir Frank Gibson, a former mayor. Thinking about the effect of the Cup and planning for it began a long time back, according to Cattalini. 'The first time Alan Bond challenged back in 1974 we knew then that one day we'd have the America's Cup in Fremantle. It's been at the back of our minds all that time,' he explains. Cattalini is a tall, thin man with a quick smile at the front edge of great nervous intensity.

'The Cup presents some incredible opportunities for Fremantle. It's the first city in Western Australia and has gone through a number of stages. We had the gold rush days when an enormous number of people landed in Fremantle before they made their way up to the goldfields. The buildings you see now in what we call the heritage area of the West End are a direct result of the gold rush.

'The opportunity we are facing is to add another period like that to the city. For the past decade or so Fremantle has been looking at itself, assessing its assets and virtues. We believe that building on the architectural heritage of the West End and keeping the human scale of the city is going to be our biggest asset.' What really preserved the fine, solid merchants' buildings of the West End was the fifty-year doldrums that followed the First World War. When the gold rush petered out and the boom of the war years ended there was simply not enough finance being generated to redevelop any of these sites. With the Australian passion for bulldozers and new buildings one can be certain that it was not a love of stucco or admiration for a mansard roof that kept the West End intact. It was poverty. The pioneer businessmen like Lionel Samson who came ashore from HMS *Challenger* in rowing boats and set up shop on the sand were tough and unsentimental. Their descendants, like great-grandson Bill Samson, who still runs the wholesale liquor business in Cliff Street two hundred yards from the beach where Lionel landed, think likewise. 'People are worried about some of the projects and spending that are under way because of the Cup,' explains Samson. 'If they are not viable when the Cup goes – and the chances are we won't keep it – who carries the can?' Historic Samson sites around Cliff Street are being sold. 'We have real estate which we are looking at selling and we're doing so only because of interest in the America's Cup. We are pragmatists.' According to Samson the city has faced a dilemma over the past decade: keep everything low-key, folksy, and become more uneconomic every year; or begin to encourage businesses to open the town up. He believes Fremantle is set on a course that would never have happened without the Cup. Yet success could strangle the company. Samson is concerned that pedestrian and vehicle traffic could grow to such an extent that moving trucks in and out to the warehouse will become impossible. 'If we start getting traffic jams in the city we'll have to look at sentiment and business and think about relocating, if only temporarily, out near the airport.' When Lionel Samson set up shop 157 years ago he couldn't have foreseen being driven out by a yacht race.

For some elderly local inhabitants the coming of the Cup has rekindled a touch of the spirit of Fremantle as it was three generations ago – when hourly trams ran to South Beach, the most popular bathing spot in metropolitan Perth because of its unique and innovative shark-net, when the stream of steamers and mail-packets into the docks made Fremantle the window on the world, and when the language of scores of nationalities could be heard on the streets. Margaret Sloss was born in a tiny, weatherboard house in South Fremantle in 1902. She still lives there. Mrs Sloss's parents came over from a country town in Victoria to join the rush to the goldfields. She remembers the hot stink of a camel train going past loaded with supplies for the diggings and the exodus each Monday morning of hundreds of men setting out to walk hundreds of miles with a wheelbarrow, a brace of shovels and a swag to sleep in. Her own father thought better of a miner's life and took work locally. According to many in Fremantle the weekend influx of gawpers and good-timers is spoiling the city, but it sounds to have been wilder in Margaret's day.

'Friday night was carnival night. All the shops stayed open late and the Scots band would march down the High Street followed by all the schoolchildren. We had a cinema show once a week,' she recalls. 'I can remember the King's Theatre used to be next to the Sail and Anchor pub. They had a revolving stage and one of their shows featured a stage coach and six horses.' It seems strange but infinitely pleasant for Margaret to see the city turning back towards the harum-scarum pioneer days of her youth. The introduction of the steam train that now runs south through three new stations past the yacht harbours and finishes at Robb's Jetty within sight of the Sloss home is a potent image for her. The last regular passenger train she can remember on the line, which has long ago been turned over to goods, was also steam-powered and used to take her to school in the city each day. A member of the Western Australian Railway History Society, Mrs Sloss regards the reprise of the steamer as an enormous boon. 'The council is spending money on things that desperately needed doing, like new signalling,' she announces firmly.

Features on the local twelve-metre sailors and the rigours of sailing eight hours a day aboard a full-on racing machine impress Mrs Sloss not a jot. 'I have always loved sailing so I never miss the TV coverage – the Cup and the cricket are the only things worth watching,' she says. 'We used to sail on the river as a family in an eighteen-foot Evelyn and they were pretty fast boats. I can remember being stranded on the beach under the cliffs at Attadale waiting for a storm to pass. There were no houses in Attadale then.' It is now an exclusive and very expensive riverside suburb.

Unfortunately, the elderly population of Fremantle is not composed entirely of people like Mrs Sloss – full of vim, vigour, and enchanting memories. The city has traditionally been the location for dozens of lodging houses, known in Australia as hotels, which provide a room, cooking facilities and, most of all, companionship for the single elderly. The hotels are rudimentary, cheap – and disappearing. They tend to be the type of buildings that lend themselves to rapid and inexpensive renovation – white walls and new washbasins – in preparation for use as Cup accommodation. The elderly residents, mostly men, have no rights as tenants. As the Cup comes closer, almost every week sees the emptying of another hotel by owners eager to participate in an event which offers the commercial possibilities of a lifetime. One of the poignant examples occurred on Christmas Eve of 1985, when twenty-seven residents were evicted from the Imperial Bedrooms prior to the owners redeveloping the property. Some went into the dwindling number of alternative lodging houses, others were provided with neat, modern flats by the State Housing Commission (recently renamed Homeswest in one of those cosmetic changes bureaucrats are so fond of). Margaret Healy was a social worker involved with 'decanting' the men.

'Even getting them into flats wasn't the success story it sounds because although these boarding houses are grotty and not the sort of life you or I would want to lead, there is a support system within them,' she explains. 'One man moved into an SHC flat and was dead within months because he didn't have the support and encouragement of his mates. He was found in an overflowing bath with broken bones. He died in hospital still in a coma. If he'd had his friends around him they would have encouraged him to look after himself better.' Physical harm is not the only risk. 'There are other men who've been put in flats in suburbs miles from Fremantle and they just sit in their smoky little rooms full of ashtrays drinking themselves to death. It's too far for their mates to go out and visit them. The social network is broken.'

Perth has little inner-city life that is not connected to the business district. The residential suburbs are leafy streets connecting residents with the local shopping mall. Neither area is welcoming to old people, either derelict or affluent, who want to walk about a little, sit in the sun chatting with friends, drink a little beer in a pub they've used for years. Fremantle has, in the past, been the sort of town where that almost European style of promenading and agreeable passing of the day was possible. Almost all of its facilities – ranging from the hospital, to the library, to the Commonwealth Bank that cashes pension cheques – are within walking distance – even on sticks – from the main square. But as the city smartens up, gears up for the jet-set, the yachtie-set and the international media, the working-class elderly find that they are no longer a welcome part of the street scene.

'There are lodging houses in east Fremantle being offered A$20,000 for ten weeks at the height of the Cup. It makes economic sense to put these people out and tart the accommodation up a little,' expounds Mrs Healy. 'It's absurd to think that these people are being forced out of this grotty housing. They have no hope of getting a better grade of accommodation and there's nothing lower down. There is virtually nowhere for them to go. This is the presentation that is being encouraged in Fremantle now. There's a whole clean-town image. Even their usual slightly shabby haunts are being cleaned up. These people just aren't as welcome as they used to be anywhere in town. As the price of a cup of coffee goes up and up, they can no longer enjoy even the small pleasures.'

It was partly the pleasure of sitting in a pavement café enjoying a cappuccino as the world meanders by that began to attract young professional people to Fremantle well before the winning of the Cup. Because of a high Italian and Portuguese proportion in the population (almost a half of the 20,000 people are from one of these two ethnic groups), street and café life is highly developed, a bonus for sensitive and languorous Anglo-Saxon Australians whose own predominant culture is tending increasingly to the suburban shopping mall and the walk-in freezer. The establishment in the mid-seventies of Murdoch University some five miles east of Fremantle was an important influence on the town. Increasing numbers of staff and students chose to live in the town, increasing a noticeable and pleasant tendency towards the Bohemian. Limestone cottages with hardwood jarrah floors and corrugated-iron roofs are abundant and cheap. Fremantle was a community ripe for the kind of gentrification that everyone who knows Camden Town or Greenwich Village is familiar with. It got under way quickly; but even if the effects were highly visible, the numbers of people involved were small.

'The Cup is accelerating processes that were already under way,' says social planner Fred Robinson, seconded by the state government to look at pressures on Fremantle and ways of alleviating them. 'Changes that would have taken two decades are going to happen in three years. You get all your casualties at once. It's like setting off a bomb rather than knocking them off with snipers.

'We are seeing the middle-class invasion of Fremantle – people like me, for instance, a middle-aged, middle-class public servant who moved here when his marriage broke up.' Robinson is too shrewd not to realise the ironies of his own position. He embodies many of the contradictions of the town. Getting up at dawn to go jogging he encounters workmen setting off on foot for the foundry, young girls heading for a hot day spent feeding the hot, insatiable ovens of the biscuit factories. Fremantle in recent years has been a town offbeat enough to encompass such oddities without visible strain.

'Freo's always been a typical Australian town, but with a lot of ethnic feeling incorporated in it,' says Mayor Cattilini. Arranging an interview with him is an uncertain business. One was cancelled with a regretful phone call from the pharmacy to the mayoral parlour. A fisherman had come in with a split hand and he was applying first aid. 'It's a working-class town so everybody seems to get on with everybody. It doesn't matter where you are in the social scale, there's an amazing unity. Everybody is in it together – there seems to be no division between people. That's what gives it its character and solidarity and why I'm proud to raise my family here.'

However, as the Cup comes closer divisions have begun to appear in the town. One of the first was between those who owned their homes and those who were tenants. The difference was not one of status. Despite having one of the highest home-ownership rates in the world, Australia has also a huge private rental market. Many affluent professional people choose not to buy a house because of the mobility and free capital that leasing provides; it is the free market economy beloved of classical economists. No rent controls, tenant security laws, or other statutory obligations interpose themselves between landlord and lessee. Several thousand houses are rented in Fremantle, a very limited supply. In classical economics, when an inelastic supply meets an elastic demand prices go through the roof.

The average increase has been to a factor of around ten. A house fetching A$100 a week will be priced at A$1,000 per week during the Cup. New leases routinely contain provisos that the tenants will have to move out from November 1986 to February 1987. During the year preceding the Cup those people living in leased accommodation lived in apprehension of every letter and phone call from their landlords. Many were evicted months before the competition so that renovations and redecorations could begin.

'We didn't find any great rent increases immediately,' explains Les Geevors, adviser at the government-funded Tenancy Advice Centre in Fremantle. 'Then the mood began to change. Some of the more notorious estate agencies began to push leaflets through people's doors asking them to move out for the Cup. The same agents took out advertisements in the local papers saying "Landlords, are you getting enough for your property?" Then talk of A$1,000 a week for any old dump started to appear. A sort of hysteria just swept through the place.' The apogee of unrealistic greed was probably reached when the French company Louis Vuitton, sponsor of the challenger series, was offered a totally undistinguished apartment for A$300,000. Understandably, French representative Bruno Trouble, a former America's Cup helmsman, assumed that the owner was trying to sell him the property. When it was explained to him that this was the proposed rent per month he exploded with rage and the story appeared in the local newspaper.

'It would have been much more expensive than any hotel in the world,' said Trouble. 'The impression we get is that people in Western Australia are crazy about making money from the America's Cup.' The *West Australian* followed up with a stinging editorial wondering just what had happened to the friendly and fair Western Australia of pre-Cup days. 'Since planning for the Cup defence began there has been a risk that the whole thing could get out of hand,' ran the leader. 'Now it appears that some property owners have been so blinded by dollar signs that they expect people to pay more to rent a property for a month than it should cost to buy it.' Amid the graffiti shouting 'Don't Let the Cup Make You Homeless' a lot of ordinary Fremantle people were wondering the same thing. At one public meeting called in South Fremantle to discuss the effects of the Cup, plans were laid to create a 'Tent City' in the grounds of the state parliament. It was an idea taken from the shameful 'Hoovervilles' that surrounded Washington in the depression of the 1930s. At the same time politicians such as America's Cup minister Des Dans and premier Brian Burke were able to say that they saw no evidence of a housing crisis.

'Dans is forever saying that no one has come into his office with any problems like this,' explains a weary Geevors. Branded a dangerous radical for his espousal of such issues as tenants' rights, from street level he looks more of a helpless and overworked pragmatist. 'How many people go to a politician's office when they are being evicted?' The Tenants Advice Centre started out being able to offer little and could soon do nothing. It was funded with A$40,000 from the state government's America's Cup department. 'I think the politicians expect us to be a Band Aid, but we simply can't direct people to houses which are not there. We cannot find them anywhere else to live. All we can do is try to draw public attention to what has been going on. Because of that we tend to be cast as the screaming radicals.'

The Labour state government has received two reports from internal working parties urging tenancy law reform, with special reference to the America's Cup. Detailed studies were made of the short-life legislation used in California to ensure that the Los Angeles Olympics did not become a cause of homelessness and accommodation rip-offs. The Fremantle branch of the Australian Labour Party put three motions in a year to the state executive urging action before it was too late. 'The government has to tackle this,' says branch president Norm Marlborough. 'Rent rises because of the America's Cup are forcing people out of Fremantle.' Yet tenancy legislation is a nettle that, even after an electoral triumph in early 1986, the pragmatic Burke government has feared to grasp. It is already under fire from some quarters for the extent of its involvement in the Cup. After all, runs the argument, in 132 years at Newport all the US government ever did was to lend the odd coastguard cutter as a regatta guardship. 'The Americans get quite upset at the government involvement here,' confirms Des Dans. 'They tend to think, "Christ. A Labour government, they're going to socialise the Cup. We might need the marines to actually get it back." '

'Housing is the biggest single problem,' agrees Fred Robinson, almost certainly the first social worker ever appointed to a yacht race. 'It's very difficult politically in Australia because the tradition is that if you've got money to invest you buy a second house and rent it out. It's visible and appealing to ordinary people compared with stocks and shares. There's been no regulation: no effective landlord tenant legislation, no rent control, just pure entrepreneurship. It's going to be very hard to intervene in a politically acceptable way.'

Des Dans is a buff, clubbable Labour politician of the old school. A trade unionist and former president of the Fremantle Labour Party, he became responsible for Cup matters almost by chance. Dans was in Newport with premier Burke shortly after the Cup was won. Burke told him that when they got back home he could start looking after matters to do with yachting. 'I have some idea – he may have said it, but I wouldn't hold him to it – that it was only a clink-and-drink exercise,' laughs Dans, a heavily jowled man who eats and drinks with relish. By the end of the Cup the state government will have spent A$52 million on the conduct of the defence. 'When I got back they were sitting on their hands over the first marina. I speeded things up, may have stood on a few conservationist toes, but you see the result today.

'I'm responsible for seeing that everything is in place, from sewerage to ASIO – our secret service. We want people to receive a good impression of Western Australia and take that good impression home with them. That involves minimising the stuff-ups. I'd be some kind of prophet in my own time if I said that there weren't going to be any. My job is simply to see that Murphy's Law doesn't ride high every day.'

Through the decision to link a multi-million-dollar tourist promotion to the America's Cup, the Western Australian state government took a decision to view the event as one of macro-economic importance. If its prime importance was going to be to generate jobs and revenue throughout metropolitan Perth and, to a lesser extent, the country areas, then, *de facto*, the problems of Fremantle could not be seen as overridingly important. And, of course, where one observer sees turmoil another sees market forces and the 'invisible hand' imposing a new order. 'Low-income people living in the centre of a city – Fremantle or anywhere else – will get hurt by expansion, whether it's for the America's Cup or a grand prix like they had in Adelaide,' says Warren Jones, executive director of the Bond syndicate. 'Events of this nature act as a catalyst. Something will come along and make the city too busy for low-income earners to live in. Fremantle was always a port foremost, but as shipping tonnages went down it went to sleep for a while. Sooner or later something else would have come along. Now it's going to be a marvellous tourist city and a marvellous waterfront city – I'm very excited by it.'

In the final year before the Cup elimination series it has been almost impossible to live in Fremantle and not be excited by the energy of the city. Every street seems to have a crane and a building project. They range in size from turning the Esplanade, a grubby but historic gold rush pub facing the harbour, into a 140-room, five-star international hotel, to putting a new shopfront on a corner delicatessen. Developers with style and imagination have had a field day. Wayne Donaldson, a businessman who had resurrected the decaying Fremantle markets ten years before and turned them into the weekend hub of the port, bought the dying Oddfellows Hotel just across the road from the markets. With the application of love, money and the skill of the Rajneeshi builders, it was transformed into the Norfolk, a semi-English pub with hanging sign (the coat of arms includes a twelve-metre yacht) and the motto 'Why Not?' 'Great events make places more interesting and Fremantle needed a change,' says Donaldson. 'The change started ten years ago when middle-class people started moving in from Perth.' His family have lived for the past three generations in the leafy and affluent Perth suburb of Nedlands, on the north shore of the Swan River. 'The Cup is making things happen in two years that were going to happen in ten anyway.'

If nothing else, the Cup has worked wonders for Fremantle's drinkers. The city's pubs were as undistinguished a clutch of rundown alehouses as could be found anywhere in the country. Prior to becoming the unofficial twelve-metre social centre, the Auld Mug had been the Cleopatra Hotel, a pub so rough that policemen habitually walked in with a hand already on their staffs. The Freemasons, another dive, became the Sail and Anchor, with a brewery on the premises and a fine restaurant upstairs. The restoration of the Victorian bar interior won national design and architectural awards. Across the road Papa Luigi', for years Freo's gossip and coffee centre, moved up four doors from a corner shop with a lino floor to a huge complex with blue awnings out over the pavements, air-conditioning and a restaurant. There may no longer be poker machines in the back room, and locals insist there is no character to the place any more and prefer to go down the road to Gino's, but the tills run hot at Papa's.

It is in the faces of retail shops that the changes in Fremantle are most visible. After all, a pub is always going to be a pub, smartened up or not. But when an ironmonger's becomes a boutique selling designer jeans, something is happening. In one row of shops, as a butcher and a family jeweller's prepares to close, Benetton – Princess Diana's favourite ready-to-wear clothes shop – prepares to open its first store in Western Australia.

Just a few yards down the street Dunkerton's the jeweller's held its closing-down sale. Jeff Dunkerton decided that with a rent increase from A$3,640 a year to A$17,000 per annum, plus a shift of taxes and charges from landlord to tenant, the business was no longer viable. It seems a shame to a lot of locals. Jeff's grandfather started the business in 1907, selling wedding rings made of Kalgoorlie gold to generations of Fremantle bridegrooms. The first shop stood directly opposite the one that has now closed. His father moved the business, having a hunch that the other side of the street was busier and better for trade. After thirty-five years in the jewellery trade Jeff plans to move away from Fremantle and take a part-time job. Business hasn't been too great in recent years. Competition from suburban shopping malls has been getting tougher all the time. There was pressure to open longer hours. 'I wouldn't advise my sons to go into small retailing. You are too vulnerable as a business,' said Jeff as he cleared the shop. He wrote appealing for help to Des Dans and received a vague, sympathetic reply. 'I remember some politicians stating that they would not allow anything of this sort to happen,' Dunkerton recalled, with a touch of melancholy anger. He plans to renew the lease and then sell it to a fashion business, or perhaps a restaurant.

Six doors farther up Market Street, Warren Dunne is preparing to close down his butcher's shop. It isn't the biggest or most popular shop in town, but he has loyal customers who like the traditional atmosphere and his personal service. Unfortunately, there aren't enough of them to finance a rent increase from A$30 a week to A$211 a week. Dunne has the same landlords, Manning Estates, as his neighbour Jeff Dunkerton. Dunne is a realist and is at least as worried about the consumer's move away from red meat as he is about the effect of the America's Cup. But it is the latter that has forced him to move at the difficult age of forty-one. Dunne says he thinks of having to re-train, although having worked for yourself it's not always easy to settle into something new.

Henderson's, the estate agents who manage the retail properties for Manning Estates, say that the rent increases are nothing to do with the Cup. It is a phrase that one hears remarkably often in Fremantle. 'Rents were ridiculously low and a lot of traders were living on cloud nine. They were tenants week-to-week rather than taking out leases and were trading inefficiently,' says a spokesman for the agents. He adds that rents have been going up steadily for the past three years and tenants seem to find them fair. The extra revenue would go to paint the shops and improve the frontages. The owners also had a desire to install new lavatories for the lessees. Repetition of misfortune becomes tedious and dulls the receptive sense. But on the same block the city centre's only wet fish shop (excellently run by Vietnamese refugees) has seen its rent increase from A$8,000 to

A$24,000 plus new service charges, and is preparing to move. Cobbler Charlie Head has found that soling and heeling cannot provide the cash-flow necessary to survive in the new Fremantle, and is quitting. So too is another butcher, a friendly rival to Dunne.

'There is a great variety of shopping in Fremantle that you don't find in shopping centres,' says Mayor Cattalini. 'Lots of little speciality shops, coffee shops and so forth. Shopping can become an entertainment almost.' Ray Costello's High Street shop is about as specialised as one could find anywhere. He sells darts, boards and the trophies that go with winning at 301. Costello's rent has gone up from A$285 a month to A$491. He is struggling to pay the new rate, but is not optimistic in the long term. 'Everyone around here is really worried,' he reports. 'Businesses like ours are small and it is hard to justify paying this much rent. A twelve per cent increase would have been natural, but not sixty-seven per cent.' A spokesman for the agents once again says the rent increases have nothing to do with the America's Cup. They are just part of a natural financial cycle.

'Small businesses are vital to the charm of the whole city. It is imperative that they survive and do well,' says Mayor Catallini. 'I hope they will be able to band together, present a united front and do some research into their future. There's not all that much evidence of big rent increases. I don't see it happening on any great scale.' The mayor believes that commercial property owners are alive to the unique ambience of Fremantle and will not be tempted to kill the small business geese that lay the golden eggs.

Rent increases are not the only pressures that have forced businesses out of Fremantle. Just opposite the beautifully restored Norfolk Hotel an oriental rug store has signs in the window: 'Moving To A Cup-Free Zone'. The building, once the city's synagogue and still sporting the Star of David on the roof pediment, is owned by the council and there has been no rent increase. 'Fremantle is changing more to be a pleasure town. Walking down here every second shop is an eating place – pizza joint, ice cream parlour, whatever,' says rug importer John Montgomery. 'I run a fairly exclusive business in the sense that a lot of the items I have are not available anywhere else in Western Australia.' His customers are not browsing around town looking for something to buy, they come because they want a certain type of Kashmiri or Tabriz rug. 'On Saturdays now I get more people through the store, but they buy nothing,' adds Montgomery, an experienced wholesaler and importer in his mid-fifties. The shop has now moved to modern, somewhat soulless premises on the edge of a new suburban shopping complex five miles towards Perth. 'A lot of the more, shall we say, *businesslike* retailers, as opposed to pleasure places, are actually moving out of Fremantle.' People like Montgomery are not opposed to the Cup – indeed, he confesses himself incurably excited by the waterfront activity and the twelve-metre yachts – but are disappointed by what they see as the failure of the authorities to protect the special nature of their city for the years beyond 1987.

'I think the council ought to have done more to protect this town, and the mayor, being a small businessman, should have gone out of his way to keep people like me and this business here,' says Montgomery. 'If anything goes wrong and we don't keep the Cup all we're going to have left is a lot of fast-food outlets. A lot of the specialised businesses that have attracted people to the city have gone and won't come back.'

The government investment in the physical infrastructure of Fremantle has been staggering. A completely new yacht harbour, slightly to the north of Fishing Boat Harbour, has been constructed especially for the Cup at a cost of A$7 million. It will house four syndicates and the ocean annexe of the Royal Perth Yacht Club. Across the road and within the basin of Fishing Boat Harbour six new docks and compounds have been built for lease by syndicates. The plan is that they will be available for use after the Cup by the local fishing industry. Right behind the new jetties a badly needed lobster-processing factory has been created. Behind the actions of the Western Australian government lies the philosophy, and surely the right one, that whatever is built or created to enable the Cup defence to take place should be of maximum use when the circus leaves town. It is a 'worst case' plan – that is to say, all projections and decisions have been made on the assumption that the America's Cup will be lost – to North America, Europe or New Zealand – and that Western Australia will have to make the most of its brief shining moment. Thus the A$30 million of Commonwealth government money from Canberra has been allocated only to projects that will help the community to cope with the impact of the Cup: new roads, housing, and so on. The decision not to allocate any public money to the syndicates trying to defend the Cup has become a controversial one – at least with the yachtsmen. But there was never any sign that taxpayers wanted their money given to what most perceive as a rich man's game.

Brian Burke, always regarded as a shrewd interpreter of what the mortgage belt regard as important, has flatly refused to help the syndicates. Sounding like a French general declaring '*Ils ne passeront pas!*', he has said that the twelve-metre teams would get 'not one cent'. Critics of the policy argue that to inject A$82 million into infrastructure but invest nothing in ensuring that it will be used a second time is economic madness. 'Holding a circus but forgetting to pay the clowns,' says the Bond syndicate's Warren Jones. Malcolm Bailey, chief executive of the Kookaburra syndicate, is irate at the suggestion they have been asking for hand-outs. The syndicates' proposal was that the government should forgo the more than A$1 million that each syndicate would pay in sales tax and import duty in order to build its yachts. 'We are striving for respite from both these duties. If we didn't choose to defend the Cup and build twelve-metres the money would never find its way into the Treasury anyway,' says Bailey.

With the Kookaburra team expecting to spend A$19.7 million by February 1987, and the Bond camp not far behind, the sums requested from the government are not highly significant in relative terms – five per cent or so of a very large budget. What the teams want most of all is a public arm around the shoulder; and that is what the politician in Burke is too shrewd to give. On the day *Australia II* won the America's Cup it was fine for Prime Minister Bob Hawke to be doused in champagne at the Royal Perth Yacht Club and, *extempore*, create a national holiday. Three years have passed since then. While all can agree that the Cup is going to be the biggest circus, the most expensive, the most *everything* yachting event in the world, there is growing evidence that many Western Australians are not that happy at having it thrust on top of them. Des Dans uses events such as the launching of *Kookaburra II* to depict those with doubts as unpatriotic whingers; but as time passes every poll and newspaper *vox pop* shows that public doubts are growing.

In the mid-1970s Fremantle became a base for artists. It had cheap housing, and large empty warehouse and wool-stores which could be rented for studio space. Many of the Italian and Portuguese immigrants had become affluent and were culturally disposed to helping artists. 'These people were understanding to artists,' says painter Sam Abercromby. 'They respected them and acknowledged that artists had a valuable place in society. They have a greater tradition of art as part of a culture.'

The arrival of the Cup has spelt trouble for the artists – a change of values, both financial and spiritual. Abercromby has already left for Portugal. His studio rent had gone up, but it was not a prime reason for departing. 'There's nothing left of the Fremantle we came to. It's tinsel-town, Disneyland,' laughs Abercromby over his shoulder en route to Lisbon. One colleague has lost his studio to a syndicate sail-loft; another's will store 40,000 tins of food for the French Kiss syndicate. 'I've been approached twenty-six times to do mediocre chocolate-box pictures of yachts. I've never painted pictures of yachts and I'm certainly not going to start now.' Abercromby is thirty-nine. Robert Holmes à Court buys his pictures. 'People in power in Perth and Fremantle have a fantasy that Freo can be Pioneer Village [a Western Australian tourist attraction] crossed with Disneyland – and ninety-nine per cent of them have never been there, so they don't even know what it is like. They are destroying everything that doesn't conform to that fantasy. There was a working party for a year on a Fremantle cultural centre. What happened to it? Footpaths for American tourists. Cattalini dreams of having a sixteen-storey office block on the site of his chemist's shop. That's where his head is at.'

The people in Fremantle most directly affected by the Cup are the fishermen. Three to four hundred boats work out of the port, and many big trawlers that fish up to the north of Australia make Fremantle their maintenance base. Working boats and the ultimate pleasure craft are not the optimum partners for one small, congested harbour. Shrewdly, the marine and harbour department of the Western Australian government have lobbied to ensure that much of the new infrastructure – such as quays, lifting bays, fuel points and hard-standing – will be of long-term benefit to the fishing industry. But inevitably many of the new facilities have been angled more to the pleasure-boat industry than to the more mundane needs of a marginally profitable fishing boat. Professional seafarers find themselves having to move seven miles south to the facilities at Jervoise Bay, an efficient but bleak spot lacking the charm of a fishing town.

'The overall effect of the Cup has been to change a quietly efficient fishing boat harbour into a tourist attraction – with rising costs for the fisherman,' says veteran Renwick Momber, who fishes from a hand-line boat. The new car park has doubled the space available for trucks to queue and load the catch, but it is often choked with tourists' cars, even in the early morning. According to Tony Pensabene, president of the Fremantle Fisherman's Association, the increase in the number of people around the harbour, and the growing fleet of private luxury craft, has made it a honeypot for marine crime. Fifty skippers, concerned at the thefts of echo-sounders, outboard motors and other valuable gear, have gathered together into a syndicate, and now pay for a private security firm to patrol the harbour area six times each night. It was established following a weekend when £10,000 worth of gear was stolen on one Saturday night alone. Prior to the Cup Fremantle's fishermen worried more about the strength of the Japanese yen against the Aussie dollar than about theft.

'A person can get AIDS. A town gets the America's Cup,' drawls George Haynes, one of Australia's foremost painters and a long-time resident of south Fremantle.

Afterword

Slaves of the Circus

It is late April 1986. By the time this book appears much may have changed among the competitors for the Cup. Reports are beginning to filter in to the Fremantle waterfront of crises among the syndicates, either over finance or personnel. In Canada True North suspended operations for a limited period and began merger discussions with the Canada I organisation. From Rome came rumours that Azzurra, the most glamorous and affluent syndicate of them all, is in trouble with defecting helmsmen and a recalcitrant crew. In Boston, yachtsmen hear tales that Leonard Greene is considering suspending the building of a new *Courageous*.

What makes the America's Cup such a fine event is the dedication of sailors and their design teams to producing yachts which represent the pinnacle of their art and skill, almost regardless of fiscal or human cost. Yet that obsessive participation could mark the beginning of the end of the contest as it now exists. The teams that are now in trouble have been sending boats and crews half-way round the world at staggering expense years before the contest itself begins. To maintain motivation and cohesion in such circumstances becomes at best difficult, in many cases impossible.

Cino Ricci is a distinguished Italian yachtsman and operations director of the Azzurra syndicate. He helmed the first *Azzurra* at Newport in 1983. At the end of his second southern summer in Perth, with the races still eight months away, Cino can see that his team may be in big trouble. He is a man of passion and thoughtfulness, and he knows that the problems are not just to do with having a slow boat that needs modifications.

'There is absolutely less pleasure in this Cup,' says Cino, sitting tanned and weary in the Azzurra sail-loft. Outside on the hoist the powder-blue yacht sits waiting for another day's trials. 'The ambience is changing. Now it is all organised. There is not the possibility to have fun with the other teams. In Newport we played soccer on many, many occasions with the British, the Canadians and the Americans. Now we have not time.

'There is more and more pressure from the sponsors. They need that we have the world championships and then the America's Cup and then the world championships again. I don't know how much longer we can work like that, only the professional can do it. Months and months, years and years, the amateur cannot neglect his profession. If you cut out the amateur the myth of the America's Cup is finished.

'You cannot pay people to have the enthusiasm and the passion. It is too repetitive. It is like a job in a bank or other job for clerical people. Always you go to sail the boat; alone with the computer or with the other boat from your syndicate. The routine becomes everything and the people – if they have not something inside, the myth of the America's Cup – they are paid and just working.' Cino glances out at the beautiful, sleek boat dangling in the bright Australian sunshine.

'Now we are obsessed. Syndicates want to prepare for the next America's Cup before this one is finished,' he adds sadly. 'We begin to be slaves of this circus.'

Index

HOW A TWELVE-METRE YACHT IS CREWED

A "twelve" is undercrewed when compared to other racing yachts of similar size. The eleven crew on board must work to their limits if the boat is to perform.

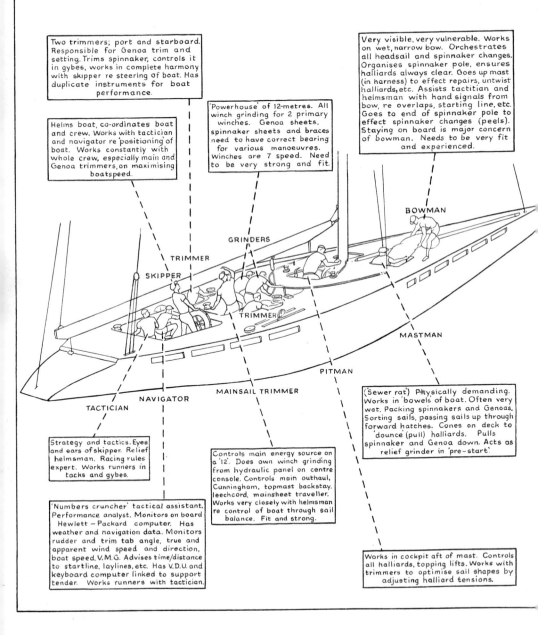

Two trimmers; port and starboard. Responsible for Genoa trim and setting. Trims spinnaker, controls it in gybes, works in complete harmony with skipper re steering of boat. Has duplicate instruments for boat performance.

Very visible, very vulnerable. Works on wet, narrow bow. Orchestrates all headsail and spinnaker changes. Organises spinnaker pole, ensures halliards always clear. Goes up mast (in harness) to effect repairs, untwist halliards, etc. Assists tactitian and helmsman with hand signals from bow, re overlaps, starting line, etc. Goes to end of spinnaker pole to effect spinnaker changes (peels). Staying on board is major concern of bowman. Needs to be very fit and experienced.

Helms boat, co-ordinates boat and crew. Works with tactician and navigator re 'positioning' of boat. Works constantly with whole crew, especially main and Genoa trimmers, on maximising boatspeed.

'Powerhouse' of 12-metres. All winch grinding for 2 primary winches. Genoa sheets, spinnaker sheets and braces need to have correct bearing for various manoeuvres. Winches are 7 speed. Need to be very strong and fit.

BOWMAN

GRINDERS

TRIMMER

SKIPPER

TRIMMER

MASTMAN

PITMAN

NAVIGATOR

MAINSAIL TRIMMER

TACTICIAN

Strategy and tactics. Eyes and ears of skipper. Relief helmsman. Racing rules expert. Works runners in tacks and gybes.

Controls main energy source on a '12'. Does own winch grinding from hydraulic panel on centre console. Controls main outhaul, Cunningham, topmast backstay, leechcord, mainsheet traveller. Works very closely with helmsman re control of boat through sail balance. Fit and strong.

('Sewer rat') Physically demanding. Works in 'bowels of boat. Often very wet. Packing spinnakers and Genoas. Sorting sails, passing sails up through forward hatches. Comes on deck to 'dounce' (pull) halliards. Pulls spinnaker and Genoa down. Acts as relief grinder in 'pre-start'.

'Numbers cruncher' tactical assistant. Performance analyst. Monitors on board Hewlett – Packard computer. Has weather and navigation data. Monitors rudder and trim tab angle, true and apparent wind speed and direction, boat speed, V.M.G. Advises time/distance to startline, laylines, etc. Has V.D.U. and keyboard computer linked to support tender. Works runners with tactician.

Works in cockpit aft of mast. Controls all halliards, topping lifts. Works with trimmers to optimise sail shapes by adjusting halliard tensions.